DISCARDED

Insights into Human Development:
Commentaries

Insights into Human Development:
Commentaries

KENNETH URIAL GUTSCH AND
LARRY L. THORNTON

University Press of Mississippi
Jackson
1978

This Volume is Authorized
and Sponsored by
DELTA STATE UNIVERSITY
Cleveland, Mississippi

Copyright © 1978 by the
University Press of Mississippi
Manufactured in the United States of America
Designed by Barney McKee

Library of Congress Cataloging in Publication Data

Gutsch, Kenneth Urial.
  Insights into human development.

  "Authorized and sponsored by Delta State University, Cleveland, Mississippi."

  1. Psychology—Abstracts. 2. Mental health—Abstracts. 3. Psychologists—Biography. 4. Mental health personnel—Biography. I. Thornton, Larry L., joint author. II. Delta State University. III. Title.
  BF121.G87   158'.08   77-17020
  ISBN 0-87805-043-4
  ISBN 0-87805-044-2 pbk.

*To Nancy and Judy, our wives,
who share our quest for insight, humanness,
and never-ending growth.*

*To Kenda, Matt, and Leigh Ann, our children,
who make such a quest worthwhile.*

Contents

PREFACE   xix
ACKNOWLEDGMENTS   xxi

AUTHORS

Adler, Alfred   3
    The Individual Psychology of Alfred Adler
    Problems of Neurosis
    Superiority and Social Interest
Allport, Gordon Willard   5
    Personality: A Psychological Interpretation
    The Nature of Prejudice
    Becoming: Basic Considerations for a Psychology of Personality
    Personality and the Social Encounter
Anastasi, Anne   7
    Differential Psychology: Individual and Group Differences in Behavior
    Fields of Applied Psychology
    Individual Differences
    Psychological Testing
Arbuckle, Dugald Sinclair   9
    Student Personnel Services in Higher Education
    Guidance and Counseling in the Classroom
    Counseling: An Introduction
    Pupil Personnel Services in American Schools
    The Self of the Counselor
    Counselor, Social Worker, Psychologist
    Counseling: Philosophy, Theory, and Practice
Axline, Virginia M.   12
    Play Therapy: The Inner Dynamics of Childhood
    Mental Deficience—Symptom or Disease?
    Play Therapy Experiences as Described by Child Participants
Beers, Clifford Whittingham   14
    A Mind That Found Itself: An Autobiography

CONTENTS

Berdie, Ralph Freimuth   15
    A Training Program in Counseling
    Counselor Attitude
    Roles and Relationships in Counseling
    The State-wide Testing Programs
    After High School—What?
    Counseling for Physically Disabled Students
    Improving Evaluation in Student Recruitment and Selection
    Some Principles and Problems of Selective College Admissions
    Minnesota Studies in Student Personnel Work
    The Movement of Men
    Strong Vocational Interest Blank Scores of High School Seniors and Their Later Occupational Entry

Berne, Eric Lennard   20
    Transactional Analysis in Psychotherapy: A Systematic Individual and Social Psychiatry
    Games People Play: The Psychology of Human Relationships
    Principles of Group Treatment

Bingham, Walter Van Dyke   22
    Aptitudes and Aptitude Testing

Bordin, Edward S.   23
    Counseling Points of View, Non-directive and Others
    Developments in Interviewing Techniques
    Psychological Counseling
    An Articulated Framework for Vocational Development
    True or False? Tests Tell the Story

Borow, Henry   26
    Vocational Planning for College Students: A Sequential Project Method
    Man in a World of Work
    The Adolescent in the World of Work
    Career Guidance for a New Age

Cattell, Raymond B.   28
    Personality and Motivation Structure and Measurement
    Objective Personality and Motivation Tests: A Theoretical Introduction and Practical Compendium
    Abilities: Their Structure, Growth, and Action

CONTENTS

Coleman, William E.   30
  Motivating Factors in In-Service Training of Faculty Counselors
  Basic Steps in Developing a Guidance Program
  Susceptibility of the Minnesota Teachers Attitude
  Some Criteria for Evaluating Elementary School Guidance Services
  Intelligence and Achievement: The 'Jangle Fallacy' Again
  Comparison of Davis-Eells and Kuhlmann-Finch Scores of Children from High and Low Socio-economic Status
  Conducting Teacher-Parent Conferences
  Assisting Teachers in Using Test Results
  Advantages and Disadvantages of Large Scale Testing Programs

Cottingham, Harold Fred   34
  Roles, Functions, and Training Levels for College Personnel Workers
  Guidance in Elementary Schools
  Guidance in the Junior High School
  Counseling and Accountability

Drakeford, John W.   35
  Psychology in Search of a Soul
  The Awesome Power of the Listening Ear
  Integrity Therapy
  Farewell to the Lonely Crowd

Dugan, Willis Edwin   37
  Counseling in the Modern Secondary School Program
  Counseling Points of View
  The Impact of NDEA upon Counselor Preparation

Ellis, Albert   39
  Reason and Emotion in Psychotherapy
  How to Prevent Your Child from Becoming a Neurotic Adult
  Sex Without Guilt

Erikson, Erik Homburger   41
  Childhood and Society
  Young Man Luther: A Study in Psychoanalysis and History
  Insight and Responsibility: Lectures on the Ethical Implications of Psychoanalytic Insight
  Gandhi's Truth: On the Origins of Militant Nonviolence
  In Search of Common Ground

CONTENTS

Eysenck, Hans Jurgen — 44
  Uses and Abuses of Psychology
  Sense and Nonsense in Psychology
  Behavior Therapy and the Neuroses
  Experiments in Behavior Therapy
  The Causes and Cures of Neurosis
  Encyclopedia of Psychology
Frankl, Viktor E. — 46
  The Doctor and the Soul: From Psychotherapy to Logotherapy
  Man's Search for Meaning: An Introduction to Logotherapy
  Psychotherapy and Existentialism: Selected Papers on Logotherapy
  The Will to Meaning: Foundations and Applications of Logotherapy
Freud, Sigmund — 49
  A General Introduction to Psychoanalysis
  New Introductory Lectures on Psychoanalysis
  Collected Papers
Fromm, Erich — 50
  Escape from Freedom
  Man for Himself
  Psychoanalysis and Religion
  The Sane Society
  The Art of Loving
  The Anatomy of Human Destructiveness
Gesell, Arnold Lucius — 54
  The First Five Years of Life: A Guide to the Study of the Preschool Child
  The Child from Five to Ten
  Developmental Diagnosis: Normal and Abnormal Child Development
  Youth: The Years from Ten to Sixteen
Glanz, Edward Coleman — 56
  An Introduction to Personal Adjustment
  The Freshman Psychology Courses as the Basis for a Student Personnel Program
  Developing a Research Program for Curriculum Validation
  Groups in Guidance

CONTENTS

Hall, G. Stanley 59
 Adolescence: Its Psychology and Its Relations to Physiology, Anthropology, Sociology, Sex, Crime, Religion, and Education
Hardee, Melvene Draheim 60
 Counseling and Guidance in General Education
 The Faculty in College Counseling
 The Sad Case of the Bigger Lost Sheep
 Faculty Advising in Contemporary Higher Education
Hatch, Raymond N. 62
 Guidance Services in the Elementary Schools
 Administration of Guidance Services: Organization, Supervision, Evaluation
 Guidance Services in the Secondary School
Hitchcock, Arthur Allen 63
 Can Teachers Make Accurate Estimates of Reading Ability
 Milestones in the Development of Personnel Services in Education
 Guidance
Hoppock, Robert 66
 Group Guidance: Principles, Techniques, and Evaluation
 Pretesting Equated Groups
 A Twenty-seven Year Follow-up on Job Satisfaction of Employed Adults
 Occupational Information
Horney, Karen 67
 The Neurotic Personality of Our Time
 New Ways in Psychoanalysis
 Self Analysis
 Our Inner Conflicts
 Neurosis and Human Growth
Hummel, Raymond Charles 70
 Vocational Development and Guidance Practice
 Ego-Counseling in Guidance: Concept and Method
James, William 71
 Principles of Psychology
 Talks to Teachers on Psychology: And to Students on Some of Life's Ideals

CONTENTS

    The Varieties of Religious Experiences: A Study in Human Nature
Jones, Arthur J.   73
    The National Picture of Pupil Personnel and Guidance Services in 1953
    Principles of Guidance
Jung, Carl Gustav   75
    Psychological Types
    Modern Man in Search of a Soul
    Psychology and Religion
    Psychological Reflections: An Anthology of the Writings of C. G. Jung
    The Collected Works of C. G. Jung
    Memories, Dreams, Reflections
Kitson, Harry Dexter   78
    How to Find the Right Vocation
    How to Use Your Mind
    I Find My Vocation
    Vocations for Boys
Korzybski, Alford Habdank   80
    Science and Sanity: An Introduction to Non-Aristotelian Systems and General Semantics
Krumboltz, John Dwight   81
    Learning and the Educational Process
    Revolution in Counseling: Implications of Behavioral Science
    Behavioral Counseling: Cases and Techniques
Lewin, Kurt   83
    A Dynamic Theory of Personality
    Principles of Topological Psychology
Lifton, Walter M.   85
    Group Classroom Techniques
    Can Teachers Serve as Counselors?
    Group Therapy in Educational Institutions
    The Role of the Teacher and the Instructor in the Guidance Program
    Automation and Counseling
    Working with Groups
Maslow, Abraham H.   87
    Principles of Abnormal Psychology: The Dynamics of Psychic Illness

CONTENTS

    Motivation and Personality
    New Knowledge in Human Values
    Toward a Psychology of Being
    Religions, Values, and Peak Experiences
Mathewson, Robert Hendry   90
    Educational Problems of Veterans—and Other Civilians
    Guidance Policy and Practice
    Provisions of Adult-Guidance Services
    Graduate Training for School Counselors
    General Guidance Counselor
    Evaluating a Program of Counselor Training Through Group Conferences
    Analysis of Unstructured Self-Appraisal: A Technique in Counselor Education
    Strategy for American Education
    Manpower or Persons?
Menninger, Karl A.   93
    Man Against Himself
    Love Against Hate
    The Human Mind
    A Psychiatrist's World: The Selected Papers of Karl Menninger
    The Vital Balance: The Life Process in Mental Health and Illness
Meyer, Adolf   96
    The Commonsense Psychiatry of Dr. Adolf Meyer: Fifty-two Selected Papers
Mowrer, O. Hobart   97
    Learning Theory and Personality Dynamics
    Psychotherapy Theory and Research
    The New Group Therapy
    Morality and Mental Health
Murphy, Gardner   100
    Experimental Social Psychology
    Personality: A Biosocial Approach to Origins and Structure
    Historical Introduction to Modern Psychology
    Human Potentialities
    Encounter with Reality
Murray, Henry Alexander   102

CONTENTS

Explorations in Personality
Manual of Thematic Apperception Test
Assessment of Men
Norris, Willa   105
  The Information Service in Guidance
  Occupational Information in the Elementary School
North, Robert Davidson   106
  Educational and Psychological Measurement
  Guidance Services
Oates, Wayne E.   108
  Religious Factors in Mental Illness
  Where to Go for Help
  The Religious Dimensions of Personality
Paterson, Donald Gildersleeve   110
  Use of New Type Examination Questions in Psychology
  Physique and Intellect
  The Measurement of Man
  Student Guidance Techniques
  The Conservation of Human Talent
Patterson, Cecil Holden   111
  A Guide for Counselors
  Counseling the Emotionally Disturbed
  Counseling and Psychotherapy: Theory and Practice
  Methods of Assessing the Vocational Adjustment Potential of the Mentally Handicapped
  Methodological Problems in Education
  Counseling: Vocational or Therapeutic? We Must Communicate Better with Our Guidance Colleagues
  Relationship Counseling and Psychotherapy
Pepinsky, Harold Brenner   114
  Counseling Theory and Practice
  Research on the Student in His Educational Setting
Porter, Elias Hull, Jr.   116
  An Introduction to Therapeutic Counseling
  On the Nature of Psychotherapeutic Interpretation
  Clients: Evaluations of Services at the University of Chicago Counseling Center

CONTENTS

Raimy, Victor Charles   117
  Training in Clinical Psychology
  Projective Pictures as Interview Devices
  Stimulus Functions of the Szondi Cards
Rank, Otto   119
  Art and Artist: Creative Urge and Personality
  Trauma of Birth
  Beyond Psychology
  Will Therapy and Truth and Reality
  Psychology and the Soul
Robinson, Francis Pleasant   122
  Effective Study
  Principles and Procedures in Student Counseling
  Psychology in Education
Roe, Anne   124
  A Rorschach Study of a Group of Scientists and Technicians
  New Light on Heredity: Adult Adjustment of Foster Home Children
  Psychological Examinations of Eminent Biologists
  A Psychological Study of Physical Scientists
  Group Rorschachs of University Faculties
  The Psychology of Occupations
  Graduate Education in Psychology
Roeber, Edward Charles   127
  Organization and Administration of Guidance Services
  Occupational Information
  Guidance and Counseling
  The School Counselor
Rogers, Carl Ransom   129
  Measuring Personality Adjustment in Children Nine to Thirteen
  The Processes of Therapy
  Electrically Recorded Interviews in Improving Psychotherapeutic Techniques
  Therapy in Guidance Clinics
  The Development of Insight in a Counseling Relationship
  A Teacher-Therapist Deals with a Handicapped Child
  Recent Research in Non-directive Therapy and Its Implications
  Significant Aspects of Client-Centered Therapy

CONTENTS

    Some Observations on the Organization of Personality
    Some Implications of Client-Centered Counseling for College Personnel Work
    The Role of Self Understanding in the Prediction of Behavior
    The Attitude and Orientation of the Counselor in Client-Centered Therapy
    A Basic Orientation for Counseling
    Client-Centered Therapy
    Communication: Its Blocking and Facilitation
    Personality Change in Psychotherapy
    The Necessary and Sufficient Conditions of Therapeutic Personality Change
    On Becoming a Person
Sanderson, Herbert Z.   135
    Norms for 'Shock' in the Rorschach
    Card Titles in Testing the Limits in Rorschach
    Basic Concepts in Vocational Guidance
Schaefer, Vernon George   137
    Industrial Organization
    Job Instruction
    Safety Supervision
Shartle, Carroll Leonard   138
    A Clinical Approach to Foremanship
    Fitting Workers to Jobs
    Developments in Occupational Classification
    Executive Performance and Leadership
    Occupational Information
Shertzer, Bruce E.   140
    Guidance: Techniques for Individual Appraisal and Development
    Fundamentals of Counseling
    Fundamentals of Guidance
    Careers in Counseling and Guidance
Shoben, Edward Joseph, Jr.   142
    The Psychology of Adjustment
    Viewpoints from Related Disciplines: Learning Theory
Skinner, Burrhus Frederic   144
    The Behavior of Organisms: An Experimental Analysis

CONTENTS

  Walden Two
  Science and Human Behavior
  Verbal Behavior
  Beyond Freedom and Dignity
Snygg, Donald   147
  Individual Behavior: A Perceptual Approach to Behavior
Stoops, Emory   148
  Principles and Practices in Guidance
  Guidance Services: Organization and Administration
Strong, Edward Kellogg, Jr.   149
  Introductory Psychology for Teachers
  Vocational Interest Blank Manual
  Vocational Interests of Men and Women
  Weighted Versus Unit Scales
  Ten-year Follow-up of Vocational Interest Scores of 1950 Medical College Seniors
Sullivan, Harry Stack   151
  Conception of Modern Psychiatry
  The Interpersonal Theory of Psychiatry
  The Psychiatric Interview
Super, Donald Edwin   154
  The Dynamics of Vocational Adjustment
  The Psychology of Careers
  Appraising Vocational Fitness
  Goal Specificity in the Vocational Counseling of Future College Students
Symonds, Percival Mallon   156
  The Dynamics of Human Adjustment
  Adolescent Fantasy: An Investigation of the Picture-Story Method of Personality Study
  The Ego and the Self
Thorne, Frederick Charles   158
  Critique of Recent Developments in Personality Counseling Theory
  An Operational Approach to the Diagnosis of Levels of Personality Integration or Psychopathology
  If Clinical Psychology Should Come of Age
Tiedeman, David Valentine   160

CONTENTS

Teacher Competence and Its Relation to Salary
Guidance: The Science of Purposeful Action Applied Through Education
Tolman, Edward Chase   161
   Purposive Behavior in Animals and Men
   Collected Papers in Psychology
Traxler, Arthur Edwin   162
   Guidance in Public Secondary Schools
   Case Study Procedures in Guidance
   Techniques of Guidance
Tyler, Leona Elizabeth   164
   Test and Measurements
   The Psychology of Human Differences
   The Work of the Counselor
Van Kaam, Adrian Leo   166
   The Art of Existential Counseling
   The Demon and the Dove: Personality Growth Through Literature
   The Emergent Self
Willey, Roy DeVerl   167
   Modern Methods and Techniques in Guidance
   Administration and Organization of the Guidance Program
   Guidance in Elementary Education
Williamson, Edmund Griffith   169
   How to Counsel Students
   Counseling and Discipline
   Counseling Adolescents
   Value Orientation in Counseling
   Student Personnel Work
Wrenn, Charles Gilbert   171
   Student Personnel Work in Colleges
   The Counselor in a Changing World
   The World of the Contemporary Counselor
Zeran, Franklin Royalton   173
   Life Adjustment Education in Action
   Guidance Services in Elementary Schools

ABOUT THE AUTHORS   175

Preface

Insights into Human Development is a unique collection of materials compiled and annotated over a period of fifteen years. We refer to them as insights primarily because they are self-styled impressions delicately blended into interpretations arrived at after considerable review. Although some of the commentaries may appear to be evaluations rather than constructive statements, it should be recognized that such a bias was never intended. The editing and styling of the materials took two years. This does not mean that the presentation is perfect, nor does it mean that the method used to introduce the material is best. What it does mean is that we have simply elected to share with readers—who are interested in psychotherapy, research, psychology, social work, religious counseling, or any other area of the behavioral sciences—resource materials that can expedite their work and enhance their understanding.

The usefulness of such a book, though not easily defined before the fact, will be in the contributions it makes to both lay and professional groups who study the behavioral sciences. At its best it will help such people to locate concise, complete, and accurate information in the shortest time possible. At worst, it will suffer from the same deficiencies so obvious in encyclopedias and other resource materials, which do not carry all the information you may want. It should be remembered, however, that the selection of this material was based on the personal bent of the authors and that each contribution was viewed in terms of breadth, literary appeal, content diversification, ease of styling, and organizational sophistication. Since the book is not a who's who in the behavioral sciences, all contributors in the field were not included. In fairness to those who weren't, it must be said that the final selection was personal and based primarily on the criteria listed for selection. When a contributor has failed to be included, it means only that we felt other materials were more important. When a contributor has been included, it means only that we both agreed that what he did was interesting, inspirational, innovative, and/or creative. Actually, the recency and the extensiveness of the material have little to do with our impressions of these contributors. Some who are included modified their theories or

PREFACE

conceptualizations very little over their productive years; others are more diversified. Throughout all of their contributions, however, there is a theme of understanding that makes them truly unique. Obviously, a reader cannot make a choice of materials unless he knows what materials are available. The value of this book is that it offers the reader, *i.e.*, the busy researcher, scholar, or behavioral scientist, the opportunity to gain a quick overview of a vast area of information. Except for the dictionary and the encyclopedia, there are few resource materials providing such a service. Within the behavioral sciences such a resource, until now, was simply not available.

KENNETH URIAL GUTSCH
LARRY L. THORNTON

Acknowledgments

A resource book such as this could not have been produced without drawing, directly or indirectly, upon a multitude of writers. We feel a deep sense of gratitude and express here a blanket appreciation to the eighty-one authors whose publications made such a manuscript possible. We include, also, our thanks to writers of secondary sources, who provided much factual data.

Many typists at Delta State University and the University of Southern Mississippi spent hours in the revisions of this manuscript over the last ten years. All their names are not known, but we do mention, to symbolize our gratitude to all of them, Sheron Carpenter Coats and Diane Peets Selby, who typed the last major drafts.

Very special thanks go to Delta State University, the sponsoring institution for this book, the members of its press committee, and to Barney McKee, director of the University Press of Mississippi. Their cooperation in working out necessary details proved to be nothing less than super.

A final note of gratitude is expressed to Marie G. Carmichael, whose final editing of the book for the University Press of Mississippi added to its overall improvement. It is amazing how a completed manuscript still includes minor errors unseen by the authors but clearly seen by a professional editor.

Although these helpful persons contributed to the final draft, we assume full responsibility for any inaccuracies and "honest errors" that remain. Some decisions became difficult to make when we found disagreement in specific information, such as dates and places. When no other option became available, we chose the primary source over secondary ones, especially in those cases when the author has been deceased for a long time.

Insights into Human Development: Commentaries

Adler, Alfred

BIRTH: February 7, 1870, Vienna, Austria
PRESENT STATUS: deceased; May 28, 1937, Aberdeen, Scotland
BACKGROUND: *Educational* M.D., University of Vienna, 1895
Professional physician, Vienna General Hospital and Polyclinic, 1895-97; private practice, general practitioner and nerve specialist, 1897-1927; founder, *Journal of Individual Psychology*, 1914; attached to Austrian army in Vienna and Krakow, 1914-18; organized the first child guidance center in Vienna, 1919; lecturer, Pedigogical Institute of Vienna, 1924; lecturer, Columbia University, New York City, 1927; clinical director, Mariahilfer Ambulatorium, Vienna, 1928; visiting professor of medical psychology, Long Island College of Medicine, New York, 1932; founder, *Journal of Individual Psychology* in the United States, 1935; practicing psychiatrist and professor of medical psychology, Long Island College, 1935-37
Field of Work founder of the school of individual psychology
Affiliations Vienna Psychoanalytic Society, Society for Free Psychoanalytic Research, Society for Individual Psychology

SUMMATION OF CONCEPTS:

As the founder of the school of individual psychology, Adler directed most of his writings toward the idea that human beings are not dominated by irrational instincts operating on an unconscious level but rather by a conscious drive to express and fulfill themselves as unique individuals. Personality is determined as one reaches out toward goals. It is then that one struggles with feelings of superiority and inferiority and ultimately forms his "life-style." Normal development concerns itself with striving for the common good of all human beings, whereas unhealthy and/or neurotic behavior results when one aims toward selfish interests rather than social interests.

ANNOTATED BIBLIOGRAPHY:

Adler, Alfred. *The Individual Psychology of Alfred Adler.* Edited and annotated by Heinz L. and Rowena R. Ansbacher. New York: Basic Books, 1956. 503 pp.

This is perhaps the most valuable book for a serious student of Adlerian psychology. The editors, by making a systematic presentation of the main body of Adler's writings, have put together the equivalent of a textbook on individual psychology. Included is a historical account of the fundamental differences that led to the separatism between Sigmund Freud and Adler. Excerpts were selected to show the development of Adler's thinking from 1907 to 1937, to present his views and methods of child guidance, and to state his thoughts on mental disorders, psychotherapy, and personality development. The editorial comments accompanying each selection of an Adlerian idea help to clarify the material.

_____. *Problems of Neurosis*. Edited by Philippi Mairet. Introduction by Heinz L. Ansbacher. New York: Harper Torchbooks, 1964. 180 pp.

A composite of thirty-seven case studies, this book presents a cross section of situations encountered during his years of practice. Emphasis is placed on the neurotic life-style, the family constellation, social feelings, and the goals of superiority—all-important aspects of the Adlerian philosophy. Interspersed in these case studies are Adler's personal comments relative to his therapeutic approach to neurosis.

_____. *Superiority and Social Interest*. Edited by Heinz L. and Rowena R. Ansbacher. Evanston: Northwestern University Press, 1964. 432 pp.

Another collection of Adler's writings, this work supplements *The Individual Psychology of Alfred Adler* and presents twenty-one papers that had not heretofore appeared in book form. Whereas the first book was aimed at showing the systematic development of Adlerian thought, this volume is a presentation of his approach and style. In essence, it becomes an in-depth reflection of the thought of the man one associates with the terms "will to power" and "inferiority complex." The book is a contribution in which Adler's thoughts become a more highly definitive part of his entire theoretical structure. Perhaps one of the most important concepts, that of striving, takes on a more profound meaning here, for it is seen as man's movement toward success by surmounting general difficulties rather than climbing over people. Adler saw this movement as a common good for all mankind.

GORDON WILLARD ALLPORT

Allport, Gordon Willard

BIRTH: November 11, 1897, Montezuma, Indiana

PRESENT STATUS: deceased; October 9, 1967, Cambridge, Massachusetts

BACKGROUND: *Educational* A.B., Harvard University, 1919; A.M., Harvard University, 1921; Ph.D., Harvard University, 1922; additional graduate studies as a Sheldon Traveling Fellow, Universities of Berlin and Hamburg (Germany), 1922-23, and Cambridge University (England), 1923-24

Professional instructor in English, Robert College, Istanbul, Turkey, 1919-20; instructor in social ethics, Harvard University, 1924-26; assistant professor in psychology, Dartmouth College, 1926-30; assistant professor of psychology, 1930-36, associate professor, 1936-42, professor, 1942-67, Harvard University

Field of Work psychological counseling, personality theory and development, group conflict and prejudice, and theories and processes of learning

Affiliations Fellow, American Psychological Association, Divisions of Personality and Social Psychology, the Society for the Psychological Study of Social Issues, and Maturity and Old Age (recipient of the Gold Medal award, 1963); Honorary Fellow, British Psychological Society; honorary member, Spanish and Italian psychological societies

SUMMATION OF CONCEPTS:

Most of Allport's writings reflect his desire to prevent the placement of premature limits upon the concept of man and his capacities for growth and development. He has, it seems, emphasized the importance of personal uniqueness, the delicate but potent interplay of expressive behavior in interaction, and the ordered thrust of individuals toward a more perfect definition of their major values. Throughout his writings, he has fought the cruder forms of behaviorism, trait psychology, and social determinism because each seems inadequate to deal with individuality. Further, he has opposed those gross positivisms that imply that individuals comprehend little more than the bare and unrelated externals of one another's behavior. To Allport, personality is not irreperably conditioned during the first three to five years of life and therefore is not adequately explained through psychoanalytic theories.

ANNOTATED BIBLIOGRAPHY:

Allport, Gordon Willard. *Personality: A Psychological Interpretation.* New York: Holt and Co., 1937. 588 pp.

After a brief outline of a number of historical approaches to the study of personality, Allport introduces concepts regarding the development of personality and new approaches to analyzing and understanding personality. Although he sees the individual as a whole person, his earlier contemporaries, the traditionalists of the time (1937), attempted to analyze certain behavior traits by measuring them and putting them together in the form of a psychograph. To Allport, this was of course an approach that needed considerable revision.

———. *The Nature of Prejudice*. Cambridge, Mass.: Addison-Wesley, 1954. 537 pp.

In this, one of Allport's earlier works, he reflects conditions of our modern age that have brought nations and people closer together and thus, in essence, established a frame of reference for the very existence of prejudice. He believes that, until recently, prejudice had a religious base, but that present-day prejudice appears to draw from such sources as economic exploitation, social structure, mores, fear, and aggression. Perhaps one of Allport's most knowledgeable statements regarding this area of prejudice is that "prejudice is a pattern of hostility in interpersonal relations which is directed against an entire group, or against its individual members; it fulfills a specific irrational function for its bearer."

———. *Becoming: Basic Considerations for a Psychology of Personality*. New Haven: Yale University Press, 1955. 106 pp.

Allport compares present-day theories of personality growth and change with the opposing views of John Locke and G. W. Leibnitz in an effort to point out the current dilemma of modern psychology. Lockean tradition pictures the mind as a *tabula rasa*, a mere passive recipient of stimuli and conditioning from the outside, whereas the Leibnitzian tradition sees the human mind as having an active, self-propelling center of its own. Allport reflects the position that a person is free to "become" and that such concepts as those by Freud and Adler—which state that the set pattern of pathological conditions of personality are established by the time a child is three to five years old—are not entirely correct and that the individual is not irreparably conditioned by that age.

———. *Personality and the Social Encounter*. Boston: Beacon Press, 1960. 386 pp.

This interestingly speculative group of essays explores the belief that personality is "both a self enclosed totality . . . and social in nature, wide open to the surrounding world." Allport deals here with such contemporary problems as race relations, the functions of social service and public health in our culture, the role of expectancy in relation to war, and areas for research in international relations. These essays are primarily valuable for the attention given to relevant psychic mechanism, but perhaps of less value in their appreciation of the relevant social structure. Although Allport offers no panacea for current social conflicts, he emphasizes that education and religion, mass media and legislation, child training and psychotherapy, in concert with other channels of human effort, must be followed if we are to produce a race of men who will seek their own salvation not at the expense of their fellowmen but in cooperation with them.

Anastasi, Anne

BIRTH: December 19, 1908, New York City

PRESENT STATUS: professor of Psychology, Fordham University

BACKGROUND: *Educational* A.B., Bernard College of Columbia University, 1928; Ph.D., Columbia University, 1930; honorary Litt.D., University of Windsor in Canada, 1967

Professional lecturer, Bernard College, 1929–30; instructor of psychology, Bernard College, 1930–39; assistant professor, Queens College of the City University of New York, 1939–46; associate professor, Fordham University, 1947–51; professor of psychology, Fordham University, 1951–; chairman of Psychology Department, Fordham University, 1968–74

Field of Work differential psychology, psychological testing, test construction, and statistical methodology

Affiliations Fellow, American Psychological Association (president, 1971–72), Divisions of General Psychology (president, 1956–57) and Evaluation and Measurement (president, 1965–66); Eastern Psychological Association (president, 1946–47); American Psychological Foundation (president, 1965–67); Psychometric Society; Phi Beta Kappa; Sigma Xi

SUMMATION OF CONCEPTS:

Anastasi's work reflects a devoted effort to contribute to the psychological study of individual differences. Most of her research is directed toward the development and use of tests for the measurement of a person's uniqueness. She believes that objective and quantitative data, such as factor analysis and similar statistical methods, provide a springboard to fulfill more completely the basic goals of differential psychology.

ANNE ANASTASI

ANNOTATED BIBLIOGRAPHY:

Anastasi, Anne. *Differential Psychology: Individual and Group Differences in Behavior.* 3rd rev. ed. New York: Macmillan Co., 1958. 664 pp.

A survey of the major areas within the domain of differential psychology, this is, in essence, an objective and quantitative investigation of individual differences. Attention is focused on the basic concepts of heredity and environment, sex differences, social class differences, and race differences. When dealing with the question of heredity and environment. the author concludes that the question is not an "either/or," but rather it is a "both/and" operation in which these two major factors of behavior are inextricably intertwined. A research finding of interest is that foster children perform above the level of expectancy; *i.e.*, they usually turn out better than what one might logically expect by looking at their family backgrounds.

_____. *Fields of Applied Psychology.* New York: McGraw-Hill Book Co., 1964. 621 pp.

Although much of her writing is in the area of differential psychology, here Anastasi has changed pace, moving to the area of applied psychology. By doing so, she presents a comprehensive picture of the professions within the field of psychology that seek to implement and/or apply psychological principles gained through research. Examples of these professions include counseling psychology, engineering psychology, consumer psychology, clinical psychology, and school psychology. In discussing clinical psychology, she explains clinical diagnosis, reviews various methods of therapy, and then focuses on the specialized research contributions in this field. Further, she explains the relationships between clinical and experimental psychology and between clinical and counseling psychology.

_____. *Individual Differences.* New York: John Wiley and Sons, 1965. 301 pp.

One of the trends in psychology has been toward presenting research in the form of a scholarly series. This book is one of a series of original works written for students in the behavioral sciences who are interested in a historical perspective of major themes and ideas in psychology. Anastasi seems the logical writer for a book of this nature and does much to place the psychological study of individual differences in historical perspective. Beginning with the early work of Francis Galton, James McKeen Cattell, and Alfred Binet, Anastasi's passages span nearly a century of research. Significant areas, such as quantitative research, behavior genetics, cultural deprivation, and the study of genius and creativity, are discussed.

———. *Psychological Testing.* 3rd rev. ed. New York: Macmillan Co., 1968. 665 pp.

This is recognized as one of the most comprehensive books in the area of psychological testing. Primarily a college textbook, it has also been designed for anyone seeking a broad view of current tests and testing problems. Anastasi clearly states in the preface that her major objective is to enable a student to evaluate any type of psychological test and to interpret test data correctly. This work could easily serve as a source book, for its content ranges from a historical overview of the history of testing to the social implications of test data, and it contains excellent descriptions of, and discussions about, the major psychometric instruments used in measuring mental ability, aptitude, personality, and interest.

Arbuckle, Dugald Sinclair

BIRTH: June 28, 1912, Estevan, Saskatchewan, Canada

PRESENT STATUS: director of counselor education and professor of education, Boston University

BACKGROUND: *Educational* B.Sc., University of Alberta, 1940; B.Ed., University of Alberta, 1942; Ph.D., University of Chicago, 1947

Professional teacher, Alberta schools, 1932-41; instructor, city of Edmonton and University of Alberta, 1941-43; educational officer, Royal Canadian Air Force, 1943-45; educational consultant, International Harvester Company, 1946-47; director of counselor education and professor of education, Boston University, 1947-; consultant and visiting professor, Washington State College, Central College of Washington, Brigham Young University, New York University, University of Hawaii, University of Texas, Oregon State University, Arizona State University, University of Southern California, and Harvard University

Field of Work counseling theory and practice, pupil personnel services, and philosophical psychology

Affiliations Fellow, American Psychological Association, Division of

DUGALD SINCLAIR ARBUCKLE

Counseling Psychology; American Personnel and Guidance Association (president, 1959); American College Personnel Association; Student Personnel Association for Teachers (president, 1955); Association for Counselor Education and Supervision; American Education Research Association

SUMMATION OF CONCEPTS:

To Arbuckle, guidance is seen as a pattern of services that should be made available to all students who desire such services. The individual is seen as a responsible person who has eminence in the counseling relationship. The author reflects a client-centered philosophy in which the keynote to understanding the client appears to be the establishment of a warm, accepting, and permissive atmosphere. He believes that the eclectic point of view, if this point of view is to exist at all, must be a reflection of the attitude held by the counselor who purports to use such an approach. To Arbuckle, certification may not be essential since counseling has gained professional status and can rest on its own merits. He feels that in counselor training more emphasis should be placed on the practical aspects of counseling.

ANNOTATED BIBLIOGRAPHY:

Arbuckle, Dugald S. *Student Personnel Services in Higher Education*. New York: McGraw-Hill Book Co., 1953. 352 pp.

Arbuckle introduces the idea that college administrators need to reexamine their student personnel programs in an effort to focus attention on the recipients of such services. He feels that many such programs have been initiated without due consideration to the qualifications of those responsible for these services. A portion of the book discusses orientation, vocational, counseling, religion, health, and housing services and student aid, *i.e.*, all components of the total student personnel program. Some space is also devoted to student activities that the author refers to as co-curricular activities. Here he places great emphasis upon student participation in planning and executing the student personnel program. The appendices suggest ways to successfully establish student personnel services within the college setting.

———. *Guidance and Counseling in the Classroom*. Boston: Allyn and Bacon, 1957. 397 pp.

Much of what the author says is based upon his own personal feelings and is relative to his own unique definitions. One position that he takes is that "the teacher *can* function as a counselor, in many modern schools he *is* functioning as a counselor, and if our children are to undergo the educational experiences that should be a part of their living in a democratic society, then he *must* function as a counselor." He attributes much of the success of the teacher to his personality and his professional teacher training. Some emphasis is placed on the client-centered approach, and much consideration is given to the need for organizing guidance activities so as to better acquaint the teacher with basic guidance principles.

_____. *Counseling: An Introduction.* Boston: Allyn and Bacon, 1961. 349 pp.

Arbuckle attempts to bring to the fore the various points of view of outstanding authorities regarding the role of the counselor. Through his own experiences and his understanding of that of others, he seeks to establish a pattern of traits that seem to be reflected by successful counselors. Arbuckle feels that a counselor is first an educator and that an understanding of the school setting is essential to effective counseling. He directs some of his attention toward counselor certification, ethics of the counselor, and the physical setting in which the counselor works. Arbuckle feels that, if counseling is to be accepted by those concerned with the educational community, a good communication system is necessary within the school and throughout the community.

_____. *Pupil Personnel Services in American Schools.* Boston: Allyn and Bacon, 1963. 417 pp.

In one of his most interesting books, Arbuckle discusses pupil personnel services and their relation to the total school setting. Great emphasis is placed on semantics, and distinctions are made among such terms as counseling, group counseling, group guidance, group therapy, and multiple counseling. He stresses the counseling continuum and brings forth points regarding the eclectic approach that are seldom if ever mentioned and many times overlooked.

_____. "The Self of the Counselor." *Personnel and Guidance Journal,* 44 (April, 1966), 807–12.

Arbuckle investigates the difficulty of self-examination by the counselor as it applies to the necessary empathic attitude exhibited in the counseling relationship. This empathy is equated to freedom in the relationship whereby the essential rudiments of openness, honesty, and genuineness must be observed prior to the development of counselor self-inspection and transference to the counselee's frame of reference.

_____. "Counselor, Social Worker, Psychologist." *Personnel and Guidance Journal*, 45 (February, 1967), 532–40.

A historical overview of the academic training, acknowledged areas of responsibility, and potential cooperation of the counselor, social worker, and psychologist is analyzed respective to a proposed "ecumenical movement" applied to the public school setting. Arbuckle cites lack of professional cooperation among the professions and proposes a mutual atmosphere of enlistment of services at the initiative of the school counselor.

_____. *Counseling: Philosophy, Theory, and Practice*. Boston: Allyn and Bacon, 1970. 445 pp.

Although Arbuckle's earlier contributions seem to lean toward an eclectic point of view, his position here appears to be more existential than anything else. His approach to counseling is introduced in four parts: Part One, "The Philosophy of Counseling"; Part Two, "The Counselor"; Part Three, "The Nature of Counseling"; and Part Four, "The Counseling Experience." It seems obvious from the preface that the book was intended for anyone interested in human relationships. However, the text itself seems more appropriate for counselors and, specifically, for those who practice as school counselors. Much of his attention is devoted to the lack of human relations between students and teachers. He feels that the school system shapes counselors, no matter how ambitious, into the mechanics of the system. As a result, the school remains an academic empire without a humanistic champion.

Axline, Virginia M.

BIRTH: unlisted

PRESENT STATUS: private practice and clinical professor, Department of Child Psychiatry, Ohio State University School of Medicine

BACKGROUND: *Educational* B.S., Ohio State University, 1931; M.A., Ohio State University, 1941; Ed.D., Columbia University Teachers College, 1950

Professional elementary schoolteacher, Columbus public schools, 1931–44; lecturer and clinician, 1942–44; research associate, University of Chicago,

VIRGINIA M. AXLINE

1944–48; visiting lecturer to associate professor, Columbia University, 1948–55; associate professor of educational psychology, New York University, 1955–58; associate professor, School of Medicine, New York University, 1958–60; director, Blind Child Research Project, New York University–Bellevue Institute of Physical Medicine and Rehabilitation, 1957–60; private practice, 1960–; clinical professor, Department of Child Psychiatry, Ohio State University School of Medicine, 1967–

Field of Work   group-centered play therapy, parent education, and research in child behavior with emphasis on handicapped children

Affiliations   American Psychological Association, Division of Psychological Aspects of Disability

SUMMATION OF CONCEPTS:

In play therapy, Axline uses what might be referred to today as a group-centered approach. She refers to it as nondirective play therapy and attempts, through using this technique, to create a permissive atmosphere in which the child grows and gains an understanding of himself and the world in which he lives. Axline believes that only as the child comes to know himself can he become a free individual.

ANNOTATED BIBLIOGRAPHY:

Axline, Virginia M. *Play Therapy: The Inner Dynamics of Childhood.* Boston: Houghton Mifflin Co., 1947. 379 pp.

This presents Axline's nondirective approach to play therapy and the theory of personality that serves as its basis. She describes the general working atmosphere to which the child is exposed and makes recommendations regarding this approach. A most interesting aspect is the presentation of ideas taken directly from the group therapy setting.

————. "Mental Deficiency: Symptom or Disease?" *Journal of Consulting Psychology,* 13 (October, 1949), 313–27.

Perhaps one of the most interesting studies done in the exploration of intelligence, this study seems to reflect the influence of emotional constraint upon test performance. The study involved fifteen children who were given intelligence tests before and after play therapy. Results indicated that one-third of the group displayed a large increase in scores.

————. "Play Therapy Experiences as Described by Child Participants." *Journal of Consulting Psychology,* 14 (February, 1950), 53–60.

This article is based on an analysis of the remarks made by children during and after play therapy. It appears to show their insight into better self-understanding, how such insights emerge, and how these self-understandings assist in bringing about emotional control.

Beers, Clifford Whittingham

BIRTH: March 30, 1876, New Haven, Connecticut
PRESENT STATUS: deceased; July 9, 1943, Providence, Rhode Island
BACKGROUND: *Educational* Ph.B., Yale University, 1897; honorary M.A., Yale University, 1922
Professional worked in a tax collector's office and with a life insurance company, 1897–1900; suffered from a mental disorder (diagnosed as a manic-depressive reaction) and attempted suicide by jumping from a fourth-floor bedroom window, 1900; institutionalized in mental hospitals, 1900–03; returned to business life in New York City and began a vigorous crusade for reform in the treatment of the mentally ill, 1904–06; published his remarkable autobiography, *A Mind That Found Itself*, 1908; founder, Connecticut Society of Mental Hygiene, 1908; founder, National Committee for Mental Hygiene, 1909; secretary, National Committee for Mental Hygiene, 1909–39; founder and secretary, American Foundation for Mental Hygiene, 1928–43; organized and became secretary-general, first International Congress on Mental Hygiene, 1930; founder and general secretary, International Committee for Mental Hygiene, 1930; founder and secretary, International Foundation for Mental Hygiene
Field of Work founder of the mental hygiene movement in the United States
Affiliations National Institute of Social Sciences (awarded the highest honor, the Gold Medal, for distinguished services for the benefit of mankind in 1933); honorary memberships in the American Psychiatric Association, the American Orthopsychiatric Association, and the British National Council for Mental Hygiene; awarded the Cross of Chevalier of Legion of Honor by the French government in 1933 in recognition of international work in mental hygiene

SUMMATION OF CONCEPTS:

As founder of the mental hygiene movement in America, Beers engaged in a personal crusade against the inhuman treatment of the mentally ill. Although his only major work, *A Mind That Found Itself*, is historically viewed as a literary classic in content and composition, it was Beers's own life experiences that gave irreproachable proof that a patient could recover from a severe mental illness and make a positive contribution to his society. Beers held firmly that mental illness is not a sin but a sickness that is treatable, often curable, and possibly preventable. He placed much emphasis on improving institutional conditions and insisted that methods of physical punishment used to control mental patients minimized their chances for recovery, for he believed that the insane's greatest need was friendship. His greatest emphasis was on changing the public's attitude toward mental illness, bringing about institutional reform, and stimulating greater interest in prevention. This he attempted through a national movement to inform the American public of the nature and prevention of mental illness.

ANNOTATED BIBLIOGRAPHY:

Beers, Clifford W. A *Mind That Found Itself: An Autobiography.* Garden City: Doubleday, Doran, and Co., 1945. 402 pp.

In this compilation of his experiences as a patient in several mental institutions, Beers shares those desultory life patterns during which he moved from the role of a patient to a truly great leader in the mental hygiene movement. He describes the inhuman treatment and physical conditions under which the mentally ill lived and shows how the doors of a mental institution may potentially swing out as well as in. The epilogue of 150 pages includes supplementary materials that provide the details of the founding of the national and international committees for mental hygiene and the American Foundation for Mental Hygiene. Letters to Beers from such notables as William James, Adolf Meyer, and Booth Tarkington are presented as examples of the interest shown in this movement by significant and influential Americans.

Berdie, Ralph Freimuth

BIRTH: June 21, 1916, Chicago, Illinois
PRESENT STATUS: deceased; August 21, 1974, St. Paul, Minnesota
BACKGROUND: *Educational* B.A., University of Minnesota, 1938; M.A., University of Minnesota, 1939; Ph.D., University of Minnesota, 1942
Professional assistant to the director of the Testing Bureau, University of Minnesota, 1941–42; counselor and assistant professor of psychology, University of Minnesota, 1942–43; psychologist, United States Naval Reserve, 1943–46; associate professor of psychology, George Peabody College, 1946–47; director, Student Counseling Bureau, University of Minnesota, 1947–66; from

associate professor to professor of psychology, University of Minnesota, 1947–74; Fulbright Resident Fellow to Australia, 1956–62; director, Student Life Studies, University of Minnesota, 1966–74

Field of Work counseling psychology, student personnel work, psychometrics, and the impact of higher education

Affiliations Fellow, American Psychological Association, Divisions of Evaluation and Measurement, Educational Psychology, and Counseling Psychology (president, 1958–59); American Personnel and Guidance Association (president, 1970–71); American College Personnel Association (president, 1965–66); Phi Beta Kappa; Phi Delta Kappa

SUMMATION OF CONCEPTS:

Berdie's basic concept of student counseling is concerned with the process of identifying students with varying potentials and increasing the probability of each student's obtaining the training most appropriate for him. He has also given consideration to conditions that result in a student's formulating a given plan.

ANNOTATED BIBLIOGRAPHY:

Berdie, Ralph Freimuth, ed. "A Training Program in Counseling." *American Psychologist*, 5 (May, 1950), 140–42.

This is devoted to the objectives of counseling courses taught by staff members of the Student Counseling Bureau at the University of Minnesota and is a result of ten years of evaluation. In each course the instructor seeks to provide: (1) knowledge of the educational and sociological side of counseling; (2) experience with occupational information materials; (3) observation of counseling done by experienced staff members; (4) critical analysis of observed counseling interviews; (5) supervised practice in counseling; (6) group and individual discussion of practice work; (7) discussions of case histories illustrating the dynamics of behavior; and (8) clarification of the philosophy of counseling. Students devote half their time to library work and half to laboratory training. Each student is expected to carry out at least fifty supervised interviews before completing the course. Emphasis is placed on a discussion of the tests and prediction batteries that are used at the University of Minnesota; and each student participates in at least one role-playing situation, followed by comments, suggestions, and criticisms from instructors and students in the class. Staff members present cases illustrating the comprehensive, longitudinal counseling approach used in actual counseling situations, and graduate students are then asked to present their own cases.

———. "Counselor Attitude." *Education and Psychology Measurement*, 11 (1951), 349–54.

This article is directed toward understanding the significance of the counselor's attitudes toward clients. It is interesting to note that Berdie promotes the idea that behavior observed in a counseling interview is an expression of the counselor's attitude as perceived by the counselee and of the counselee's attitude as perceived by the counselor. When one considers how some clients, perhaps grossly mishandled by therapeutic techniques, respond favorably to counseling interviews, it seems apparent that this effectiveness may be the result of factors not related to counseling but rather to the way in which the counselee perceives the counselor as a person who offers assistance and understanding.

———. *Roles and Relationships in Counseling*. Minnesota Studies in Student Personnel Work, No. 3. Minneapolis: University of Minnesota Press, 1953.

Consisting of three papers presented at the Second Annual Conference of Administrators of College and University Counseling Programs, this publication provides information about such semantically challenging areas as clinical psychology, counseling, and teaching. The report also exemplifies a phenomenon of our times—the development of new professional groups eager to provide experiences aimed at helping man.

———. "The State-Wide Testing Programs." *Personnel and Guidance Journal*, 32 (April, 1954), 454–59.

This describes statewide testing programs in forty states. The testing programs provided the basis for advisory services. The results served to assist students to find desirable types of training and faculty members to better understand students. Berdie feels that, when such information is provided by tests, the school is one step nearer meeting the needs of the students and each student is in position to make more effective use of the resources found in the school.

———. *After High School—What?* Minneapolis: University of Minnesota Press, 1954. 240 pp.

A report on the factors that condition the attendance or nonattendance at college of youths who would be able to profit from such an experience, this study attempts to determine why some high school students go on to college while others, equally qualified, drop out. It provides data on a number of circumstances that seem to be determining factors in planning for future high school seniors in Minnesota. Berdie has done much to point out that such factors as ability, high school achievement, age, sex, financial resources, paternal occupation, family background, nationality origin, religion, geography, extracurricular activities, and attitudes of students are important to final decisions. From a series of interviews with high school seniors, recurring themes and patterns have been found, which lead the author to form four hypotheses: (1) an inordinate waste of talent characterizes our educational system; (2) ecological factors are related to the waste of talent; (3) psychological factors are related to this waste of talent; and (4) both the economic and the cultural levels of the home are closely related to a child's plan for education after high school. The author concludes that the conditions that result in the formulation of a given plan by a student also tend to be those that determine the extent to which he is able to follow those plans.

———. "Counseling for Physically Disabled Students." *Journal of Higher Education*, 26 (December, 1955), 475–78.

Rehabilitation of physically disabled students is not the responsibility of the counselor alone. Berdie feels that counseling can do much to assist disabled students if the counselor who works with them has the necessary experience and utilizes those techniques that are essential to counseling disabled students.

———. "Improving Evaluation in Student Recruitment and Selection." *Personnel and Guidance Journal*, 34 (April, 1956), 481–86.

Berdie is concerned with evaluation relative to the worth of the individual for higher education. He feels that it is important for each student to receive appropriate training, regardless of how high or low his I.Q. score is. Recruitment and selection are continuous parts of the same process designed to identify students with varying potentials and thus help them to acquire the training most appropriate. It appears, at present, that the most consistent method of recruitment and selection is the student's previous record. Although other methods are used, it must be realized that no method is perfect and that considerable energy must be directed toward better selection methods.

---. "Some Principles and Problems of Selective College Admissions." *Journal of Higher Education,* 31 (April, 1960), 191–99.

Berdie deals here with the problem of selective admissions. He considers two questions that seem basic to the problem. The first concerns the kind and number of students to be admitted, the probable ratio of success of these students, and the effect of admissions on size of enrollment. The second question concerns values. The logic underlying selective admissions seems obvious, since it is a desire by colleges to admit students with the greatest potential for academic success. Although it is reasonably simple to raise and lower admission requirements, the immediate threat from such activity is that the requirements that eliminate poor students will also eliminate good students, thus making selective admissions a challenging problem for the researcher.

---, ed. *Who Goes to College?* Minnesota Studies in Student Personnel Work, No. 12. Minneapolis: University of Minnesota Press, 1962.

This study covers a long time span, focusing upon aptitudes and abilities of several generations of high school and college students. It provides a profound background of information for counselors and administrators who seek to assist students interested in higher education. Berdie applies his psychological knowledge to the field of education in an effort to compare college aptitude test scores, high school percentile ranks, and scores on English tests over a period of thirty years. The results show that there is no tendency for college freshmen to be more capable academically than the freshmen of earlier years. In essence, Berdie seems to feel that the intellectual ability of the Minnesota college students at the time of this study was no different from what it had been thirty years before.

---. "The Movement of Men." *Teachers College Record,* 66 (November, 1964), 113–22.

This article traces the rise in the application of objective measurement techniques consistent with the changing educational and occupational posture of our society. Much consideration is given to the decisions made from objective measurement. Arguments over the pros and cons of personality and intelligence testing are introduced, with some focus of attention not only on the problems involved with test design but also on the men who are to be measured.

---. "Strong Vocational Interest Blank Scores of High School

Seniors and Their Later Occupational Entry." *Journal of Applied Psychology*, 49 (June, 1965), 188-93.

To study the predictive validity of the SVIB, a sample was taken that consisted of 130 university graduates who had received degrees in dentistry, mechanical engineering, architecture, or journalism and who had taken the SVIB while seniors in high school. Interest scores and profiles for the four groups were compared at preprofessional and professional time periods, and comparisons were made between each of these four groups and three groups studied earlier. The SVIB scores for each of the groups of university graduates tended to parallel stated interests when members of these groups were high school seniors. The comparative analysis revealed that SVIB scores and later occupational choices were statistically significant.

Berne, Eric Lennard

BIRTH: May 10, 1910, Montreal, Canada

PRESENT STATUS: deceased; July 15, 1970, San Francisco, California

BACKGROUND: *Educational* B.A., McGill University, 1931; M.D., C.M. (master in surgery), McGill University, 1935; student, New York City Psychoanalytic Institute, 1941-43; student, San Francisco Psychoanalytic Institute, 1947-56

Professional intern, Yale Psychiatric Clinic, 1936-38; private practice, New York City and Norwalk, Connecticut, 1940-43; served in Medical Corps, United States Army, 1943-46; private practice, San Francisco and Carmel, California, 1946-70; adjunct psychiatrist, Mount Zion Hospital, San Francisco, 1952-70; consultant to surgeon general, U.S. Army, 1951-56; lecturer on psychiatry, University of California Medical School, 1960-70; consultant in group therapy, McAuley Clinic, San Francisco, 1962-70

Field of Work originated the concept of transactional analysis, an approach to group psychotherapy

Affiliations diplomate, American Board of Psychiatry and Neurology; Fellow, American Psychiatric Association; chairman of the board, International Transactional Analysis Association; American Medical Association

SUMMATION OF CONCEPTS:

Through transactional analysis, a form of psychotherapy, most of Berne's work reflects an endless effort on his part to explain personality in terms of the ego states that lie behind social responses. In very simplified form, Berne suggests that in all social interactions, called transactions, one responds as a Parent, an Adult, or a Child (PAC). In therapy each participant is made aware of the PAC responses he makes that tend to reveal his attitudes and inner feelings. This theory attempts to explain the psychology of human relationships, hypothesizing that all transactions between persons, whether they are constructive or destructive, reflect these inner relationships. Berne believes that the simplicity of this approach provides an avenue of perception wherein an individual may gain deep insight into the "root" thoughts and feelings that produce the fruits of behavior.

ANNOTATED BIBLIOGRAPHY:

Berne, Eric. *Transactional Analysis in Psychotherapy: A Systematic Individual and Social Psychiatry.* New York: Grove Press, 1961. 320 pp.

The term "transactional analysis" was described initially in 1956. (Read Eric Berne, "Ego States in Psychotherapy," *American Journal of Psychotherapy.* 11 [1957], 293-309. This volume contains the clinical and theoretical material upon which transactional analysis is based as well as a fine-line distinction between it and Freudian, neo-Freudian, Jungian, or Adlerian systems. Transactional analysis has as its goal the establishment of open and authentic communication between the emotional and intellectual dimensions of the personality.

_____. *Games People Play: The Psychology of Human Relationships.* New York: Grove Press, 1964. 192 pp.

Eric Berne's *Games People Play* and David Reuben's *Everything You Always Wanted to Know About Sex** (1969) are isolated examples of popular books written by psychiatrists that made and remained on the best-seller list for an extended period. *Games* attempts to reveal in simple, lay terminology some basic insights into a practical understanding of human behavior. The theory for the analysis and clear understanding of the games is summarized, followed by descriptions of the individual games. The thesaurus of games includes marital games, party games, and sexual games.

_____. *Principles of Group Treatment.* New York: Oxford University Press, 1966. 379 pp.

Based on many years of personal experience, this book captures Berne's feelings about group settings, supervision of groups, and the advisement and training of other group therapists. Berne prefers the term "group treatment" to group therapy. He carefully delineates and clarifies differences among supportive therapy, psychoanalytic therapy, group-analytic therapy, and transactional analysis. Much of the material has been introduced in Berne's earlier works.

Bingham, Walter Van Dyke

BIRTH: October 20, 1880, Swan Lake City, Iowa
PRESENT STATUS: deceased; July 8, 1952, Washington, D.C.
BACKGROUND: *Educational* attended the University of Kansas, 1897–98; B.A., Beloit College, 1901; attended University of Chicago, 1905–06, and the University of Berlin, 1907; M.A., Harvard University, 1907; Ph.D., University of Chicago, 1908; awarded S.C.D. (honorary) degrees from Beloit College, 1929, and Illinois Wesleyan University, 1950

Professional associate in the Psychology Department, University of Chicago, 1906–07; instructor in educational psychology and assistant to E. L. Thorndike, Columbia University Teachers College, 1908–10; assistant professor of psychology, Dartmouth College, 1910–15; professor of psychology and head of the Division of Applied Psychology, Carnegie Institute of Technology, 1915–24; executive secretary, Committee on Classification of Personnel in the U.S. Army, 1917–18; lieutenant colonel, Personnel Branch of the General Staff, U.S. Army, 1918–19 (during World War I, he became part of a committee of seven to prepare the first group psychological tests for army use, *i.e.*, the army alpha and beta tests); chairman, Division of Anthropology and Psychology for the National Research Council, 1919–20; director, Personnel Research Federation, Inc., 1924–34; president of the board, the Psychological Corporation, 1926–28; professorial lecturer in psychology, Stevens Institute of Technology, 1930–40; consultant, Occupational Information Service, U.S. Office of Education, 1938–39; chief psychologist, Adjutant General's Office, War Department, 1940–47 (during this period, he assisted in the development of the army's general classification test); consultant, 1947–52

Field of Work occupational psychology with a strong emphasis on psychological measurement and evaluation

Affiliations Fellow, American Psychological Association, Division of Measurement and Evaluation; American Association of Applied Psychology (president, 1941); Psychometric Society; International Musical Society; Phi Beta Kappa; Sigma Xi

SUMMATION OF CONCEPTS:

Bingham directed his attention toward assisting well-adjusted persons to achieve to the best of their ability. His efforts were expended in designing tests to measure vocational aptitudes. He felt that such instruments might help individuals to adjust to the world of work.

ANNOTATED BIBLIOGRAPHY:

Bingham, Walter Van Dyke. *Aptitudes and Aptitude Testing.* New York: Harper and Brothers, Publishers, 1937. 390 pp.
This is an interesting presentation of early attempts at aptitude testing and the objectives of such a testing program. Bingham did much to help present-day psychometricians understand the problems involved in designing a test that will help people estimate their own potentials in making vocational selections. His early attempts in test construction had as a focus of attention the discovery of unsuspected talents, the discovery of alternative fields that would lend themselves well to the individual's present aptitudes, the discovery of strengths and weaknesses, and the discovery of "self" and the ability to relate this self to the world of work.

Bordin, Edward S.

BIRTH: November 7, 1913, Philadelphia, Pennsylvania

PRESENT STATUS: professor of psychology and chief of Counseling Division, Bureau of Psychological Services, University of Michigan

BACKGROUND: *Educational* A.B., Temple University, 1935; M.S., Temple University, 1937; Ph.D., Ohio State University, 1942

Professional administrative Fellow and assistant coordinator of Student Personnel Services, University of Minnesota, 1939–40; assistant to the director of the Testing Bureau, University of Minnesota, 1940–42; instructor and counselor, University of Minnesota, 1942–43; assistant professor and counselor, Student Counseling Service, University of Minnesota, 1943–44; civilian consultant, War Department, Washington, D.C., 1944–45; acting director, University Counseling Bureau, University of Minnesota, 1945–46; director of Student Counseling Center and associate professor of psychology, Washington State College, 1946–48; chief of the Counseling Division, University of Michigan, 1948–; director of the doctoral program in clinical psychology, University of Michigan, 1951–63; associate professor of psychology, 1948–55, and full professor, 1955–, University of Michigan; editor, *Journal of Consulting Psychology,* 1959–64

Field of Work research theory in counseling and psychotherapy, personality development with emphasis on the adolescent period, and the development of vocational interests

EDWARD S. BORDIN

Affiliations Fellow, American Psychological Association, Divisions of Evaluation and Measurement, Clinical Psychology, Counseling Psychology (president, 1955), and Community Psychology; American Association for the Advancement of Science

SUMMATION OF CONCEPTS:

Bordin believes that the ideas of man are relative to the setting from which they emerge. In essence, he believes that the seed of understanding lies in observation and that counselor training must include not only academic knowledge as absorbed from formal statements but also observation of therapeutic situations. Further, he feels that the premise from which an understanding of personality theory will eventually evolve will be relative to practical therapeutic experiences. This is to say that personality theory will depend upon facts brought out in therapy and that therapy will depend upon personality theory to examine and inculcate these findings from one generation to the next.

ANNOTATED BIBLIOGRAPHY:

Bordin, Edward S. "Counseling Points of View, Non-Directive and Others." In *Trends in Student Personnel Work*. Minneapolis: University of Minnesota Press, 1949. Pp. 120-29.

Bordin here enters the challenging area of semantics and entertains the idea that much confusion stems from the word *counseling*. The issues posed concern two basic questions that are considered major problems even today—namely, who is responsible in the counseling situation and at what level will the client respond within this setting? Bordin feels that the client-centered approach is more suitable for certain persons than for others. He believes that in the future counseling will best lend itself to the eclectic approach.

————. "Developments in Interviewing Techniques." In *Trends in Student Personnel Work*. Minneapolis: University of Minnesota Press, 1949. Pp. 105-13.

Perhaps one fairly consistent trend in interviewing during the past quarter century has been toward establishing new methods. This constant search for better methods seems to give impetus to the counseling movement in the United States and might well be one factor that has assisted in bringing counseling closer to the status of an applied science.

The article includes a discussion of research supporting the belief that counseling services are of value.

———. *Psychological Counseling.* New York: Appleton-Century-Crofts, 1955. 405 pp.

The author applies a unique approach to meeting the needs of the novice counselor. To accomplish this end, the book has been divided into three sections: (1) "Introduction to Psychological Counseling," (2) "Theoretical Foundations," and (3) "The Process of Psychological Counseling." The book has also been designed to give graduate students interested in counseling a more sophisticated look at the field. Bordin assumes that the reader will already have as a background a familiarity with the principles of psychology. Some discussion of recorded interviews is included and may well add great interest for any person interested in counseling.

———. "An Articulated Framework for Vocational Development." *Journal of Counseling Psychology,* 10 (Summer, 1963), 107–17.

The major current approaches to the problems of occupational choice are compared with regard to theories of personality, their structural characteristics, and their assumptions regarding the process of choice. Bordin proposes a new framework, which is a series of dimensions, traceable to infantile physiological functions, that will account for all of the gratifications that work can offer. It is then illustrated that any occupation can be described in terms of the relative strengths of these component dimensions and their relation to a series of modifying characteristics. The problems of finding the dimensions and the application of the theoretical framework to job analysis and other issues are discussed.

———. "True or False? Tests Tell the Story." *PTA Magazine,* 59 (January, 1965), 4–6.

Various areas of measurement are reviewed with respect to their effectiveness in measuring specific traits. I.Q. tests are viewed as measuring many in- and out-of-school experiences limited by specific perception of what traits actually compose intelligence. Ability testing is reported as measuring specific abilities related to the child's present and future vocational success. The nature of changing scores is investigated with the conclusion that the earlier the child is evaluated the greater the tendency of score change. Tests are seen as only part of the picture; the more information gained about the individual, the greater is the likelihood of accurately assessing the child's potential.

Borow, Henry

BIRTH: May 31, 1917, Philadelphia, Pennsylvania
PRESENT STATUS: professor of psychological studies, General College and College of Education, University of Minnesota
BACKGROUND: *Educational* B.A., Pennsylvania State University, 1939; M.S., Pennsylvania State University, 1942; Ph.D., Pennsylvania State University, 1945
Professional Personnel Research Division of the Engineering, Science, and Management War Training Program, Pennsylvania State University, 1942-44; instructor of psychology, Pennsylvania State University, 1944-46; civilian expert, U.S. Department of the Army, Japanese Universities Institute on Student Personnel Services, Japan, 1951-52; faculty, University of Minnesota, 1949-; professor of psychological studies, University of Minnesota, 1955-; research associate, Mann-Lincoln Institute of School Experimentation, Teachers College, Columbia University, 1959-60; lecturer, NDEA Counseling and Guidance Institutes, 1959-66; lecturer or visiting professor, eighteen universities and colleges throughout the United States
Field of Work vocational guidance, counseling psychology, and mental health
Affiliations American Personnel and Guidance Association; National Vocational Guidance Association (president, 1967-68); Fellow, American Psychological Association, Divisions of Counseling Psychology, Educational Psychology, and Evaluation and Measurement; American Men of Science; Phi Beta Kappa

SUMMATION OF CONCEPTS:

Most of Borow's work reflects an endless effort to help people master themselves and conduct their lives more humanely. Having the humanistic social philosophy that one should learn to stand on his own feet and master his own destiny in spite of limitations and barriers, Borow has focused on the area of occupational psychology and the attendant issues of career development to make that philosophy a reality. He views work as a way of life that needs the very best career planning possible. His concern is with helping the individual to develop a realistic appraisal of his abilities and interests. Work-related experiences and psychological testing assist in making this appraisal.

ANNOTATED BIBLIOGRAPHY:

Borow, Henry, and Robert V. Lindsey. *Vocational Planning for College Students: A Sequential Project Method.* Englewood Cliffs: Prentice-Hall, 1959. 186 pp.

The subtitle touches on its purpose. Essentially the book serves as a structured method of introducing an occupational course to students who want to explore the world of work and to make realistic plans for the future. As a philosophical basis for the exploration, the authors present three basic questions: (1) Who am I? (2) Where am I going? (3) How am I going to get there? They believe that achieving vocational independence is a major step toward a productive life. Emphasis is placed on understanding the world of work, understanding vocational interests, values, and aptitudes, recognizing human likenesses and differences, and exploring specific occupations. The authors conclude that an occupational choice is not something one solves at once. Rather, it is viewed as a continuing process.

―――, ed. *Man in a World of Work.* Boston: Houghton Mifflin Co., 1964. 606 pp.

This is a classic in the field of vocational guidance. The contributors are people who have committed themselves to implementing the guidance philosophy. Persons such as Donald Super, Anne Roe, C. Gilbert Wrenn, and others offer a wealth of experience to the student who is seeking an understanding of occupational behavior and the research that supports such understanding. With a continuity seldom found in a compilation of separate articles, this book reflects the historical and philosophical foundations of vocational guidance and the meaning of human work experiences.

―――. "The Adolescent in the World of Work." In James F. Adams, ed. *Understanding Adolescents: Current Developments in Adolescent Psychology.* Boston: Allyn and Bacon, 1968. Pp. 337–60.

In capsule form Borow looks at the impact of work on the contemporary American teen-ager. Discussion centers on some of the basic concepts of career development, the theories of vocational choice, and the occupational outlook for youth. Borow discusses the motives underlying vocational choice and cites the work of Morris Rosenberg, who has identified helping people, earning extrinsic rewards, and self-expression as the three value systems around which vocational decisions tend to cluster. Borow feels that one of the counselor's major functions is to assist the student in making a realistic occupational choice.

———, ed. *Career Guidance for a New Age.* Boston: Houghton Mifflin Co., 1973. 348 pp.

As always, Henry Borow does an excellent job of bringing together some information that should be highly significant to career counselors. He attempts here to draw from the past, examine the present, and look toward the future. To do this, he covers both the philosophy of work and its implications for counseling. Contributors include such distinguished authors as Gilbert Wrenn, John Krumboltz, Donald Super, and Donald Blocher. Although each contribution stands by itself, Borow creates a continuity between contributions by introductory commentaries, which add cohesiveness to the entire book. As a collection of well-written articles related to career guidance, the book should serve a variety of specialists who work in that area.

Cattell, Raymond B.

BIRTH: March 20, 1905, West Bromwich, Staffordshire, England

PRESENT STATUS: research professor of psychology, emeritus, University of Illinois (Urbana), and director, Institute of Personality and Ability Testing

BACKGROUND: *Educational* B.S., King's College, University of London, 1924; Ph.D., University of London, 1929; M.A., University of London, 1931; D.Sc., University of London, 1939

Professional lecturer, University College of the South West, Exeter, England, 1927–32; director, City of Leicester Child Guidance Clinic, 1932–37; research associate to E. L. Thorndike, Teachers College, Columbia University, 1937–38; G. Stanley Hall Professor of Genetic Psychology, Clark University, 1938–41; lecturer and Fellow, Harvard University, 1941–44; civilian consultant on personnel research, Adjutant General's Office of the War Department, 1944–45; research professor in psychology and now professor emeritus, University of Illinois, 1945–; chief consultant, Institute of Personality and Ability Testing, 1948–73; director, 1973–

Field of Work factor analysis of personality, measurement of motivation, group and cultural behavior pattern analysis, and statistical methodology

Affiliations Sigma Xi; British Psychological Society; Eugenics Society; Human Genetics Society; American Psychological Association, Division of Personality and Social Psychology; awarded Darwin Research Fellowship, 1935

RAYMOND B. CATTELL

SUMMATION OF CONCEPTS:

Dedicated to the idea that human motivation and personality can be studied through the use of quantitative, mathematical, and multivariate experimental methods, Cattell has committed most of his efforts to analyzing personality characteristics into surface and source traits. "Factor analysis" has been used primarily as a means of discovering source traits of personality, and "cluster (correlation) analysis" has been used in finding a set of surface traits. His investigations are similar to the work of H. J. Eysenck in that both use mathematical models for analyzing personality components. His position also resembles that of Gordon Allport in that both of their personality theories may be accurately labeled trait theories. Surface traits are defined as the clusters of observable, behavioral events. Source traits are classified as the deep, genuine influences that help guide, direct, determine, and explain human behavior. These latter traits are, in Cattell's opinion, the more important. Cattell's investigations have resulted in the development of several personality questionnaires for various age levels, *e.g.*, the Sixteen Personality Questionnaire (16 PF), the High School Personality Questionnaire (HSPQ), the Early School Personality Questionnaire (ESPQ), and the Children's Personality Questionnaire (CPQ). These and other standardized instruments developed by the Institute of Personality and Ability Testing are designed to enable students of human behavior to explore personality theory and the idea of human behavior in given situations.

ANNOTATED BIBLIOGRAPHY:

Cattell, Raymond B. *Personality and Motivation Structure and Measurement.* New York: World Book Co., 1957. 948 pp.

This is a survey of the development and progress of personality-oriented research based on factor-analytic techniques. Cattell's stated purpose is to integrate for the busy professor and student the results of fragmentary and widely scattered research in the field of personality assessment. His discussions focus on (a) basic principles of personality research, (b) present knowledge of personality source-trait structures, (c) formal models and the theoretical integration of structured measurement, (d) the measurement of attitudes, motivation, and conflict adjustment, (e) personality change, and (f) resultant new test techniques in clinical, educational, and industrial psychology. An impressive appendix presents research in the recognition and summarization of both surface and source traits.

──────, and Frank W. Warburton. *Objective Personality and Motivation Tests: A Theoretical Introduction and Practical Compendium.* Chicago: University of Illinois Press, 1967. 687 pp.

This is a resource book designed primarily as a reference for students seeking more sophisticated insight into the theoretical structure of personality testing. Drawing from the knowledge of many persons trained in this area, the beginning student of psychometrics may find the work irrelevant for his immediate needs. One interesting inclusion in this volume is a listing of 612 personality tests from which 2,364 variables have been derived.

──────. *Abilities: Their Structure, Growth, and Action.* Boston: Houghton Mifflin Co., 1971. 608 pp.

Included here is a sociological and historical appraisal of the role of abilities in group settings. Abstract theories are applied to practical areas of intelligence and ability testing. Cattell clearly discusses his theory of fluid and crystallized intelligence. The chapters are divided into sections, each of which may serve as a self-contained teaching unit. An interesting study is related to investigating the myths and facts associated with genius and creativity.

Coleman, William E.

BIRTH: May 30, 1921, Utica, New York

PRESENT STATUS: president of Coleman and Associates; industrial consultant and university lecturer

BACKGROUND: *Educational* B.A., Ohio State University, 1942; M.A., Ohio State University, 1946; Ph.D., Ohio State University, 1949

Professional teaching assistant and counselor, Ohio State University, 1946–47; instructor, University of Tennessee, 1947–49; coordinator of guidance and assistant professor, University of Tennessee, 1949–51; director of testing and guidance, University of Tennessee, 1951–56; social scientist, Rand Corporation, 1958–60; visiting lecturer, University of Wisconsin, 1960; director of psychological services, Ward J. Jenssen, Inc., 1960–61; consultant in measurement, Houghton Mifflin Company, 1957–63; vice-president, Trans-Pacific Management Service, 1961–63; lecturer, UCLA Extension, 1962–; vocational

consultant, Social Security Administration, 1963–; consultant, U.S. Department of Labor, 1964–; president, Coleman and Associates, 1963–
  Field of Work educational and psychological measurement, industrial psychology, and counseling techniques
  Affiliations Fellow, American Psychological Association, Divisions of Counseling Psychology and Evaluation and Measurement; American Personnel and Guidance Association; National Employment Counselors Association; National Vocational Guidance Association; American Educational Research Association

SUMMATION OF CONCEPTS:

Coleman is an experimenter who believes in using scientific investigation in education. One of his most interesting ideas is his belief that the intellectual factors and emotional factors cannot be dichotomized. He implies a need for counselors to remain cognizant of emotional dimensions even though they are dealing with clients who appear to have an educational or vocational problem. Coleman introduces the concept that guidance is designed to provide an environment in which the child can develop into a socially desirable, personally happy, and completely wholesome individual. It is in such an environment that the person is encouraged to develop traits of self-direction, self-control, and self-appraisal and can thus avoid the stigma of being told what to do and how to do it. He implies that general faculty counseling is more desirable than the centralization of student personnel services and that the decentralized approach can be introduced through in-service training programs designed to collect and utilize information about children. Coleman also emphasizes the need for better evaluative techniques and a guidance point of view. He believes that learning, discipline, and pupil-teacher relations might best be handled in terms of the attitudes of teachers and that the total guidance program will depend on the extent to which faculty members can accept students.

ANNOTATED BIBLIOGRAPHY:

Coleman, William. "Motivating Factors in In-Service Training of Faculty Counselors." *Educational and Psychological Measurement*, 11 (1951), 747–51.
  Coleman presents the idea that a decentralized plan of student personnel services on university and college campuses seems to be a forthcoming trend. He feels that, if such a trend is to be effective, staff

members must be oriented in the area of student personnel services through such means as staff meetings and case conferences.

_____. "Basic Steps in Developing a Guidance Program." *Clearing House*, 26 (April, 1952), 474–79.

Coleman introduces the steps that he considers necessary for initiating guidance services in the secondary school. He presumes that such steps will eventually lead to a sound guidance program based on student needs and realistic objectives.

_____. "Susceptibility of the Minnesota Teachers Attitude Inventory to 'Faking' with Experienced Teachers." *Educational Administration and Supervision*, 40 (April, 1954), 234–37.

An interesting study, this research is concerned with the Minnesota Teacher Attitude Inventory, which was administered to seventy-six elementary and secondary teachers in an effort to determine if experienced teachers could make better scores by faking. The inventory was administered twice, the first time with standard instructions and the second time, five to seven days later, with modified instructions requiring that teachers answer the questions as administrators might in a school system having a pupil-centered point of view. The score obtained in the readministration differed from the first at the .01 level of significance.

_____. "Some Criteria for Evaluating Elementary School Guidance Services." *Elementary School Journal*, 55 (September, 1954), 247–48.

Coleman introduces some criteria that appear suitable for the self-evaluation of a guidance program at the elementary school level. These criteria are presented in the form of a questionnaire and are to be answered by faculty members, administrators, or observers.

_____, and Edward E. Cureton. "Intelligence and Achievement: The 'Jangle Fallacy' Again." *Educational and Psychological Measurement*, 14 (1954), 347–51.

This article is the result of a study that closely parallels a previous one by T. L. Kelley. The design of the research was to determine the overlap between group intelligence tests and school achievement tests. Used were the Otis Quick-Scoring Test Beta, Forms CM and DM, and the word meaning, paragraph meaning, and arithmetic computation subtests of the Stanford Achievement Test, Forms DM and EM. The study indicates a 95 percent overlap between one test of verbal intelligence and specific subtests of achievement.

———, and A. W. Ward. "Comparison of Davis-Eells and Kuhlmann-Finch Scores of Children from High and Low Socio-Economic Status." *Journal of Educational Psychology,* 46 (December, 1955), 465–69.

The purpose of this study was to test the claims made for the Davis-Eells games with respect to the cultural fairness of the test. The Davis-Eells and Kuhlmann-Finch tests were administered to 194 children from high and 200 from low socioeconomic homes in three cities. The data obtained did not support the claims for the Davis-Eells test.

———. "Conducting Teacher-Parent Conferences." *Understanding the Child,* 25 (October, 1956), 117–18.

Here the author establishes a frame of reference in which to work when attempting to establish teacher-parent conferences. One point that Coleman feels is essential to the well-being of such a conference is that it be introduced before any trouble arises. Coleman also places emphasis on the necessity of proper communications with parents.

———. "Assisting Teachers in Using Test Results." *Personnel and Guidance Journal,* 36 (September, 1957), 117–18.

This report was prepared to assist classroom teachers in using test results more effectively. One suggestion is that manuals be written specifically for test users and that short courses be developed so that teachers might better understand how to select and administer tests and how to interpret test results.

———. "Advantages and Disadvantages of Large-Scale Testing Programs." *California Journal of Secondary Evaluation,* 35 (January, 1960), 56–60.

In this study, which presents the advantages and disadvantages of a large-scale testing program, Coleman seeks to help schools determine their need for a specific type of program. Advantages of such a testing program are machine scoring at a lower cost, better norms, and competent consultants. The disadvantages are forced conformity, inappropriate norms, increased scoring costs, and slow service. These advantages and disadvantages must be weighed by each school system in view of immediate objectives.

Cottingham, Harold Fred

BIRTH: December 11, 1913, Charleston, Illinois
PRESENT STATUS: professor of education, Florida State University
BACKGROUND: *Educational* B.Ed., Eastern Illinois University, 1935; M.A., University of Iowa, 1940; Ed.D., Indiana University, 1947
Professional teacher in the Illinois secondary schools, 1936–42; instructor in education, Indiana University, 1942–44; director of guidance, William Woods College, 1944–45; director of guidance and research, Moline public schools, 1945–48; head of Department of Guidance and Counseling, Florida State University, 1948–68; associate professor and professor of education, Florida State University, 1948–
Field of Work counselor training, elementary guidance, and the nature of the guidance function in education
Affiliations American Personnel and Guidance Association (president, 1964–65); National Vocational Guidance Association (president, 1962–63); Association of Counselor Education and Supervision; Fellow and diplomate, American Psychological Association, Division of Counseling Psychology

SUMMATION OF CONCEPTS:

Cottingham appears to believe that the guidance point of view is an educational attitude that focuses the attention of the entire staff, from janitors to supervisors, on the needs of pupils in the school setting. He maintains that, in order to understand guidance, one must see it as a point of view or an educational philosophy, as an experiential process, and as a pattern of services

ANNOTATED BIBLIOGRAPHY:

Cottingham, Harold F. "Roles, Functions, and Training Levels for College Personnel Workers." *Personnel and Guidance Journal,* 33 (May, 1955), 534–38.

Cottingham attempts to clarify the roles and functions of different student personnel workers at the high school and college levels. An interesting aspect of this article is his grouping of personnel people into the four categories of educational advisers, general personnel workers, personnel counselors, and personnel technicians.

_____. *Guidance in Elementary Schools.* Bloomington, Ill.: McKnight and McKnight Publishing Co., 1956. 325 pp.

Cottingham introduces the idea that guidance in the elementary school should have the following objectives: personality adjustment, social adjustment, and academic integration. He further maintains that the four specific approaches to guidance at this level are through administration and curricular policy, community resources, instructional procedures, and selected professional activities. The purpose of such an approach is to assist the child in gaining the background of understanding that will help him as he enters new environmental situations. Cottingham feels that at this level much can be done by teachers and counselors to utilize such subjective methods of appraisal as anecdotal records, observations, interviews, and autobiographies. He believes that, as the concepts of mental hygiene, counseling, and therapy become increasingly important, the referral responsibilities of the classroom teacher to these services will more clearly emerge.

———, and William E. Hopke. *Guidance in the Junior High School.* Bloomington, Ill.: McKnight and McKnight Publishing Co., 1961, 390 pp.

The authors introduce material that seems to lend itself well to counselor education programs, workshops, or in-service training programs. Much emphasis is placed on the philosophy of guidance services in the junior high school and the systematic patterns through which such services might logically be implemented. The authors also introduce what they feel are good guidance practices at the junior high school level.

———, H. D. Bruck, and R. C. Reardon. *Counseling and Accountability.* Elmsford, N.Y.: Pergamon Press, 1973. 279 pp.

This book deals with research in the areas of counseling and psychotherapy. The authors have exercised great initiative in bringing together basic understandings about how to approach and improve research. Thirteen examples of published counseling research are reproduced.

Drakeford, John W.
BIRTH: September 26, 1914, Sidney, Australia
PRESENT STATUS: professor of psychology and counseling and director of the Marriage and Family Counseling Center, Southwestern Baptist Theological Seminary, Fort Worth, Texas
BACKGROUND: *Educational* B.A., University of Sidney, 1949; Dip.Edn.,

JOHN W. DRAKEFORD

Sidney Teachers' College, 1950; B.D., New South Wales Baptist Theological Seminary (Australia), 1953; M.A., Texas Christian University, 1958; Th.M., Brite Divinity School of Texas Christian University, 1960; D.R.E., Southwestern Baptist Theological Seminary, 1958; Ed.D., Southwestern Baptist Theological Seminary, 1967

Professional minister, Baptist church, 1937–42; chaplain, Australian army, 1943–45; minister, Baptist church, 1945-49; youth director, New South Wales Baptist Union, 1949–54; professor, Southwestern Baptist Theological Seminary, 1954–; Lilly Fellow, Department of Psychology, University of Illinois, 1964; certified psychologist, Texas State Board of Examiners of Psychologists

Field of Work psychology of religion, group therapy, and marriage and family counseling

Affiliations American Psychological Association, Texas Psychological Association, Association for Clinical Pastoral Education, American Association of Marriage Counselors

SUMMATION OF CONCEPTS:

Drakeford's writings reflect a strong interest in bridging the gap between psychology and religion. He views these two disciplines as friends rather than enemies. Strongly emphasizing the "psyche" as the third dimension of man's personality, he believes that psychologists and counselors must not ignore this dimension in assisting persons who experience intrapersonal and interpersonal conflicts.

ANNOTATED BIBLIOGRAPHY:

Drakeford, John W. *Psychology in Search of a Soul.* Nashville: Broadman Press, 1964. 301 pp.

The author attempts to present a survey of the themes associated with the psychology of religion. Psychological definitions and insights are drawn from outstanding psychologists, such as Sigmund Freud, Carl Jung, and William James, and from religious students of human behavior, such as Leslie Weatherhead, Wayne Oates, and Elton Trueblood. Drakeford presents some basic psychological facts along with the idea that the role of modern psychology includes healing man's troubled soul.

———. *The Awesome Power of the Listening Ear.* Waco, Texas: Word Books, 1967. 126 pp.

The process of counseling is generally viewed as having many facets. This book emphasizes the implications involved in only one dimension, the art of listening, recognized as a major tenet of the Rogerian, client-centered counseling approach. Drakeford believes that effective listening is not an easy art and that its mastery requires time, effort, perseverance, and discipline. The "open ear" is presented as a more effective counseling technique than the "open mouth."

―――. *Integrity Therapy.* Nashville: Broadman Press, 1967. 153 pp.

Integrity therapy is described as "a new direction in psychotherapy." It stresses the place of values in human experience and contends that emotional disturbances are sometimes the result of transgressing values and becoming secretive about their failure. Integrity therapy, associated with Hobart Mowrer, does not call for new or different moral values, but for greater fidelity in those already accepted but poorly followed. Drakeford has found the principles of integrity therapy, used essentially with small groups, successful with marital problems because of its emphasis on openness, confession, group interaction, and personal responsibility.

―――. *Farewell to the Lonely Crowd.* Waco, Texas: Word Book Publishers, 1969. 144 pp.

In this book dealing with the illnesses of modern society, Drakeford analyzes seven groups that strive to help troubled individuals. These "self-help" groups, which emphasize both group support and individual responsibility, are Alcoholics Anonymous, for alcoholics who acknowledge their condition; Synanon and Daytop Lodge, for drug addicts; Seven Steppers, for former prisoners; TOPS, for the overweight; Recovery Incorporated, for former mental patients; Yokefellows, a religious fellowship designed for personal growth; and Integrity Therapy, a new approach to marriage counseling. Drakeford concludes, "The self-help principle can be applied to almost every area of human experience and all forms of group life."

Dugan, Willis Edwin

BIRTH: August 31, 1909, Rippey, Iowa

PRESENT STATUS: executive director emeritus, American Personnel and Guidance Association

BACKGROUND: *Educational* B.E., St. Cloud State College, 1937; M.A., University of Minnesota, 1939; Ph.D., University of Minnesota, 1942

WILLIS EDWIN DUGAN

Professional elementary and secondary schoolteacher, 1927–34; assistant director, National Youth Administration in Minnesota, 1935–38; counselor, University High School, Minneapolis, 1938–42; director of student personnel and assistant professor, College of Education, University of Minnesota, 1942–43; assistant national director of personnel, American Red Cross, 1943–46; assistant professor, 1946–47, associate professor, 1947–50, and professor, 1950–66, University of Minnesota; executive director, American Personnel and Guidance Association, 1966–72; executive director emeritus, American Personnel and Guidance Association, 1972–

Field of Work preparation of educational counselors and psychological workers, plus the evaluation of school guidance and counseling

Affiliations American Personnel and Guidance Association (president, 1963–64); Association of Counselor Education and Supervision (president, 1961–62); National Vocational Guidance Association; Student Personnel Association for Teacher Education (president); American Psychological Association, Division of Counseling Psychology

SUMMATION OF CONCEPTS:

From the author's writings, it appears that he favors guidance services at every level of education and the support of such services through well-established teacher-counselor relationships. Much of his research has been directed toward improving guidance services and developing within the reader an awareness of the future challenges facing the world. Perhaps his philosophy in counseling is defined most accurately as eclectic, since he has long maintained the idea that each situation may well offer the possibility of a different approach.

ANNOTATED BIBLIOGRAPHY:

Dugan, Willis E. "Counseling in the Modern Secondary School Program." *National Association of Secondary School Principals Bulletin*, 35 (January, 1951), 9–78.

This article covers seven chapters and seems quite comprehensive. Dugan attempts to define such terms as counseling and guidance and to outline in detail such aspects of counseling as the objectives of counseling within the institutional setting, the needs of youth, the levels of counseling, the interview, and the relationship in counseling. Dugan focuses on three basic concepts that he believes are essential to counseling: the final decision in any counseling situation rests with the client; no uniform approach in counseling will fit all situations; and counseling is performed at different levels of complexity. The article might serve well to orient the novice counselor to the guidance point of view.

———, ed. *Counseling Points of View.* Minneapolis: University of Minnesota Press, 1958. 48 pp.

An interesting discussion between Carl R. Rogers and Edmund G. Williamson, this booklet presents two contrasting approaches to counseling. It is a booklet that those interested in counseling will find stimulating and challenging.

———. "The Impact of NDEA upon Counselor Preparation." *Personnel and Guidance Journal,* 39 (September, 1960), 37–40.

The author devotes much of this article to the future of counseling and the need for quality counselors. His primary focus of attention is on the growth of guidance from 1960 to 1965 and the need for training programs that offer the counselor-trainee practical counseling experiences.

Ellis, Albert

BIRTH: September 27, 1913, Pittsburgh, Pennsylvania

PRESENT STATUS: executive director, Institute of Rational Living, and director of clinical services, Institute for Advanced Study in Rational Psychotherapy

BACKGROUND: *Educational* B.B.A., City College of New York, 1934; M.A., Columbia University, 1943; Ph.D., Columbia University, 1947

Professional free-lance writer, 1934–38; personnel manager, Distinctive Creations, 1938–48; clinical psychologist, New Jersey State Hospital at Greystone Park, 1948–49; instructor, Department of Psychology, Rutgers University, 1948–49; instructor, Department of Psychology, New York University, 1949; chief psychologist, New Jersey State Diagnostic Center, 1949–50; New Jersey Department of Institutions and Agencies, 1950–52; private practice, psychotherapy and marriage counseling, 1953–68; executive director, Institute for Rational Living, 1959–; director of clinical services, Institute for Advanced Study in Rational Psychotherapy, 1968–

Field of Work marriage and family counseling, human sexuality, and rational-emotive psychotherapy

Affiliations Fellow, American Psychological Association; American Sociological Association; American Association of Marriage Counselors; American Orthopsychiatric Association; American Association of Applied Anthropology; American Academy of Psychotherapists; American Group Psychotherapy Association; American Association for the Advancement of Psychotherapy

ALBERT ELLIS

SUMMATION OF CONCEPTS:

As the founder of the rational-emotive method of psychotherapy, Ellis directs his most significant writings toward the development of his psychotherapeutic system. His formulations to a great degree repudiate the tenets of classical psychoanalysis and the social psychological approaches. The core of the rational-emotive system is based on the hypothesis that a person's human emotions are caused and controlled by his thought pattern. Emotional problems are viewed as the result of unrealistic, negative, illogical, and self-defeating thoughts. Thus, negative feelings, which result from negative thoughts, may be changed to positive feelings by changing one's internalized sentences or "self-talk." Ellis believes that a person is constantly talking to himself and that, when he discovers what he is saying, he may replace negative patterns with positive ones. The role of the therapist is to assist an individual discover what comprises his self-talk, to question the rationality of this silent monologue, to dispel the negative input, and to substitute positive and realistic thoughts for the negative ones.

ANNOTATED BIBLIOGRAPHY:

Ellis, Albert. *Reason and Emotion in Psychotherapy.* New York: Lyle Stuart, 1963. 442 pp.

This is perhaps Ellis' most significant book, for it is here that he explains the theoretical foundation for rational-emotive psychotherapy. His underlying theme is that human emotion is intrinsically an attitudinal and cognitive process. Ten irrational ideas that cause and sustain emotional disturbances are presented, *e.g.*, "the idea that one should be competent, adequate, achieving in all possible respects if one is to consider oneself worthwhile." The essence of rational therapy (RT) is to review realistically ideas and notions that lead to hostile, anxious, defensive, and ineffective behavior and then through logic and reason to overcome these thoughts that tend emotionally to disintegrate an individual. Ellis illustrates how rational therapy is used in treating frigid and impotent persons, fixed homosexuals, schizophrenics, and psychopaths, and he also considers some of the objections raised by his critics.

───────. *How to Prevent Your Child from Becoming a Neurotic Adult.* New York: Crown Publishers, 1966. 247 pp.

Ellis attempts to inform parents about factors associated with neurotic behavior. He describes a person's neurosis as disrupted communication and/or ineffective communication with himself and others. Believing that early childhood teaching is only part of the story of behavior, Ellis states that children seem to inherit a predisposition to behave neurotically. This predisposition may lead to a troubled adult life if parents do not try to counter this tendency. He presents suggestions on how this may be accomplished.

─────. *Sex Without Guilt.* New York: Lancer Books, 1966. 192 pp.

This book reviews various forms of sexuality, ranging from masturbation to adultery. Very liberal in his views on sexuality, Ellis presents the pros and cons of premarital sexual relations. Unlike other writers on sex and marriage relations, including David Mace, Evelyn Duvall, and Pitirim Sorokin, he rejects the idea that premarital intercourse is bad for all persons at all times under all circumstances. Also, he suggests that an invariant rule for all persons relative to adultery is invalid, for some are able to benefit in this form of relationship and others are not. For the person seeking the arguments supporting liberal sex views, this book is a useful source.

Erikson, Erik Homburger

BIRTH: June 15, 1902, Frankfurt, Germany

PRESENT STATUS: professor of human development and lecturer on psychiatry, Harvard University

BACKGROUND: *Educational* clinical training in psychoanalysis under Anna Freud and August Aichhorn, resulting in a formal degree from the Vienna Psychoanalytic Institute; honorary M.A., Harvard University, 1960; honorary LL.D., University of California (Berkeley), 1968

Professional research assistant, Yale University, 1936–39; lecturer and research associate, child welfare, 1939–49, lecturer in social welfare, 1945–49, lecturer in psychiatry at the Medical School, 1947–49, University of California (Berkeley); training psychoanalyst, San Francisco Psychoanalysis Institute, 1942–50; professor of psychology and research associate, University of California (Berkeley), 1949–50; senior staff member, Austen Riggs Center, Stockbridge, Mass., 1951–60; professor of psychology, Departments of Psychiatry (Medical School) and Psychology, University of Pittsburgh, 1951–60; professor of human development and lecturer on psychiatry, Harvard University, 1960–

ERIK HOMBURGER ERIKSON

Field of Work   a leading figure in psychoanalysis and an outstanding researcher of human development with an emphasis on the psychosocial development of the human life cycle

Affiliations   American Psychoanalytic Association; American Academy of Arts and Sciences; Society for Applied Anthropology; Fellow, American Psychological Association, Division of Developmental Psychology

SUMMATION OF CONCEPTS:

Although Erikson received extensive psychoanalytic training in Vienna, he is frequently thought of as an ego analyst along with Heinz Hartmann, Anna Freud, and David Rapaport. Erikson's contributions concern the development of important new extensions of psychoanalytic theory. His best-known modification of psychoanalysis is the substitution of eight psychosocial stages for the five psychosexual periods. Erikson's approach seems to add much to Freud's work by clarifying operationally some of the ideas about energy force. Both the psychosocial and psychosexual periods are developmental theories, stressing early childhood experiences and the continuity of human evolvement. As the term psychosocial suggests, emphasis is placed on the variable role of the environment and social interaction in the process of growth and development. Erikson believes that the healthy individual solves problems as he faces them and that he emerges from his inner and outer struggles with an added sense of inner unity and an increased capacity to face new conflicts in the human life cycle. In essence, the best way one may face and conquer future crises is to handle the present struggles successfully, if growth is in fact the side product of this struggle.

ANNOTATED BIBLIOGRAPHY:

Erikson, Erik H. *Childhood and Society.* New York: W. W. Norton and Co., 1950. 397 pp.

The major contribution of this, Erikson's first book, is his presentation of several stages of identity crises, vitally important in a person's psychosocial development. It is hypothesized that personal identity is achieved through a long process of resolving critical problems faced at different periods. Erikson elaborates on this and outlines the sequence of the human life cycle, which he labels the eight stages of man. These are basic trust versus basic mistrust, autonomy versus shame and doubt, initiative versus guilt, industry versus inferiority, identity versus role confusion, intimacy versus isolation, generativity versus self-absorption, and ego integrity versus despair.

———. *Young Man Luther: A Study in Psychoanalysis and History.* New York: W. W. Norton and Co., 1958. 288 pp.

Initially Erikson planned his study of Martin Luther to be limited to a chapter concerning the emotional crises in late adolescence and early adulthood, but decided to expand the study into this book. Luther is discussed from the point of view of presenting his identity crisis in psychosocial terms. Erikson cites areas in which he believes Sigmund Freud and Luther agreed, although they used different language. Erikson feels that Freud and Luther both concluded that the child is in the midst of the man—individually, collectively, and historically.

———. *Insight and Responsibility: Lectures on the Ethical Implications of Psychoanalytic Insight.* New York: W. W. Norton and Co., 1964. 256 pp.

In this book is a series of lectures given by Erikson on three different continents. On each occasion, addressing people of varied cultural backgrounds, he focuses on the responsibility of each generation to those who follow. The first chapter, entitled "The First Psychoanalyst," is an address commemorating Sigmund Freud's hundredth birthday, and Erikson leaves little doubt of his deep-seated appreciation and gratitude for Freud's ideas. Implementing the ideas that he proclaimed in these lectures, Erikson takes the insight and knowledge gained from previous writers and then modifies and extends these insights for those who follow.

———. *Gandhi's Truth: On the Origins of Militant Nonviolence.* New York: W. W. Norton and Co., 1969. 475 pp.

Unlike many psychological writers, Erikson devotes much of his book to the application of his principles of human relations. Erikson's interest in Mahatma Gandhi and Martin Luther may have been influenced by Freud. As one may recall, it was Freud who carried a manuscript of Moses with him when he was exiled from his country in 1938. (Read "The First Psychoanalyst" in *Insight and Responsibility.*) Erikson attempts to follow Gandhi's life chronologically in a search for the meaning of what Gandhi called Truth. Erikson dedicates this book to the memory of Martin Luther King, the man who applied Gandhi's Truth so effectively on the American soil.

HANS JURGEN EYSENCK

———. *In Search of Common Ground*. New York: W. W. Norton and Co., 1973. 143 pp.

These are edited transcripts that resulted from two meetings between Erik Erikson and Huey P. Newton. Each states his fundamental position on the role of the black man in modern America. Erikson discusses his concept of the identity crisis and how it relates to the modern black movement. This is contrasted with Newton's position, and the book remains a struggle for common ground.

Eysenck, Hans Jurgen

BIRTH: March 4, 1916, Berlin, Germany

PRESENT STATUS: professor of psychology at the Institute of Psychiatry, University of London; director, Psychological Department, Maudsley Hospital; and senior psychologist, Bethlem Royal Hospital

BACKGROUND: *Educational* early education in Germany, France, and England; Ph.D., Department of Psychology, University of London, 1940; D.Sc., University of London, 1964

Professional senior research psychologist, Mill Hill Emergency Hospital, 1942–45; senior psychologist and director, Psychological Department, Maudsley Hospital, 1946–; senior psychologist, Bethlem Royal Hospital, 1948–; visiting professor, University of Pennsylvania, 1949–50; reader in psychology, Institute of Psychiatry, University of London, 1950–54; visiting professor, University of California (Berkeley), 1954; professor of psychology, Institute of Psychiatry, University of London, 1955–

Field of Work attitude research, body types, psychotic-neurotic behavior, factor analysis, learning theory, and scientific research in human personality

Affiliations Fellow, American Psychological Association, Division of Personality and Social Psychology

SUMMATION OF CONCEPTS:

As an advocate of empirical, scientific personality research, Eysenck has tirelessly investigated and reported his statistically controlled findings in the area of human behavior. He has openly attacked nonscientific formulations, projective tests, psychiatrists, psychotherapy generally, and especially the psychoanalytic approach. Although Eysenck does not claim to have formulated a theory of personality, his interests in factor analysis and learning theory have directed him toward the area of behavior therapy. He feels that neurotic symptoms are learned behavior patterns, requiring the use of learning theory, since psychotherapeutic methods have failed. Psychotherapy, he insists, needs methodology, for without it one must strain to call psychotherapy a science. Probably Eysenck's greatest controversy has centered on his claim that untreated neurotics experience the same rate of remission as do neurotics who are treated through the use of psychoanalysis or eclectic psychotherapy.

ANNOTATED BIBLIOGRAPHY:

Eysenck, H. J. *Uses and Abuses of Psychology.* Baltimore: Penguin Books, 1953. 317 pp.

Eysenck scrutinizes the claims of psychology as a science of human behavior. Areas of discussion include intelligence testing, psychotherapy, national differences, racial intolerance, and other aspects of human behavior. In each of these areas, psychological abuses are evaluated, and a clear distinction is made between the use of psychology when research supports the action and the abuse of psychology when personal opinion rather than scientific research has been utilized.

————. *Sense and Nonsense in Psychology.* Baltimore: Penguin Books, 1957. 349 pp.

This book is a sequel to *Uses and Abuses of Psychology,* although it is designed to be read independently. Eysenck deals with such interesting subjects as hypnosis, telepathy, clairvoyance, and the interpretation of dreams. He raises valid questions and draws conclusions relative to the scientific usefulness of some forms of psychological measurement, *e.g.*, the interpretation of dreams in the treatment of mental disorders. In the usual Eysenck spirit of searching criticism, he discusses personality measurement and seriously questions the Rorschach and thematic apperception test (TAT) "experts."

————, ed. *Behavior Therapy and the Neuroses.* Oxford, England: Pergamon Press, 1960. 479 pp.

In this group of readings in modern methods of treatment, Eysenck links learning theory to behavior therapy. To accomplish this end, he relies quite heavily on the contributions of such notables as Joseph Wolpe and A. A. Lazarus. Although the author disclaims having a full-grown "personality theory," one may draw some conclusions by noting that the book is dedicated to the memory of J. B. Watson. Attention is given to reciprocal inhibition therapy, conditional inhibition, aversion therapy, and therapy by positive conditioning and feedback control.

———, ed. *Experiments in Behavior Therapy*. Oxford, England: Pergamon Press, 1964. 558 pp.

This is a companion volume to *Behavior Therapy and the Neuroses*. Eysenck pays homage to men such as J. B. Watson, Joseph Wolpe, Neal Miller, Hobart Mowrer, and B. F. Skinner for their research in the treatment of mental disorders. The author's purpose for this book is an underlying hope that behavior therapy, based on learning theory, will someday replace orthodox methods of psychotherapy. The research "proves" that behavior therapy has been successful in the practical world of experience, although some therapists are thought to have rejected it before trying it.

———, and S. Rackman. *The Causes and Cures of Neurosis*. San Diego: Robert B. Knapp, 1964. 310 pp.

The major concern of this book is diagnosing and treating neurotic disorders, as well as determining the underlying causes for neuroses. Some attention is given to the various dimensions of personality, with emphasis on biological factors, before a deeper study is made on anxiety reactions, obsessive-compulsive disorders, and sexual disorders. Finally, attention is given to methods of behavior modification.

———, ed. *Encyclopedia of Psychology*. 3 vols. New York: Herder and Herder, 1972. 1200+ pp.

This comprehensive reference work deals with the various factors of contemporary psychology. Three hundred major articles and five thousand entries were prepared by distinguished authors from twenty nations. The major articles offer a full definition of terms, an overview of historical foundations, and a discussion of research and scientific controversies. Included is a complete bibliography.

Frankl, Viktor E.

BIRTH: March 26, 1905, Vienna, Austria

PRESENT STATUS: professor of psychiatry and neurology at the University of Vienna Medical School; head of Department of Neurology at the Poliklinik Hospital in Vienna

BACKGROUND: *Educational* M.D., University of Vienna, 1930; Ph.D., University of Vienna, 1949

Professional published his first article at the invitation of Sigmund Freud in the *International Journal of Psychoanalysis*, 1924; editor, *Der Mensch im Alltag*

VIKTOR E. FRANKL

(psychological journal), 1926–27; joined faculty at the University of Vienna as professor of neurology and psychiatry, 1947; visiting professor, Harvard University, 1961; visiting professor, Perkins School of Theology at Southern Methodist University, 1966; served as professor of logotherapy at the International University in San Diego and visiting clinical professor of psychiatry at Stanford University; guest lecturer in Argentina, Australia, Ceylon, China, India, Israel, Japan, Mexico, Puerto Rico, South Africa, and Costa Rica, excluding more than thirty lecture tours in the United States and three lecture tours around the world

Field of Work   psychiatry, existential psychotherapy, and philosophical psychology

Affiliations   Austria Medical Society for Psychotherapy

SUMMATION OF CONCEPTS:

As the originator of the school of psychotherapy known as logotherapy or existential analysis, Frankl directs his writings toward defining an approach to assist individuals with emotional problems. Unlike many European existentialists, Frankl is neither pessimistic nor antireligious. Rather, he has a positive view of man, which dictates that man has the ability to rise above himself and to find meaning in life. Believing that man's most common problem is feeling alienated, above and without identity, he feels that psychoanalysis increases man's fragmentation but that logotherapy offers man the opportunity to stress the development of spiritual and ethical values. Gordon W. Allport, the late eminent psychologist at Harvard, defined logotherapy as "the most significant psychological movement of our day."

ANNOTATED BIBLIOGRAPHY:

Frankl, Viktor E. *The Doctor and the Soul: From Psychotherapy to Logotherapy.* New York: Alfred A. Knopf, 1955. 236 pp.

Frankl believes that man lives in three dimensions: the somatic, the mental, and the spiritual. This book focuses on the reality of man's spiritual nature, which Frankl believes cannot be ignored. As the title suggests, logotherapy is intended to take in man's spiritual sphere. Logotherapy is not intended to replace religion, but is viewed as being particularly effective in assisting the nonreligious person to work through feelings of emotional stress. Examples of the technique of logotherapy include paradoxical intention and de-reflection. The former is designed to counteract anticipatory anxiety; the latter, to counteract the compulsive inclination to self-observation. Frankl concludes by referring to his therapeutic process as a medical ministry, operating along a dividing line between medicine and religion.

———. *Man's Search for Meaning: An Introduction to Logotherapy.* New York: Washington Square Press, 1963. 214 pp.

Frankl gives an account of his personal experiences in Nazi concentration camps during World War II. From these experiences, he concludes that many prisoners died primarily because of a loss of meaning for life. Frankl coins the term "noogenic neurosis," defined as a loss of meaning in human experience. He believes that the "will to meaning" is the most human phenomenon of all, one of the basic attributes distinguishing man from lower animals. Frankl believes that much wisdom is found in Friedrich Nietzsche's statement, "He who has a *why* to live can bear almost any *how!*" Using this as the basis for therapeutic growth, Frankl suggests that meaning may be discovered in one's life through performing unselfish deeds for others, through commitment to eternal values, such as love, and through purposeful suffering. He contrasts logotherapy and psychoanalysis by saying that during psychoanalysis a patient lies on a couch and tells things that are sometimes very disagreeable to tell, but in logotherapy he stands up and hears things that are sometimes very disagreeable to hear.

———. *Psychotherapy and Existentialism: Selected Papers on Logotherapy.* New York: Simon and Schuster (a Clarion Book), 1967. 242 pp.

As stated in the subtitle, this volume includes a number of reprinted papers on logotherapy. The term logotherapy, coined by Frankl in the 1920s, is a synonym for existential analysis. Among other things, Frankl explains the meaning of life in a threefold way. He sees meaning first in *what we give* to life in terms of our creative works. Second, life meaning is seen through *what we take* from the world in terms of our experiencing values. Finally, meaning is experienced through *the stand we take* toward a fate unchangeable, such as terminal cancer.

———. *The Will to Meaning: Foundations and Applications of Logotherapy.* New York: New American Library, 1969. 181 pp.

Frankl dedicates this book to the memory of Gordon W. Allport, who as editor of the *Journal of Abnormal and Social Psychology* introduced the theory of logotherapy to the American public. This book is the outcome of a lecture series presented at Southern Methodist University during the summer of 1966. He presents the foundations of his beliefs by setting forth the assumptions and tenets underlying his system. The application section discusses the treatment of noogenic neuroses, psychogenic neuroses, and somatogenic neuroses. The first treatment focuses upon helping one find meaning, the second explains neurosis in a conventional sense, and the third is treatment of somatogenic diseases in general.

Freud, Sigmund

BIRTH: May 6, 1856, Freiberg, Moravia (Czechoslovakia)

PRESENT STATUS: deceased; September 23, 1939, London, England

BACKGROUND: *Educational* entered the University of Vienna Medical School, 1873; was awarded a research grant to the Zoological Experimental Station at Trieste, 1876; made a major discovery with petromyzon, a genus of fish, 1878; received the M.D. degree, University of Vienna, 1881; attended Jean Martin Charcot's demonstrations of hypnosis in Paris and studied various aspects of hysteria, 1885

Professional resident physician at Vienna General Hospital, where he worked for several years in the physiological laboratory of E. W. von Bruecke and later in the psychiatric clinic with brain anatomist, T. H. Meynert, 1882–86; entered practice as a neurologist, 1886; professor of neuropathology, a nonteaching position, 1902–38; published *Studies in Hysteria*, in collaboration with Josef Breuer, which marked Freud's transition from physiology to psychology, 1895; published *The Interpretation of Dreams*, his first great work, 1900; invited with Carl Jung by G. Stanley Hall to be first lecturer at Clark University, Worcester, Massachusetts, 1909

Field of Work founder of the school of psychoanalysis

Affiliations received Goethe Prize, 1930; elected to the Royal Society, 1936; major influence for First International Congress of Psychoanalysis, 1908; established the International Psychoanalytic Association, 1910

SUMMATION OF CONCEPTS:

Because Freud founded the school of psychoanalysis, most of his writings were directed toward his perceptions of psychoanalysis and the utilization of such an approach in assisting patients suffering from mental illnesses. He placed much emphasis on defining specific psychoanalytic techniques and on applying them in practical situations. He appeared ready and willing to alter his perception of a situation if research indicated that he should.

ANNOTATED BIBLIOGRAPHY:

Freud, Sigmund. *A General Introduction to Psychoanalysis.* New York: Garden City Publishing Co., 1927. 405 pp.

A composite of twenty lectures, this work is philosophical in nature with the focus on Freud's major contributions up to that time. Much emphasis is placed on semantics, and such concepts as the etiology of neuroses, the instinct theory, psychosexual development, the libido theory of narcissism, and the theory of the unconscious are discussed quite thoroughly.

_____. *New Introductory Lectures on Psychoanalysis.* London: Hogarth Press, 1933. 257 pp.

Freud dwells on his concept of anxiety and on the feeling of inferiority reflected by certain women. The book is derived from a series of lectures geared to communicate Freudian concepts to the nonprofessional person. Freud has done much to clarify his position, and, for the person seeking to learn more about Freudian concepts, this book appears most suitable.

_____. *Collected Papers.* 5 vols. New York: Basic Books, 1959. 2,274 pp.

Among the most comprehensive works produced by Freud, these papers cover such broad areas as the history of the psychoanalitic movement, the technique involved in psychoanalysis, case histories in psychoanalysis, metapsychology, and applied psychoanalysis. Many readers interested in counseling will undoubtedly find these papers challenging. Regardless of how one reacts to this work, it seems apparent that it would be difficult if not impossible to read such a comprehensive coverage of unique information without feeling the dynamic overtones in some way. In essence, it might be said that this work covers every conceivable question that the novice counselor might have regarding Freudian concepts and perhaps introduces many ideas that are new, exciting, and stimulating.

Fromm, Erich
    BIRTH: March 23, 1900, Frankfurt, Germany
    PRESENT STATUS: professor of psychology, National University of Mexico

ERICH FROMM

BACKGROUND: *Educational* Ph.D., University of Heidelberg, 1922; additional study in psychoanalysis at the University of Munich and the Berlin Psychoanalytic Institute
Professional lecturer, Psychoanalytic Institute of Frankfurt, the Institute for Social Research, and the University of Frankfurt, 1929-33; International Institute for Social Research, New York City, 1934-39; guest lecturer, Columbia University, 1940-41; faculty, Bennington College, 1941-50; Fellow, William Alanson White Institute of New York City; professor, National University of Mexico, 1951-; adjunct professor, New York University, 1961-
Field of Work psychoanalysis and social psychology
Affiliations Fellow, New York Academy of Sciences; Washington Psychoanalytic Society; American Psychological Association; honorary member, Mexican National Academy of Medicine

SUMMATION OF CONCEPTS:

Unlike many writers, Fromm does not exhibit a unifying theme in his work. Perhaps one may best describe his writings as diversified and profound. His contributions range from the psychology of ethics to thoughts on foreign policy to the cold war issues. His thoughts are constantly growing and therefore constantly changing. This dynamism makes it appear that he sometimes contradicts himself. Actually, his diversification and flexibility give the reader the opportunity to witness man in the process of becoming. What Fromm views one way at one time may differ completely at a later moment. Nevertheless, to Fromm, psychology is a discipline that cannot be divorced from philosophy, religion, ethics, sociology, political science, and economics. With this in mind, one may read Erich Fromm with a clearer perspective. Fromm's theory of personality includes an optimistic view of man and the idea that society's environmental forces are the most powerful influences in molding behavior. Because man worships the products of his own hands, he is seen as the cause of his many complex problems. This idolatry of materialism places man in a perplexing dilemma—a struggle between how he lives and why he lives. Fromm feels the answer to man's troubled existence is dependent on the innate capacity to love and be loved. Five human needs must be met for man to experience healthy personality growth, *i.e.*, transcendence, identity, rootedness, frame of orientation, and relatedness. Once fulfilled, man can solve the problems he himself has created. These human needs are fulfilled through love, which is seen as the answer to the problem of human existence.

ANNOTATED BIBLIOGRAPHY:

Fromm, Erich. *Escape from Freedom.* New York: Holt, Rinehart, and Winston, 1941. 305 pp.

Fromm points out that freedom, in addition to being a political and philosophical term, is also a psychological problem. His thesis seems to be that "modern man, freed from the bonds of a pre-individualistic society, which simultaneously gave him security and limited him, has not gained freedom in a positive sense of the realization of his individual self; that is, the expression of his intellectual, emotional, and sensuous potentialities." Thus, man has gained independence and isolation at the same moment. His alternatives are either to escape from the burden of this freedom, an act that could result in dependencies and submission, or to move forward to the ultimate realization of positive freedom, an act that could lead to uniqueness and individuality.

———. *Man for Himself.* New York: Holt, Rinehart, and Winston, 1947. 254 pp.

This book is dedicated to the psychology of ethics. Fromm believes that psychology and psychotherapy must deal with morals and ethics, *i.e.*, with the "natural" and "spiritual" realms of personality. Believing that ethical relativism is contrary to human nature, Fromm is convinced that the sources of moral norms and standards are found in man's nature itself. If these moral norms are violated, then the consequences are mental and emotional disintegration. Conversely, if the moral norms that are based on man's inherent qualities are followed, then a mature and integrated personality results. This idea, labeled "humanistic ethics," is based on the principle that "good" is that which results in good for man and "evil" is that which is detrimental to man. The sole criterion of ethical value is man's welfare.

———. *Psychoanalysis and Religion.* New Haven: Yale University Press, 1950. 119 pp.

Fromm's position is that psychoanalysis is neither the enemy nor the ally of religion but concerns itself primarily with the human reality behind theological doctrines. According to Fromm, man without faith, love, and truth is incomplete, confused, and anxious. Believing that mental illness results from man's failure to develop his moral and spiritual potential, Fromm sees the psychoanalyst as the "physician of the soul." An early chapter makes a penetrating comparison between Freud's and Jung's positions on religion.

———. *The Sane Society*. New York: Holt, Rinehart, and Winston, 1955. 370 pp.

This book discusses the plight of modern man in a society whose major concern is economic productivity rather than increased human productivity. Fromm asks, "How can a society that has created a greater material wealth than any other in the history of the human race be considered sane when millions of its people have been killed through wars that are justified by religion?" He speaks of the "pathology of normalcy," suggesting that the normal behavior of the masses is not necessarily in the best interests of the human race. Fromm believes that to allow present trends to develop unchecked will result in an insane society of totally alienated persons.

———. *The Art of Loving*. New York: Harper and Row, 1956. 133 pp.

This is perhaps Fromm's most interesting and readable work. Modern man is viewed as being alienated from his fellowman, from himself, and from the One who has created him. Man has placed his faith in the things he himself has created and thus has become "object oriented" rather than "search oriented"; *i.e.*, he has become more interested in the goal than in the journey he takes to reach it. Man needs to bridge the gap to reach his full potential. Becoming is the art of loving. It is achieved when man's human needs of transcendence, identity, rootedness, and relatedness are met through brotherly love, motherly love, erotic love, self love, and the love of God. The basic elements of such love are care, responsibility, respect, and knowledge. These become manifest as man develops the capability of "loving persons" and "using things" rather than "loving things" and "using persons."

———. *The Anatomy of Human Destructiveness*. New York: Holt, Rinehart, and Winston, 1973. 521 pp.

This is a book for sophisticated thinkers. Fromm not only discusses his own theory of human nature but uses arguments designed to refute Skinnerian behaviorism (*i.e.*, the idea that man's feelings are second to the forces of conditioning) and Lorenzian aggression (*i.e.*, the idea that within man there is a spontaneous, innate readiness to fight, which is essential to survival). To make his point, Fromm covers much ground including animal studies, paleontology, anthropology, and sociology.

This knowledge and his own background as a researcher and clinician combine to bring the reader an interesting thesis on aggression and how it results from the interaction between man's existential needs and various social conditions. He uses case studies of such leaders as Adolf Hitler and Joseph Stalin in his presentation.

Gesell, Arnold Lucius

BIRTH: June 21, 1880, Alma, Wisconsin
PRESENT STATUS: deceased; May 29, 1961, New Haven, Connecticut
BACKGROUND: *Educational* B.Ph., University of Wisconsin, 1903; Ph.D., Clark University, 1906; M.D., Yale University, 1915; honorary Sc.D., Clark University, 1930; honorary Sc.D., University of Wisconsin, 1953

Professional instructor, Department of Psychology, Los Angeles State Normal School, 1908–10; assistant professor of education, Yale University, 1911–15; founder and director, Yale Psycho-Clinic (later changed to Yale Clinic of Child Development, Yale School of Medicine), 1911–48; professor of child hygiene, Yale School of Medicine, 1915–48; school psychologist, Connecticut State Board of Education, 1915–19; founder, Photographic Research and Film Library at Yale, 1925; attending pediatrician, New Haven Hospital, 1928–48; research associate, child vision research, Yale School of Medicine, 1948–50; Gesell Institute of Child Development founded in his honor, 1950; research consultant, Gesell Institute of Child Development, 1950–58

Field of Work leading authority and pioneer in child development

Affiliations American Association for the Advancement of Science, American Medical Association, American Orthopsychiatric Association, American Academy of Pediatrics, American Academy for Cerebral Palsy (president, 1952–53), American Psychiatric Association, American Pediatric Society, National Academy of Sciences, Phi Beta Kappa, Sigma Xi, Alpha Omega Alpha, Kappa Delta Pi

SUMMATION OF CONCEPTS:

Gesell's work is a significant contribution to the study of human development. The primary emphasis is on understanding behavioral patterns from birth through adolescence. The results of his tedious chronological studies have established a precedent accepted by many American parents as the normal growth pattern for children. Gesell believed that, although differences can occur, patterns of child development evolve in a predictable sequence. His general formulation is called progressive morphogenesis, that is, a process of differentiation and integration. Gesell accounted for differences between developmental stages by using the spiral growth concept. This concept attempts to explain how a child reverts to earlier forms of behavior, *i.e.*, partial regression, before he is able to surpass his previous level of performance. Gesell's pioneering ideas have received considerable criticism, but they have served to stimulate additional research and a renewed search for clearer understandings of human development.

ANNOTATED BIBLIOGRAPHY:

Gesell, Arnold, *et al. The First Five Years of Life: A Guide to the Study of the Preschool Child.* New York: Harper and Row, 1940. 393 pp.

Gesell reports on the behavior patterns of children from birth to age five. In 1925 he wrote his first major work, *The Mental Growth of the Preschool Child,* which was the predecessor of this one. Both works are dedicated to the theoretical and practical applications of psychology in the search to better understand children during their early, formative years. As an aid to understanding how growth takes place, Gesell includes a pictorial survey depicting typical behavior during each of the first five years of life. This book serves as a springboard for later manuscripts dealing with the time from birth through adolescence.

_____, and Frances L. Ilg. *The Child from Five to Ten.* New York: Harper and Brothers, Publishers, 1946. 475 pp.

The construction of this book closely parallels the form used in describing the child from one to five. Although recognizing that age norms are not absolute and that each child travels at his own tailor-made time schedule, Gesell treats each yearly age level in terms of ten major fields of behavior. These are motor characteristics, personal hygiene, emotional expression, fears and dreams, self and sex, interpersonal relations, play and pastimes, school life, ethical sense, and philosophic outlook. Gesell believes that all these areas are subject to laws of growth and that parents and teachers can best assist the development of children when they recognize these growth trends. Growth is viewed as motion, and the underlying principle of child care is viewed as assisting and guiding the child's growth, step by step, rather than attempting to mold the child behaviorally into some predetermined image.

_____, and Catherine S. Amatruda. *Developmental Diagnosis: Nor-*

mal and Abnormal Child Development. 2nd rev. ed. New York: Harper and Row, 1947. 496 pp.

This work is the result of the many years of clinical experience gained from the developmental examinations of infants and preschool children at the Yale Clinic of Child Development. Psychometric students who want to find out more about the Gesell developmental schedules will find this book helpful, since it is here that he first discusses them. Since then, they have been used to study the mental growth of the preschool child. Norms of development at different age levels are presented to provide a criterion for a differential diagnosis. Motor development, adaptive behavior, language development, and personal-social behavior are the four different aspects of growth. Normal patterns are provided, as are developmental deviations and defects, which include amentia and retardation, convulsive disorders, neurological malfunctions, blindness, cerebral injury, and environmental retardation. The examination technique used with the Gesell developmental schedules are explained in detail.

————, Frances L. Ilg, and Louise Bates Ames. *Youth: The Years from Ten to Sixteen.* New York: Harper and Brothers, Publishers, 1956. 542 pp.

This study completes the trilogy begun with *The First Five Years*, followed by *The Child from Five to Ten.* Most of the data were derived from research studies at the Gesell Institute of Child Development, founded in 1950. Rather than using a schedule of norms, Gesell uses a triple arrangement, which summarizes maturity profiles, maturity traits, and maturity trends at each of the seven age zones. The maturity profile simply characterizes the student at each age level, whereas the age traits focus on the behavioral patterns and specific problems encountered as the youngster develops. The maturity trends indicate growth gradients and sequences for each annual cycle. Both counselors and psychologists may find Gesell's trilogy of significant benefit if using bibliotherapy as a technique with clients.

Glanz, Edward Coleman
 BIRTH: December 22, 1924, Georgetown, South Carolina
 PRESENT STATUS: professor of psychology and president of Southampton College, Long Island University

EDWARD COLEMAN GLANZ

BACKGROUND: *Educational* A.B., Bates College, 1948; M.A., Columbia University Teachers College, 1949; Ed.D., Columbia University Teachers College, 1950
Professional personnel and testing consultant, David Clark Company, 1948; director, Lamport House, Evening Division, City College of New York, 1949-50; director of student personnel, Quinnipiac College, 1950-53; counselor, Vocational Counseling Service, New Haven, Connecticut, 1953-54; chairman, College of Basic Studies, Boston University, 1953-56; provost, Southampton College of Long Island University, 1963-69; professor of psychology and president, Southampton College, 1969-
Field of Work counseling, guidance, and group dynamics
Affiliations American Personnel and Guidance Association; American Psychological Association, Division of Counseling Psychology; Phi Beta Kappa; American Association of University Professors

SUMMATION OF CONCEPTS:

Glanz believes that group techniques, psychological testing, and individual counseling form the three conceptual tools that help guidance workers create for students an individualized educational atmosphere. He maintains that guidance workers should employ techniques that have emerged as effective and that emphasis in the guidance program should be on both social growth and intellectual development.

ANNOTATED BIBLIOGRAPHY:

Glanz, Edward Coleman, and Ernest B. Walston. *An Introduction to Personal Adjustment.* Boston: Allyn and Bacon, 1958. 348 pp.

With this text, the authors attempt to assist college students to better understand themselves and from this understanding to emerge as more mature and better adjusted persons. Perhaps of greatest interest to the counselor is that much of the book is concerned with the practical application of psychological theory and the utilization of test results by both students and counselors to arrive at more accurate self-concepts. The reader will undoubtedly find the appendices of considerable value in helping the student to move toward a higher level of understanding about himself and the world in which he lives.

_____, et al. "The Freshman Psychology Courses as the Basis for a Student Personnel Program." *Personnel and Guidance Journal,* 38 (December, 1959), 290-94.

The authors present one approach to teaching a required course in psychology based on the principles of dynamic adjustment processes.

They feel this approach might well be used to make counseling more effective in a college student personnel program. Emphasis is placed on a required freshman course in psychology that would serve as a vehicle for teaching the application of psychological and other principles that would help students taking the course to deal with the normal range of problems met by adolescents in college. The article covers such aspects of interest as the similarity between the role of the counselor and that of the psychology professor. A critique of the article is also included.

————, and James F. Penny. "Developing a Research Program for Curriculum Validation." *Journal of Higher Education,* 32 (January, 1961), 39–44.

The authors focus attention on the significance of and need for validation studies in the area of guidance and counseling. Much of the article is related to research designed to determine, if possible, what contribution the psychology and guidance program was making to positive student change and to discover what factors in the college as a whole were associated with student change. The research was conducted in the College of Basic Studies at Boston University. Results indicate that additional studies would be necessary and that at least one of these would have to be directed toward the influence of faculty attitude as perceived by the student.

————. *Groups in Guidance.* Boston: Allyn and Bacon, 1962. 385 pp.

This book contains numerous principles and theories subscribed to in present-day research. The author also presents a variety of research that has already been done on group procedures in guidance. Glanz points out that group procedures have "come of age" and that current personnel programs can benefit greatly from recent research. He sees group guidance as a tool that can be combined with other such tools as counseling and testing in an effort to make the total guidance program more effective. He emphasizes the leadership role and how vital such a role is to the effectiveness of the group. Much attention is placed on the need for a basic understanding of counseling approaches and the flexibility attached to such approaches. Along with this, the author stresses such points as the significance of communications within the group setting and the purposes of testing.

Hall, G. Stanley

BIRTH: February 1, 1844, Ashfield, Massachusetts
PRESENT STATUS: deceased; April 24, 1924, Worcester, Massachusetts
BACKGROUND: *Educational* B.A., Williams College, 1867; student at Union Theological Seminary, 1867-68; studied philosophy in Germany at the Universities of Bonn and Berlin, 1868-71; B.D., Union Theological Seminary, 1871; Ph.D., Harvard University, 1878 (believed to be the first Ph.D. degree in psychology awarded in America); additional psychological study in Germany with Wilhelm Wundt, Wilhelm F. von Ludwig, and Hermann von Helmholtz, 1878-80
Professional instructor of philosophy, modern languages, and English, Antioch College, 1872-76; lecturer in educational problems, Harvard University, 1880-81; professor of psychology, Johns Hopkins University, 1882-88; opened the first formal psychological laboratory in America, 1883; president, Clark University, 1888-1920
Field of Work American pioneer in experimental psychology, educational psychology, and the psychology of religion
Affiliations early leader and the first president, American Psychological Association; founder, *American Journal of Psychology*, 1887; founder, *Pedagogical Seminar*, 1891 (now the *Journal of Genetic Psychology*); founder, *Journal of Religious Psychology*, 1904 (elapsed in 1914); founder, the *Journal of Applied Psychology*, 1917; Phi Beta Kappa

SUMMATION OF CONCEPTS:

As an early American leader in the development of psychology as a separate science, Hall seemed to develop an interest in some specific area, to carry it through the pioneer stage, and then to move on to another topic. He once concluded that his intellectual life could be viewed, in his own words, as a series of "crazes," but behind each of these he left a laboratory, a journal, or an institute. He made, it seems in retrospect, his greatest contribution in educational psychology. Ultimately he possessed a deeper interest in people than in "rats and stats," two major interests of the experimentalist. Although the origin of the psychological laboratory is closely linked with his name, a close examination of his life reveals a greater fascination with the living problems of human behavior than with the founding of a laboratory.

ANNOTATED BIBLIOGRAPHY:

Hall, G. Stanley. *Adolescence: Its Psychology and Its Relations to Physiology, Anthropology, Sociology, Sex, Crime, Religion, and Education.* 2 vols. New York: D. Appleton and Co., 1904. 1,373 pp.

This monumental work is the most significant early scientific study of adolescence. Being the first great student of this developmental period, Hall is generally called the "father of adolescent psychology." *Adolescence* deals with the teen-ager and his relationship to other life experiences with a strong emphasis on education and religion. In the preface Hall states that the child and the race are each keys to the other, and he introduces a theory of recapitulation, which presupposes that the history of the race becomes a part of the genetic constitution of the individual. Adolescence is viewed as a period of storm and stress corresponding to the troubled transition that occurred when man moved from savagery to civilization. The study of the adolescent was greatly advanced by this publication, for it came at a time when there was hope that psychology could be the key to major questions in education. Hall describes the adolescent's four major concerns as self-realization, sex channelization, social reformation, and a search for God or cosmic meaning.

Hardee, Melvene Draheim

BIRTH: November 30, 1915, Clarion, Iowa
PRESENT STATUS: professor of higher education, Florida State University
BACKGROUND: *Educational* B.A., Iowa State Teachers College, 1934 (now the University of Northern Iowa); M.A., Columbia University Teachers College, 1937; Ph.D., University of Chicago, 1948
Professional counselor-teacher, Stephens College, 1943–48; coordinator of counseling, Florida State University, 1948–59; visiting professor during summer sessions at the University of Mississippi, Michigan State University, and Brigham Young University, 1948–67; lecturer at University of Denver, 1965–66, at St. Louis University, 1969, and at Boston College, 1970; professor of higher education, Florida State University, 1959–; staff consultant, Higher Education Executive Associates, 1968–
Field of Work student personnel work in higher education with emphasis on the coordination of instructional and student personnel areas
Affiliations American Psychological Association, Divisions of General Psychology and Counseling Psychology; American Personnel and Guidance Association; American College Personnel Association (president, 1962–63)

SUMMATION OF CONCEPTS:

Hardee has for many years promoted the idea of incorporating college faculty members into counseling. To her, much of what is done in the area of college counseling has as its foundation the counseling done at the secondary level. She believes that such an extension and interchange of ideas between the college and high school results in a more sophisticated program of personnel work. Further, she recognizes the need to orient future teachers in the area of counseling so that they may assist in making the personnel program more effective in their respective settings.

ANNOTATED BIBLIOGRAPHY:

Hardee, Melvene D., ed. *Counseling and Guidance in General Education.* Yonkers-on-Hudson, N.Y.: World Book Co., 1955. 424 pp.

Edited by Hardee and sponsored by the National Committee on General Education of the Association for Higher Education, this text contains a descriptive appraisal of counseling and its relationship to general education. It appears that the trend in higher education is toward general education and that the utilization of teacher talent and counselor skill will provide the fullest possible benefits for students. The team relationship formed as counselors, administrators, and faculty members work to help the student gain an ultimate benefit is focused to provide a core of unity within an essentially diversified college setting.

———. *The Faculty in College Counseling.* New York: McGraw-Hill Book Co., 1959. 379 pp.

Designed to achieve a high degree of integration between the student personnel program and the program of instruction, this book brings forth the concept that faculty members, through in-service training programs, can be trained to assume specific personnel responsibilities at appropriate levels within the student personnel program. Hardee has done much to outline specific methods and programs presently used by a variety of institutions throughout the United States. She feels that every effort should be made to establish a cooperative working relationship among deans, department heads, and coordinators or directors of counseling and that specific attention should be directed toward establishing a cooperative working relationship between teaching faculty members and staff counselors. It is her contention that relationships such as these are possible through in-service training programs designed to orient faculty members to their counseling responsibilities.

———. "The Sad Case of the Bigger Lost Sheep." *Personnel and Guidance Journal,* 38 (November, 1959), 202–06.

In this article, Hardee introduces the idea that graduate students as well as undergraduate students need assistance in setting life goals. She touches upon a subject that needs more attention in the future.

———. "Faculty Advising in Contemporary Higher Education." *Educational Record*, 42 (April, 1961), 112–16.

Hardee once again encourages a stronger unity between student personnel services and instructional services. One way of achieving this unity, she says, is through systematic advisement. Although much opposition is reflected toward presently existing types of advisement, it appears that little is done here to provide the reader with a clear-cut, functional approach to the problem. In effect, it remains an area of concentration for serious students as well as for people engaged in personnel work.

Hatch, Raymond N.

BIRTH: February 5, 1911, Plymouth, Ohio

PRESENT STATUS: professor of guidance and educational psychology, emeritus, Michigan State University

BACKGROUND: *Educational* B.S., Ashland College, 1929; M.A., Michigan State University, 1947; Ed.D., Oregon State University, 1950

Professional elementary teacher, Shelby, Ohio, public schools, 1934–38; secondary teacher and director of guidance, Shelby public schools, 1939–43; director of guidance, public schools, East Lansing, Michigan, 1943–46; associate professor of guidance, Michigan State University, 1946–52; professor and chairman of the Guidance Department, Michigan State University, 1952–54; director, Bureau of Research, College of Education, Michigan State University, 1954–56; assistant dean, College of Education, Michigan State University, 1956–60; chief of party education and planning, Michigan State University–University of Ryukus, 1962–63; Michigan State University–Thailand Project, 1964–67; chairman, Department of Counseling and Educational Psychology, Michigan State University, 1963–64; professor of guidance and educational psychology, 1968–; professor of guidance and educational psychology, emeritus, 1977–

Field of Work organization and administration of guidance services

Affiliations American Personnel and Guidance Association, National Vocational Guidance Association (president, 1957), Association of Counselor Education and Supervision

SUMMATION OF CONCEPTS:

Hatch has written in several diversified fields, and a great deal of what he believes is reflected in the annotated bibliography. At least one of his basic concepts is to have writers present guidance texts designed to meet the need for immediate application. Hatch places much emphasis on the proper organization of guidance services and on the significance of proper initiation and implementation. To help students at all, the author sees a necessity for presenting this assistance in a systematic way.

ANNOTATED BIBLIOGRAPHY:

Hatch, Raymond N. *Guidance Services in the Elementary Schools.* Dubuque: William C. Brown Co., 1951. 113 pp.

The author stresses the importance of introducing guidance services at the elementary school level. He feels that, if guidance is to assist students, it must provide a plan that will ensure continuous services for that student and continuous information about that student. This book appears to have some potential for the in-service training of teachers.

―――, and Buford Stefflre. *Administration of Guidance Services: Organization, Supervision, Evaluation.* Englewood Cliffs, N.J.: Prentice-Hall, 1958. 449 pp.

Much of the first part of the book is devoted to principles involved in the organization of guidance services and the delegation of responsibilities relative to these services. The second part of the book illustrates organizational patterns involving specific school settings.

―――. *Guidance Services in the Secondary School.* Dubuque: William C. Brown Co., 1963. 197 pp.

The author devotes much time to the development of guidance services at the secondary level. He includes a personalized philosophy of guidance and how it relates to the total school program. He introduces specific techniques that might help counselors become more effective and outlines in detail a method of operation that, to him, seems most logical for implementing guidance services.

Hitchcock, Arthur Allen

BIRTH: November 6, 1910, Albany, New York

PRESENT STATUS: professor of education, State University of New York at Albany, and consultant, U.S. Office of Education

BACKGROUND: *Educational* A.B., Wesleyan University, 1932; Ed.M., Harvard University, 1934; Ph.D., Yale University, 1948

Professional director of guidance, Bristol, Connecticut, 1938–43; training and personnel specialist, U.S. Army, 1943–46; assistant director of the Guidance Center and lecturer in guidance, Harvard University, 1946-49; professor of educational psychology and director of the Junior Division and Counseling Service, University of Nebraska, 1949-55; executive director, American Personnel and Guidance Association, 1955-66; lecturer at Temple University, George Washington University, and Michigan State University, professor of education, State University of New York at Albany, 1966-; consultant, U.S. Office of Education, 1966-

Field of Work adolescent growth, college adjustment, and an interdisciplinary approach in guidance, counseling, and psychology

Affiliations Fellow, American Psychological Association, Divisions of Counseling Psychology and the Society for the Psychological Study of Social Issues; American Personnel and Guidance Association; National Vocational Guidance Association; American Educational Research Association; American Association for the Advancement of Science

SUMMATION OF CONCEPTS:

Hitchcock appears to feel that the world today is one in which changes are taking place faster than ever before. It is because of these many and varied changes that he finds it necessary to place great emphasis on identifying able students and assisting them to their fullest development. In essence, it is his belief that through a well-planned guidance program for able students the needs of the nation will be more adequately met.

ANNOTATED BIBLIOGRAPHY:

Hitchcock, Arthur Allen. "Can Teachers Make Accurate Estimates of Reading Ability?" *Clearing House*, 29 (March, 1955), 422-24.

This is a study designed to determine whether a teacher can accurately estimate the reading ability of her students. To answer this question, a teacher of English rated her 101 eighth-grade students on their reading ability. Each student was assigned a grade placement rating in each of three areas: paragraph meaning, word meaning, and average reading ability. The teacher's ratings were based upon eight criteria. A standardized reading test was then administered to the students, and a statistical analysis of the results was made through the use of coefficients of correlation. The correlations between the teacher's ratings and the test results were so high that it appears that teachers' ratings are nearly as accurate as test ratings. It must be realized however that, although teachers of English may estimate the reading ability of their students accurately, this finding does not imply a generalization of ability in teachers of other subjects.

_____, et al. "Milestones in the Development of Personnel Services in Education." *Personnel Services in Education*. National Society for the Study of Education's 58th yearbook. Chicago: University of Chicago Press, 1959. Pt. 2, pp. 238–98.

It appears that the forces that have shaped personnel work in education are forces that have occurred gradually and now serve as the milestone of this work. Since 1850, America has made rapid strides in converting a rural way of life into an urban way of life. To the school and the curriculum such strides have posed a never-ending challenge. Each decade seems to have brought progress and new modifications with the emphasis always on the industrialization of our country and the training necessary to carry out such a philosophy of life. Interestingly enough, it was realized that people must be prepared for a great deal of flexibility in their new work responsibilities. This need for preparation created an especially strong desire for direction in planning for the world of everyday living. Once it was realized that intelligent planning was in order, personnel work in education was seen as a possible means of utilizing the best efforts of each individual. Such efforts by education have resulted in a trend toward specialization and the ability of the school to fill the demands of a growing country. The response of personnel work in education to the needs of this nation is far more than a response to a collection of techniques and instruments; it is a new way of looking at people, a new way of working with people, and a new way of stimulating people so that those who emerge from this new philosophy of life have the strength that is most readily reflected in self-understanding and satisfactory adjustment to an ever-changing way of life.

_____. "Guidance." *Compton's Pictured Encyclopedia*. Chicago: F. E. Compton and Co., 1963. Pp. 251*a*–51*d*.

Hitchcock maintains that a child is guided by the advice and influence of parents, teachers, ministers, club leaders, and many other people who come into his life. Not until recent years, however, have there been people who were trained particularly for guidance functions and who specialized in assisting students recognize and utilize specific information about themselves. The person who helps them to this level of development is recognized as a counselor. Most high schools and many elementary schools employ counselors, and ideally there should be 1 full-time counselor for every 250 students at the secondary school level. The average ratio in the United States appears to be 1 counselor to 800 students. It is the purpose of the counselor to help teachers and parents understand the child better while assisting the child to better understand himself. A frequent approach to such an understanding is through the utilization of such content as test results and school records and the observation of behavior. It is presumed that guidance counseling will help a student achieve better grades and lead to intelligent educational choices. Since complete and well-kept records are the bases for such choices, it is essential to have a well-planned testing program.

Hoppock, Robert

BIRTH: December 24, 1901, Lambertville, New Jersey

PRESENT STATUS: emeritus professor of counselor education

BACKGROUND: *Educational* B.S., Wesleyan University, 1923; M.A., Columbia University Teachers College, 1932; Ph.D., Columbia University, 1935

Professional teacher, Lambertville public schools, 1924–26; general passenger agent, Trenton Transit Company, 1926–27; vocational counselor, Rahway, New Jersey, public schools, 1927–30; field secretary, National Vocational Guidance Association, 1930–32; assistant director, National Occupational Conference, 1933–39; professor of education, New York University, 1939–74; emeritus professor of counselor education, 1974–

Field of Work occupational information, vocational counseling, teaching occupations, and group procedures in guidance

Affiliations Fellow, American Psychological Association, Division of Counseling Psychology; American Personnel and Guidance Association; National Vocational Guidance Association; Phi Delta Kappa; American Association of University Professors

SUMMATION OF CONCEPTS:

Hoppock has long maintained that occupational information is of vital importance to any person seeking employment. He has introduced the idea that, when a vocational counselor and a client enter into a working relationship, many of the decisions reached by the client may well be influenced by what the counselor says or does. Much emphasis has been placed on the counselor's ability to understand and use a theory of vocational choice. Hoppock has given much attention to the significance of testing on occupational decisions and to the influence of occupational information on final occupational selections. Much of his research concerns follow-up studies on job satisfaction.

ANNOTATED BIBLIOGRAPHY:

Hoppock, Robert. *Group Guidance: Principles, Techniques, and Evaluation.* New York: McGraw-Hill Book Co., 1949. 382 pp.

This is an early attempt by Hoppock to present his concepts of group procedures in the utilization of occupational information. He feels that students should receive knowledge about job opportunities that will assist them in job selection. Hoppock introduces the idea that the counselor's responsibility is to help his client both discover his strong and weak points and to use this knowledge as a basis for vocational selection and personal adjustment.

_____, and Edward R. Couny. "Pretesting Equated Groups." *Educational and Psychological Measurement,* 15 (Summer, 1955), 163–65.

Hoppock introduces a procedure for equating groups for research purposes.

_____. "A Twenty-Seven-Year Follow-up on Job Satisfaction of Employed Adults." *Personnel and Guidance Journal,* 38 (February, 1960), 489.

This was a study designed to determine, if possible, what factors could be attributed to job satisfaction. The research, initiated in 1932, involved twenty-three persons who were studied on a longitudinal basis.

_____. *Occupational Information.* New York: McGraw-Hill Book Co., 1963. 514 pp.

A revision of a book originally published in 1957, this volume introduces some new and refreshing concepts based on the author's long experience in the area of occupational information. Although much of his attention is focused upon the collection, filing, and dissemination of information, he introduces here his personal concepts concerning the significance of the follow-up study in occupationally oriented research. He places much importance on using the occupational information in counseling, on the significance of theories related to vocational choice, and the circumstances under which occupational information might conceivably be taught.

Horney, Karen
  BIRTH: September 16, 1885, Hamburg, Germany
  PRESENT STATUS: deceased; December, 1952, New York City

KAREN HORNEY

BACKGROUND: *Educational* M.D., University of Berlin, 1913
Professional instructor, Institute for Psychoanalysis, Berlin, 1920–32; associate director, Chicago Institute for Psychoanalysis, 1932–34; lecturer, New School for Social Research, 1935–52; instructor, New York Psychoanalytic Institute, 1934–41; dean, American Institute for Psychoanalysis, 1941–52
 Field of Work reinterpretation of psychoanalysis and personality development
 Affiliations Association for the Advancement of Psychoanalysis, American Psychiatric Association

SUMMATION OF CONCEPTS:

Horney's writings reflect a desire on her part to reinterpret and enlarge Freudian concepts. She insisted that her purpose, relative to psychoanalysis, was to modify an old system rather than to create a new one. Thus, her concepts are labeled neo-Freudian, and her teachings are linked with a group, which includes Alfred Adler, Harry Stack Sullivan, and Erich Fromm, that emphasizes the impact of social and cultural factors in personality development. Her view of man is a positive one, believing that he has the potential to evolve into a happier and healthier individual. Horney's primary concept is that of basic anxiety, which she views as the result of conflicts between a person and his environment. If these conflicts are not resolved, then a person may develop what she calls a "neurotic" personality pattern.

ANNOTATED BIBLIOGRAPHY:

Horney, Karen. *The Neurotic Personality of Our Time.* New York: W. W. Norton and Co., 1937. 299 pp.
 The main contention of this book is that neuroses are generated by conflicts and disturbances in social interpersonal relationships. Man is viewed as a product of his social interactions plus the customs and roles of his culture. For example, a rejected child may use a variety of means to cope with the anxiety created by rejection. By so doing, the child may develop some neurotic striving for affection or power. If this neurotic reaction reduces anxiety, then the child may continue to react in this way. Eventually this response pattern may become part of his basic life attitude.
 ———. *New Ways in Psychoanalysis.* New York: W. W. Norton and Co., 1939. 313 pp.

This book is the result of Horney's dissatisfaction with the therapeutic results of psychoanalysis. Each Freudian concept is carefully analyzed and reinterpreted. In a way, Horney "de-sexes" the Freudian concept that emphasizes pleasure as a motivator of human behavior and a root cause of neuroses. Rather, she believed that her clients behaved neurotically because of societal pressures, economic inadequacies, and work pressures. Much of her attention was given to changing conceptions concerning the length of analysis. She suggested that additional knowledge and research were necessary to improve any system. In conclusion, Horney believed that the more a therapist understands a psychic problem, the less time he loses in arriving at a solution.

―――――. *Self-Analysis*. New York: W. W. Norton and Co., 1942. 309 pp.

In this book Horney moves from the theoretical framework developed in her first two major works to some practical implications of analysis. The idea she presents is that man has to struggle with his own feelings and that a highly skilled professional can achieve very little success without the patient's cooperation and readiness to attack the problem. Believing that the professional therapist has the mission of helping persons develop their full potentialities, Horney feels that self-insight, which clarifies frictions and misunderstandings, can free one from crippling compulsions and lead to personality integration.

―――――. *Our Inner Conflicts*. New York: W. W. Norton and Co., 1945. 250 pp.

This is perhaps Horney's most outstanding work. In it she synthesizes her concepts and concludes that a person uses three types of reactions to deal with his conflicts and frustrations. These are: moving toward people, moving against people, and moving away from people. Suggesting that all normal persons use these three reactions in response to conflicts, she feels that only the highly neurotic individual uses one to the exclusion of the others. Thus, a neurotic is characterized as being extremely helpless, hostile, or isolated in his interpersonal relations. It is not the conflict that makes one neurotic, it is how he deals with the conflict.

―――――. *Neurosis and Human Growth: The Struggle Toward Self-Realization*. New York: W. W. Norton and Co., 1950. 391 pp.

The subtitle gives a picture of what the book is all about. Horney views man as having a conflict between his ideal self, which is the fantasized self, and the real self. The conflict results from man's alienation between these two concepts. His frustration emerges as he struggles with something that seems beyond his reach. A healthier and more realistic goal is self-realization, which lies somewhere on the continuum between the ideal and the real. Self-realization allows man to grow within the confines of his potential and permits him to set realistic goals against which his movement toward such goals can be witnessed.

Hummel, Raymond Charles

BIRTH: August 13, 1921

PRESENT STATUS: associate professor and research associate, University of Pittsburgh; research associate, Learning Research and Development Center

BACKGROUND: *Educational*   B.B.A., City College of New York, 1943; M.A., Columbia University, 1947; Ph.D., Columbia University, 1958

Professional   interpreter and personal technician, U.S. Army, 1943–46; employment counselor for fifty-two New York associations, 1947–54; researcher, Horace Mann–Lincoln Institute and Experimental School, Columbia University, 1954–56; assistant professor, Harvard University, 1956–60; lecturer in education, Harvard University, 1960–63; director of guidance, Allegheny County schools, 1963–65; chairman, Program in Counselor Education, University of Pittsburgh, 1963–65; research associate, University of Pittsburgh, 1963–; research associate, Learning Research and Development Center, 1965–

Field of Work   vocational development and counseling theory with emphasis on ego-counseling

Affiliations   American Psychological Association, Division of Counseling Psychology; American Personnel and Guidance Association; National Vocational Guidance Association

SUMMATION OF CONCEPTS:

Hummel's attention seems to be directed toward the development of a counseling approach that relates well to many disciplines and manifests itself in a united concept that he refers to as ego-counseling.

ANNOTATED BIBLIOGRAPHY:

Hummel, Raymond C. "Vocational Development and Guidance Practice." *Journal of the National Association of Deans of Women*, 18 (October, 1954), 13–18.

Hummel touches upon the relation of guidance to the individual seeking vocational assistance. He introduces a vocational development theory and the five essential areas of understanding basic to the development of such a theory—i.e., education, personality theory, vocational diagnosis, occupational information, and the role of the counselor.

———. "Ego-Counseling in Guidance: Concept and Method." *Harvard Education Review*, 32 (Fall, 1962), 463-82.

Hummel introduces the term ego-counseling, which may well become synonymous with his name, seeing it as a more functional approach to counseling. He suggests that guidance is an applied science of psychology and does much to explain his personal concept of ego-counseling and how it relates to guidance. Perhaps of greatest concern to the counselor is his paradigm of the ego-counseling process as it is experienced by both the counselor and the client. As Hummel sees it, this pattern involves the setting, relationship, analysis, reorganization and synthesis, and action.

James, William

BIRTH: January 11, 1842, New York City
PRESENT STATUS: deceased; August 26, 1910, Chocorua, New Hampshire
BACKGROUND: *Educational* entered Harvard University, 1861 (studied chemistry, comparative anatomy, and physiology); entered Harvard Medical School, 1864; traveled to Brazil with the Thayer expedition, headed by Dr. Louis Agassiz, eminent Swiss-American naturalist, 1865-66; spent eighteen months in Berlin and Dresden, Germany, which marked the starting point of his two-fold interest in psychology and philosophy of religion; M.D., Harvard Medical School, 1869; honorary doctorates from Edinburgh, Geneva, Oxford, and Padua
Professional instructor, assistant professor, and professor, Harvard University, 1872-1907 (taught psychology, philosophy, and physiology); developed first course in America on the relation of psychology to physiology and established the first American psychological laboratory, in which G. Stanley Hall was a student, 1875; commissioned to write his famous *Principles of Psychology*, 1878 (published in book form, 1890); delivered Gifford Lectures on Natural Religion, University of Edinburgh, 1901-02; visiting professor, Stanford University, 1906; delivered Hibbert Lectures, Oxford University, 1908
Field of Work American pioneer in establishing psychology as a separate science and an early student of the psychology of religion
Affiliations Society for Psychical Research

WILLIAM JAMES

SUMMATION OF CONCEPTS:

Because James was a psychologist who pioneered efforts to make his profession a separate science, his literary contributions are included in the great books of the Western world, a collection of literary material considered historically significant. Much of his psychological writings are philosophical in nature, for he emphasized an "open" rather than a "closed" approach. In essence, he plowed the ground and others followed. Known for his pragmatism, James assumed that an idea was true if it worked satisfactorily. Like Freud, he maintained that one must always be ready to alter his perception if research and experience called for it. He stated, however, that scientific evidence need not be present for a person to believe in the spiritual and supernatural. James felt that certain experiences do not lend themselves to scientific investigation, and he considered a belief in immortality valid if it makes a person's life and behavior more meaningful and significant.

ANNOTATED BIBLIOGRAPHY:

James, William. *Principles of Psychology.* 2 vols. London: Macmillan and Co., 1901. 1,393 pp.

Twelve years in preparation, these two volumes are recognized as the most formal early introduction to psychology. Thousands of students received their initial psychological insights from this famous work. James introduced the research findings of Wilhelm Wundt, Hermann von Helmholtz, Francis Galton, Alfred Binet, and other European writers associated with the "new" psychology. Opposing the structuralist school of thought, which emphasized sensations, he stressed the importance of observing behavior, a key concept of the functional school. Probably the most classical and widely discussed idea in this work was what we now call the James-Lange theory of emotions, which states that emotions are the result of rather than the cause of bodily reactions.

_____. *Talks to Teachers on Psychology and to Students on Some of Life's Ideals.* New York: Henry Holt and Co., 1924. 301 pp.

In this book, originally published in 1899, James presented some basic ideas of learning generally associated with educational psychology. He stressed the idea that knowing psychology does not guarantee that one will be a successful teacher, but he believed that it could provide the tools for a person to teach more effectively than he could without the knowledge. Emphasis was placed on the laws of habit, the association of ideas, and an explanation of memory. The book concerns itself with ideas related to human blindness and the making of a significant life and includes three talks to students.

―――――. *The Varieties of Religious Experiences: A Study in Human Nature.* New York: Modern Library, 1936. 526 pp.

Rejecting the traditional concepts of religion, James viewed God as a presence to be encountered in human experiences. Actually, he saw religion as an experience rather than a dogma. How a person's religion influenced his behavior was of greatest importance to James. This study opened a new avenue of psychological thought regarding the examination of religion. It was an approach that gave hope to many who could find little if any meaning in following only rituals and creeds. Much of James' material was derived from actual case histories, many involving persons having unusual experiences and beliefs. James suggested that the study of actual experiences could uncover facts of man's nature that could not be gained through other sources. He found that many individuals, whose mystical experiences seemed "abnormal" to the average religious person, experienced a joyous vitality more like an acute fever than a dull habit. James noted that these experiences of faith tended to unify and integrate their lives, although some experiences were extremely emotional and sudden and others occurred gradually with little outward emotion.

Jones, Arthur J.

BIRTH: March 2, 1871, Grinnell, Iowa

PRESENT STATUS: deceased; August 27, 1963, Eagle's Mere, Pennsylvania

BACKGROUND: *Educational* A.B., Grinnell College, Iowa, 1893; Ph.D., Columbia University, 1907

Professional instructor, Grinnell College, 1893-95; teacher, Central High School, Minneapolis, Minnesota, 1895-98; superintendent of schools, Redwood Falls, Minnesota, 1898-1904; professor of education, Rhode Island Normal School, 1907-11; head of the Department of Education, University of Maine, 1911-19; professor of secondary education, University of Pennsylvania, 1919-41; professor emeritus, University of Pennsylvania, 1941-63

Field of Work guidance and counseling

Affiliations Association of School Administrators, Society of College

ARTHUR J. JONES

Teachers (secretary, 1921–41), American Educational Research Association, American Personnel and Guidance Association, Vocational Guidance Association (president, 1936), Phi Beta Kappa, Phi Kappa Phi, Phi Delta Kappa, Kappa Phi Kappa

SUMMATION OF CONCEPTS:

Jones felt that such conditions as changes in the home and family pattern, in industry and labor, and in population foster guidance and that young people need assistance in coping with such changes. He did much to introduce the school as the one institution designed to help the child through this formative period of his life, and he saw guidance as the auxiliary phase of the total school program designed to provide individual and group assistance with vocational decisions, educational plans, and personal-social goals.

ANNOTATED BIBLIOGRAPHY:

Jones, Arthur J., and Leonard M. Miller. "The National Picture of Pupil Personnel and Guidance Services in 1953." *Bulletin of the National Association of Secondary School Principals,* 38 (February, 1954), 105–59.

A report of national importance, this article introduces the existing condition of guidance services in our schools and suggests what action might be taken to improve these conditions. Great consideration is given to the graphic presentation of facts such as population growth in schools, counselor-student ratios, and guidance facilities available. Although these facts are more than twenty years old, their use is almost essential if guidance is to determine the degree of progress it has experienced during that time.

———. *Principles of Guidance.* 5th ed. New York: McGraw-Hill Book Co., 1963. 305 pp.

This edition is a revision of ideas originally presented by Jones, and in it he did much to update his material and to bring it into line with modern concepts. Although many of the ideas originally introduced in his first editions served as a frame of reference for the development of guidance, this book assumes great latitude in introducing a variety of new and highly speculative concepts. For those people engaged as counselor-educators, this work might well serve as an inspiration; for students interested in counseling, it might well serve as a basic frame of reference.

Jung, Carl Gustav

BIRTH: July 26, 1875, Kesswyl-Thurgau, Switzerland
PRESENT STATUS: deceased; June 6, 1961, Kusnacht-Zurich, Switzerland
BACKGROUND: *Educational* entered University of Basel, 1895; M.D., University of Basel, 1900; published his medical dissertation, "On the Psychology and Pathology of So-called Occult Phenomena," 1902; developed interest in psychiatry and, after intensive reading, studied in Paris with Pierre Janet, Jean Martin Charcot's student and successor; honorary doctorates from universities at Geneva, Calcutta, and Allahabad (India) and from Oxford, Clark, and Harvard
Professional assistant, Burgholzi Mental Hospital, Zurich, 1900–04; senior physician, Psychiatric Clinic, University of Zurich, 1905–09; established a laboratory for experimental psychopathology at the Psychiatric Clinic, 1904–05; lecturer in psychiatry, University of Zurich, 1905–13; met Sigmund Freud in February, 1907, and this friendship formally ended in 1914 when Jung withdrew from the International Psychoanalytic Association; private practice of medicine, specializing in psychotherapy, Kusnacht-Zurich, 1909–61 (this provided a base of operations that allowed Jung to travel extensively, to write, and to see patients as his schedule and health allowed); traveled to the United States with Freud in 1909 to deliver the famous Clark University lectures, arranged by G. Stanley Hall; lecturer in psychology, Federal Polytechnical University, Zurich, 1933–40; professor, medical psychology, University of Basel, 1944–45; conducted seminars in English for English-speaking students prior to his retirement; following his academic retirement, the C. G. Jung Institute, which carries on research and trains analytical psychologists, opened in Zurich, 1948
Field of Work founder of the system of analytical psychology and early leading scientific contributor to psychiatry
Affiliations Fellow, Royal Society of Medicine, London; Swiss Academy of Medical Science; Swiss Society for Psychiatry; Swiss Society for Practical Psychology; International Medical Society of Psychotherapy (president, 1933)

SUMMATION OF CONCEPTS:

Most of Jung's writings deal with both the conscious and the unconscious processes and the impact they have on behavior. Although once influenced by Freud's ideas, Jung proved himself an independent thinker by developing his own system of thought. The one similarity to psychoanalysis may be his emphasis on the unconscious. Yet, it must also be realized that his operational definition is, in itself, quite different from Freud's. One distinctive feature of his system is his view of man.

He believed that causality, which emphasizes man's individual and racial history, and teleology, which emphasizes man's aims and aspirations, are both significant factors in the formation of behavior. His viewpoint seems a hopeful one. Rather than seeing man as deterministic and the product of isolated experiences, Jung suggested that aims, aspirations, and purposes also influence one's life. As a result, he practiced a future-oriented therapy, which stresses self-realization through purposeful goals. In contrast to Freud, he also believed that one's past includes not only experiences of this life but a cumulative deposit of racial history. He viewed this racial past as a storehouse of unconscious ideas or an accumulation of predispositions and potentialities. These components of the collective unconscious, called archetypes, were believed to make up the foundation upon which the structure of personality is built. Included in the collective unconscious are our moral, spiritual, and religious values, believed by Jung to motivate our behavior even more than do our fundamental instincts. Jung believed that man's purpose of existence is to achieve unification of his conscious and unconscious experiences.

ANNOTATED BIBLIOGRAPHY:

Jung, Carl G. *Psychological Types*. Translated by H. Godwin Baynes. London: Pantheon Books, 1923. 654 pp.

This book deals with the idea that, although many typical differences exist in human personality, there are also typical distinctions. These are what Jung has termed the "introversion" and "extroversion" types. This concept is probably his most original and best known. Personality is viewed as moving in one of two directions and as predisposed toward one or the other direction. The extrovert's life is centered on action as he moves in the direction of people and lives in an objective and nonreflective world. Conversely, the introvert's life is centered on subjectively personal experiences as an attempt to free himself from outside distractions and to enjoy the privacy of his own inner life. Jung also suggests in this book that all persons have four psychological functions, *i.e.*, thinking, feeling, sensation, and intuition. Because a person utilizes one function more easily than the others, the one that dominates becomes his superior function. Moreover, a person with any one of these major functions can be introverted or extroverted.

———. *Modern Man in Search of a Soul.* Translated by W. S. Dell and Cary F. Baynes. New York: Harcourt, Brace, and World, 1933. 282 pp.

This is one of Jung's most famous books, written at a time when militant rationalism challenged traditional faith in God. Attempting to be scientifically objective, Jung stated that man believes in God, has believed in God or a god of some sort throughout the ages, and will continue to believe in Him. Jung did not, however, discuss whether God exists as interpreted in traditional, Christian theological thought. In the concluding chapter, "Psychotherapists or the Clergy," Jung penned one of his famous quotations, which states that, if all of his adult patients possessed what the great religions had tried to give their followers, they would not have become ill. He added that in patients over thirty-five there was not one whose problem ultimately was not that of finding a religious outlook on life. He felt it safe to state unequivocally that not one of these patients fully gained inner healing without regaining his religious outlook.

———. *Psychology and Religion.* New Haven: Yale University Press, 1938. 131 pp.

This book is based on the Terry Lectures of 1937, delivered at Harvard University. Jung attempted to show the interrelationship between psychology and religion. As did most psychologists, Jung viewed religion as an experience rather than a creed. He concluded that religious experience is absolute and indisputable. Religion, he believed, is more easily experienced than discussed, and, in spite of what others think about religious experience, it has a great source of meaning for the one who possesses it. This idea was a major underlying point of division between Freud and Jung, for Freud viewed religion primarily as an illusion.

———. *Psychological Reflections: An Anthology of the Writings of C. G. Jung.* Selected and edited by Jolandi Jacobi. New York: Pantheon Books, 1953. 342 pp.

As the subtitle reflects, this book is a collection of many choice passages from the prolific pen of Carl Jung. Beginning students in the behavioral sciences may find that these passages serve as an antecedent to some of Jung's complete volumes. An indication of what lies in store is suggested by the following divisions: "The Nature and Activity of the

Psyche," "Man in His Relation to Others," "The World of Values," and "On Ultimate Things."
———. *The Collected Works of C. G. Jung*. Edited by Herbert Read, Michael Fordham, and Gerhard Adler. Translated by R. F. C. Hull. 18 vols. New York: Pantheon Books, 1957. 6,000+ pp.

This comprehensive collection of Jung's works is both impressive and delightfully entertaining. It truly complements the collected papers of Sigmund Freud, which were presented in five volumes. This accumulation of thoughts begins with his first published work, the medical degree dissertation delivered before the faculty of medicine at the University of Zurich in 1902, and concludes with books relating to the practice of psychotherapy and the development of personality. His final volume submits for consideration a bibliography, some miscellaneous works, and a general index. At his own request, Jung's memoirs, edited by Aniela Jaffe, are not included, for he did not regard his autobiography as scientific and objective.

———. *Memories, Dreams, Reflections*. Recorded and edited by Aniela Jaffe. Translated by Richard and Clara Winston. New York: Pantheon Books, 1961. 398 pp.

This autobiography, initiated by Jung after his eighty-first birthday, is extraordinary in that it personifies the happenings of his inner life. Surprising to those who know of his massive contribution to psychology and psychiatry, Jung left the impression that his life had been "singularly poor in outer happening." This personal account does not give the slightest hint of the historical events occurring during his lifetime. He concluded that he could only understand himself in light of *inner happenings*, which he believed made up the singularity of his life.

Kitson, Harry Dexter
BIRTH: August 11, 1886, Mishawaka, Indiana
PRESENT STATUS: deceased; September 25, 1959, Mishawaka, Indiana
BACKGROUND: *Educational* A.B., Hiram College, 1909; A.M., University of Minnesota, 1913; Ph.D., University of Chicago, 1915
Professional assistant in Psychology Department, University of Minnesota, 1913–14; Fellow, University of Chicago, 1914–15; instructor in psychology, University of Chicago, 1915–19; associate professor and professor, Indiana Uni-

versity, 1919–25; professor of education, Columbia University Teachers College, 1925–51; professor emeritus, University of Chicago, 1951–59
  Field of Work   occupational selection and the psychology of vocational adjustment
  Affiliations   Fellow, American Psychological Association, Division of Counseling Psychology; Sigma Xi; Alpha Tau Omega

SUMMATION OF CONCEPTS:

Kitson's writings reflect a strong interest in vocational psychology. Much of his work is directed toward the psychology of studying, buying, and advertising, as well as the proper use of tests, the dangers of prediction in vocational guidance, and the needs of youth in the world of work. He appeared to be committed to the belief that no test by itself could determine a suitable vocation for any one person and that a comprehensive understanding of a person was possible only after subjective and objective information were combined. Furthermore, he believed that such a combination permitted a selection that was realistic and effective, since it combined qualities of knowledge, interest, growth potential, and aspiration, thus encouraging change as opportunity is presented.

ANNOTATED BIBLIOGRAPHY:

Kitson, Harry Dexter. *How to Find the Right Vocation*. New York: Harper and Brothers, Publishers, 1938. 215 pp.
  Kitson does an excellent job of presenting the problems confronting individuals who are entering the world of work. He does much to point out the necessity for analyzing talents and working toward advancement. The information presented can be readily used by counselors, faculty members, or students as they work together to establish realistic student goals.
  ———. *How to Use Your Mind*. 4th ed. Philadelphia: J. B. Lippincott Co., 1951. 192 pp.
  A rather unusual book for Kitson, this text does much to introduce the basic laws of learning and the relationship of such learning to physical health. Much emphasis is given to the effectiveness of study through stronger vocabulary and increased interests. Kitson also focuses upon the concept that individuals can become more effective by realizing their capabilities and utilizing their qualities to their best advantage.

ALFRED HABDANK KORZYBSKI

———. *I Find My Vocation.* New York: McGraw-Hill Book Co., 1954. 275 pp.

This book does much to present the steps a young person frequently takes when choosing a field of work. Kitson also introduces concepts regarding problems one might encounter, information that one might need, and practices in which one might engage, as one searches within the world of work for personal happiness.

———, and Edgar Morgan Stover. *Vocations for Boys.* New York: Harcourt, Brace and Co., 1955. 361 pp.

A book designed to assist young men in understanding trades, skills, and professions in an intelligent and meaningful way, it covers skilled trades, vocations in business, professions, science and technology, government-connected work, agriculture, and transportation. Kitson provides the reader with a comprehensive source of information to help in selecting a vocation intelligently.

Korzybski, Alfred Habdank

BIRTH: July 3, 1879, Warsaw, Poland
PRESENT STATUS: deceased; March 1, 1950, Lakeville, Connecticut
BACKGROUND: *Educational* graduate study in Germany, Italy, and the United States
Professional teacher of mathematics, physics, French, and German in Warsaw before World War I; traveled to the United States as member of the Intelligence Department, Russian General Staff, 1916; secretary of the Polish-French Military Commission in the United States and Canada, 1918; recruiting officer for the Polish-French army, 1918; secretary, Polish Commission, League of Nations, 1920; president and director, Institute of General Semantics (Chicago), 1938; writer and lecturer, 1920–50
Field of Work concerned with the art and science of human engineering
Affiliations Fellow, American Association for the Advancement of Science; American Mathematical Society; Chicago Society for Personality Study; Society for Applied Anthropology; New York Academy of Psychiatry; Society for Symbolic Logic

SUMMATION OF CONCEPTS:

Korzybski placed great emphasis upon the influence of language on the functioning of a person's nervous system. He maintained that, if the modification of language is profound enough to assure appropriate changes in the evaluative processes of the nervous system, then behavior can be modified through a change of linguistic habits. It was his opinion that the usefulness of a language depends upon the similarity of its structure to the empirical world in which the individual lives. He further maintained that the world abounds in maladjustment today simply because our language structure is in conflict with the structure of our empirical world.

ANNOTATED BIBLIOGRAPHY:

Korzybski, A. *Science and Sanity: An Introduction to Non-Aristotelian Systems and General Semantics.* Lakeville, Conn.: International Non-Aristotelian Library, 1948. 806 pp.

Korzybski presents three concepts in general semantics that he considers basic to maximum predictability. The first is the principle of non-identity, which seems to imply that a word *is not* the thing it represents. In essence, the Aristotelian principle of identity leads one to believe that certain things are identical to other things. Korzybski feels that no one thing is identical to anything else and that in our evaluative processes we tend to identify our statements about facts with the facts themselves. The second concept is that of non-allness, which seems to imply that a word *does not* embrace all of the characteristics of the thing it represents. According to Aristotelian concepts, one is a failure or a success. That is to say, one is either a success or a failure by virtue of the fact that Aristotelian concepts promulgate absolutes. In contrast, Korzybski introduces the idea that infinite possibilities become apparent as one analyzes each new challenge. The third concept is that of self-reflectiveness, which for Korzybski implies that we can speak about language in language. This means that, in terms of human behavior, one can react to an event, can react to his reaction, and can then react to his reaction *ad infinitum*. Perhaps a major contribution of this book is that it presents the significance of general semantics to persons engaged in the area of counseling.

Krumboltz, John Dwight

BIRTH: October 21, 1928, Cedar Rapids, Iowa
PRESENT STATUS: professor of education and psychology, Stanford University
BACKGROUND: *Educational* B.A., Coe College, 1950; M.A., Teachers

JOHN DWIGHT KRUMBOLTZ

College of Columbia University, 1951; Ph.D., University of Minnesota, 1955
Professional counselor and teacher, West Waterloo, Iowa, High School, 1951–53; teaching assistant, University of Minnesota, 1953–54; instructor, University of Minnesota, 1954–55; research psychologist, United States Air Force, 1955–57; assistant professor, educational psychology, Michigan State University, 1957–59; associate professor, Michigan State University, 1959–61; associate professor, education and psychology, Stanford University, 1961–66; professor of education and psychology, 1966–
Field of Work counseling research and behavior modification
Affiliations American Psychological Association, Divisions of Counseling Psychology, Educational Psychology, Evaluation and Measurement, and Experimental Analysis of Behavior; American Personnel and Guidance Association (recipient of the Outstanding Research Award in 1959, 1966, and 1968); American Educational Research Association; Guggenheim Fellow, 1967–68

SUMMATION OF CONCEPTS:

As a major proponent of the behavioral counseling viewpoint, Krumboltz directs most of his writings toward the conceptualization of counseling through learning. In behavioral terms, learning is the process by which a person changes. Krumboltz interprets the counseling process as an encounter between a client and a counselor in which the counselor becomes active and often directive in the expert arrangement of learning or relearning experiences that tend to change the client's behavior in order to solve whatever problem or conflict he faces. Much emphasis is placed on the corrective and reinforcing value of experiences that occur between sessions.

ANNOTATED BIBLIOGRAPHY:

Krumboltz, John D., ed. *Learning and the Educational Process.* Chicago: Rand McNally and Co., 1965. 277 pp.

This collection of papers is an outgrowth of a summer conference held at Stanford University in 1964. An attempt was made at that time to explore recent psychological concepts of educational learning that had not been treated by researchers. Krumboltz selected from the presentations what he considered to be representative of the major topics and ideas. Two that may be of interest are a study of intrinsic and extrinsic motivation and a discussion of impulsive and reflective children.

─────, ed. *Revolution in Counseling: Implications of Behavioral Science.* Boston: Houghton Mifflin Co., 1966. 121 pp.

The significance of this book is its attempt to introduce a systematic approach to behavioral counseling. Five papers, presented initially at the Cubberley Conference at Stanford University in 1965, make up the content. The primary purpose of the conference was to explore effective and innovative ways by which school counselors could assist students in their educational growth. Emphasis is placed on counseling goals, the implications of behavioral science for counseling, and the worth of the individual. The final phase of the book deals with C. Gilbert Wrenn's attempt to establish a bridge of cordial relations between perceptual psychology and behaviorism; he suggests that both reflection and reinforcement may have a place in the counseling process.

_____, and Carl E. Thoresen, eds. *Behavioral Counseling: Cases and Techniques.* New York: Holt, Rinehart, and Winston, 1969. 515 pp.

Basically this work serves as a counseling cookbook. Attempts are made throughout the book to explain in practical terms the meaning of the term "behavioral counseling." The authors readily agree that this approach to counseling has much in common with other approaches, although it has certain distinguishing features. Krumboltz emphasizes the importance of formulating goals in counseling that may be evaluated. He states that a counseling goal must meet three criteria: it must be a goal desired by the client, the counselor must be willing to help the client achieve the goal, and it must be possible to assess the extent to which the client achieves the goal. Krumboltz denies that this theory is impersonal and static, for he believes change, improvement, and growth are virtually inevitable in the very nature of behavioral counseling.

Lewin, Kurt

BIRTH: September 9, 1890, Mogilno, Germany

PRESENT STATUS: deceased; February 12, 1947, Newtonville, Massachusetts

BACKGROUND: *Educational* Kaiserin Augusta Gymnasium, 1903–08; University of Freiburg, 1908; University of Munich, 1909; Ph.D., University of Berlin, 1909–14

Professional served in the German army, 1914–18; assistant at the Psychological Institute, University of Berlin, 1921; privatdocent of philosophy, University of Berlin, 1921–26; professor of philosophy and psychology, University of Berlin, 1926–33; visiting professor of psychology, Stanford University, 1932–33; professor of psychology, Cornell University, 1933–

35; professor of child psychology, Child Welfare Research Station, University of Iowa, 1935–44; visiting professor at Harvard University and University of California (Berkeley), 1938–40; associated with the Office of Strategic Services, 1944–45; director, Research Center for Group Dynamics, Massachusetts Institute of Technology, 1944–47

Field of Work Gestalt psychology

Affiliations American Psychological Association, Division of the Society for the Psychological Study of Social Issues; Midwest Psychological Association; American Association for the Advancement of Science; Phi Epsilon Pi; Sigma Xi

SUMMATION OF CONCEPTS:

Lewin is most frequently recognized as a leader in the area of Gestalt psychology, in which his attention seemed to be directed toward understanding the motivation of human behavior. It was this very interest that prompted him to study individuals in a group setting while working at the Massachusetts Institute of Technology and later to establish the group-training institute at Bethel, Maine. Perhaps his greatest contribution was his concept of the "field," which he referred to as life space containing the person and his psychological environment. To Lewin, behavior was relative to the present field, never to the past or the future, and the present field, in essence, was relative to the world as it was perceived by the individual. One can now see how Lewin paved the way for phenomenological psychology and how his concepts brought forth the realization that many things perceived are of little or no immediate concern to a person and, therefore, remain in his psychological background. Lewin's most interesting belief regarding perception is that objects of concern to an individual seem to have a positive or negative valence that attracts or repels interest in those objects. The positive or negative valence is, of course, relative to the way the person perceives the object. If he sees it as positive, an attracting force known as a positive vector directs him toward the object. Lewin's interest in these forces referred to as vectors eventuated a new approach in the study of behavior and motivation, which he called vector analysis.

ANNOTATED BIBLIOGRAPHY:

Lewin, Kurt. *A Dynamic Theory of Personality.* New York and London: McGraw-Hill Book Co., 1935. 286 pp.

WALTER M. LIFTON

Here Lewin discusses the conflict between Aristotelian and Galilean modes of thought in contemporary psychology. Much emphasis is placed on the mind and the significance of environmental forces in child development. He also considers some experimental investigations of the past.

———. *Principles of Topological Psychology.* New York and London: McGraw-Hill Book Co., 1936. 231 pp.

Lewin reflects his attitude toward present theories in psychology and his own personal concept of life space. Much of the text is devoted to his concept of topology, a new mathematical discipline that he felt would help make psychology a real science. Another point of interest introduced is his concept of an understandable psychological language independent of schools of psychology.

Lifton, Walter M.

BIRTH: November 2, 1918, Brooklyn, New York

PRESENT STATUS: professor of education and director of the Guidance and Counseling Program, State University of New York at Albany

BACKGROUND: *Educational* B.A., Brooklyn College, 1942; M.A., New York University, 1947; Ph.D., New York University, 1950

Professional psychiatric social worker, personnel technician, and specialist, United States Army, 1943–46; senior vocational appraiser, the Guidance Center, Hunter College, 1946–48; lecturer in education and guidance, New York University, 1946–50; assistant and associate professor of education, University of Illinois, 1950–59; director of Guidance Publications and Service Department, Science Research Associates, 1959–64; coordinator of Pupil Personnel Services, Rochester City School District, 1964–70; professor of education and director of the Guidance and Counseling Program, State University of New York at Albany, 1970–

Field of Work group counseling techniques, counselor selection, and occupational information

Affiliations Fellow, American Psychological Association, Division of Counseling Psychology; American Personnel and Guidance Association; National Vocational Guidance Association; American College Personnel Association

SUMMATION OF CONCEPTS:

Lifton recognizes an innate "spark of divinity" in each human being. He feels that this spark can become dulled or perhaps even be extinguished if man does not conscientiously pursue a path of intellectual, social, and economic freedom through greater fraternity. It is his opinion that man must avoid the type of encapsulation that so readily becomes the core of rejection. Lifton believes that to reject your fellowman is to become your own jailor—to become limited in scope, action, and effective living and, in essence, to become unfit for society. He maintains that the philosophy and function of guidance at any level, and through any means at its command, are to assist people to understand themselves and the world in which they live.

ANNOTATED BIBLIOGRAPHY:

Lifton, Walter M. "Group Classroom Techniques." *Progressive Education*, 30 (May, 1953), 210–14.

Lifton reports on a study he did to gain insight into group techniques. His approach involves permissiveness and understanding by the instructor, which are supplemented by latitude in the presentation of materials and by self-evaluation concerning the personal enrichment gained through such presentations.

———. "Can Teachers Serve as Counselors?" *Journal of Education*, 136 (May, 1954), 226–29.

The author approaches this frequently asked question by presenting those points on which teaching and counseling appear to be quite similar and those that seem to make each quite different.

———. "Group Therapy in Educational Institutions." *Review of Educational Research*, 2 (April, 1954), 156–65.

Much emphasis is placed on the necessity for defining group therapy in terms of the educational setting. Such an approach, it seems, would relate group therapy to the "normal" person and learning content to perceived personal need. Lifton also points out some distinguishing marks between therapy and counseling, group therapy and group dynamics.

———, and Harold F. Cottingham. "The Role of the Teacher and the Instructor in the Guidance Program." *Review of Educational Research*, 27 (April, 1957), 192–201.

The authors indicate a strong need for research in such areas as assessing group processes in the classroom, the effects of the curricula and texts on attitude formation and problem solving, elementary school occupational information and orientation, and teacher training and evaluation in the area of guidance. Many of the people currently working in these areas of research are listed for the convenience of those who may want to pursue these studies further.

———, and Dale J. Hart. "Automation and Counseling." *Personnel and Guidance Journal*, 37 (December, 1958), 282–86.

This article describes the authors' perception of the impact of automation and revolutionary change upon the school counselor. The authors discuss the presumed effects of leisure time and future attitudes toward work, indicating that counselors must prepare to assist in programs designed to train people and retrain displaced persons for the world of automation.

———. *Working with Groups*. New York: John Wiley and Sons, 1961. 238 pp.

This book appears to be designed to help people interested in developing a technique that is effective when working with groups. The author talks about group guidance and subject matter groups, and much emphasis is placed on resolving problems in a democratic way. Lifton believes that, once a group has faced and resolved a problem, it has experienced a method of working together that will be reflected in future efforts to resolve problems.

Maslow, Abraham H.

BIRTH: April 1, 1908, Brooklyn, New York
PRESENT STATUS: deceased; June 8, 1970, Menlo Park, California
BACKGROUND: *Educational* A.B., University of Wisconsin, 1930; M.A., University of Wisconsin, 1931; Ph.D., University of Wisconsin, 1934
Professional research assistant in social psychology, University of Wisconsin, 1929–30; assistant instructor of psychology, University of Wisconsin, 1930–34; Teaching Fellow, University of Wisconsin, 1934–35; Carnegie Research Fellow, Columbia University, 1935–37; tutor to associate professor, Brooklyn College, 1937–51; associate professor of psychology, Brandeis University, 1951–55; professor of psychology, Brandeis University, 1955–62; chairman, Department of Psychology, Brandeis University, 1951–62; Andrew Kay Visiting Fellow, Western Behavioral Sciences Institute, La Jolla, California, 1961–62; Resident Fellow, W. P. Laughlin Foundation, 1969–70
Field of Work theory of motivation, psychological health, transpersonal theory

ABRAHAM H. MASLOW

Affiliations Fellow, American Psychological Association, Divisions of Personality and Social Psychology, the Society for the Psychological Study of Social Issues, Psychology and the Arts, Clinical Psychology, and Philosophical Psychology; Massachusetts State Psychological Association; Fellow, New York Academy of Sciences; Phi Beta Kappa; Sigma Xi

SUMMATION OF CONCEPTS:

Perhaps Maslow's most significant contribution to the study of human behavior is his emphasis on healthy people rather than sick ones. Concerned primarily with growth motivation, Maslow believed that healthy growth may be gained through self-actualization. To him, this is a state of "being" experienced when everything goes right in one's personality development. The antithesis of self-actualization is personal disintegration and ultimately, therefore, psychotic behavior. It seems that Maslow was reacting against the emphasis placed on abnormal behavior and strongly suggesting that some emphasis be placed on studying the development of the healthy personality. His positive view of man's nature paves the way for his theoretical construct.

ANNOTATED BIBLIOGRAPHY:

Maslow, Abraham H., and Bela Mittelmann. *Principles of Abnormal Psychology: The Dynamics of Psychic Illness.* New York: Harper and Row, 1941. 665 pp.

This is Maslow's first major work. In it, the authors cover such areas as psychotherapy, psychopathology, and psychological syndromes. Initially a study is made of the meaning of the terms "normal" and "abnormal," and the authors use many illustrations and case studies as a means of introducing and simplifying various psychological concepts. As one would anticipate in a study of abnormal psychology, attention is given to neurotic and psychotic reactions. Also, one of the best-written sections focuses upon the psychopathic personality and character disorders. A glossary is provided, as is an appendix introducing psychometric techniques used in personality assessment, such as the Rorschach test, the thematic apperception test (TAT), and word association tests.

———. *Motivation and Personality.* New York: Harper and Row, 1954. 411 pp.

In this his chief work, Maslow proposes a personality theory based on motivational needs. He assumes that psychological health is determined by the degree to which one fulfills his need priorities and proposes the following hierarchy: the physiological needs, *i.e.*, water, air, and physical comfort; the safety needs, *i.e.*, freedom from fear and insecurity; the belongingness and love needs, *i.e.*, desire to be somebody who loves others and is loved in return; the esteem needs, *i.e.*, high evaluation of oneself, such as self-respect or self-esteem, and the esteem of others; the need for self-actualization, *i.e.*, desire to become everything one is capable of becoming; and the aesthetic needs, *i.e.*, order, symmetry, closure, and completion of an act. Maslow suggests that fulfilling these needs in sequence is the direction man follows in his effort to develop an integrated personality. As one quickly detects, the theory presents an optimistic view of human nature.

———, ed. *New Knowledge in Human Values*. New York: Harper and Brothers, Publishers, 1959. 268 pp.

Maslow attempts to bring together in one volume several addresses by some of the foremost authorities in the realm of human values. The papers are from a conference, "New Knowledge in Human Values," sponsored by the Research Society for Creative Altruism, at which man's moral direction was spotlighted. Starting from the premise that the "moral transformation of man and the man-made universe is the most important item on today's agenda in history," men such as Pitirim A. Sorokin, Gordon W. Allport, Erich Fromm, Paul Tillich, and Kurt Goldstein addressed themselves to the theme of human values.

———. *Toward a Psychology of Being*. Princeton: D. Van Nostrand Co., 1962. 214 pp.

This book is a sequel to *Motivation and Personality*, although it is more philosophical. Linking himself with such writers as Carl Rogers, Rollo May, and Alfred Adler, Maslow presents his optimistic psychology, often called "the third force" because it contrasts sharply with the Freudian and behavioral schools of psychology. Using case studies of psychologically healthy persons, Maslow demonstrates from the lives of average people that human beings can be loving and creative and are capable of pursuing high aspirations and meaningful values. Maslow admits, although he is not opposed to the scientific approach, that he structured his position out of "pilot researches, bits of evidence, personal observations, theoretical deduction, and on sheer hunch."

———. *Religions, Values, and Peak Experiences*. Columbus: Ohio State University Press, 1964. 123 pp.

ROBERT HENDRY MATHEWSON

Perhaps one of the most helpful psychological theses on religious experiences, this lecture by Maslow speaks to both the organized church and conventional atheism. To the atheist Maslow suggests that "religion is easy to criticize but difficult to explain." Believing that some psychologists, *e.g.*, Sigmund Freud, have so reduced religion that they have overlooked its potential therapeutic value, Maslow feels that they have thrown out too much. Moreover, he implies that the churchmen have failed to acknowledge the possibility that "peak religious experiences" can occur outside religious or mystical contexts. An interesting conclusion noted by Maslow is that "the Truth" is not dependent on man.

Mathewson, Robert Hendry

BIRTH: September 13, 1899, Bridgeport, Connecticut

PRESENT STATUS: professor emeritus of education, City University of New York

BACKGROUND: *Educational* B.S., University of Connecticut, 1922; M.A., Columbia University, 1932; Ph.D., Yale University, 1940

Professional assistant in the College of Education and alumni secretary, University of Connecticut, 1923–25; staff member, American consulate general, Stockholm, Sweden, 1925–27; editor, Simmons-Boardman Publishing Company and Radford Publishing Company, New York City, 1927–32; youth and adult counselor and lecturer, YMCA, and adult education program, Norwalk, Connecticut, 1933–35; educational supervisor, Connecticut State Department of Education, 1935–45; lecturer, Harvard University, 1943–45; associate professor, Graduate School of Education, Harvard University, 1945–48; director of the Guidance Center, Harvard University and Tufts College, 1945–49; professor of education, City University of New York, 1950–64; visiting Fulbright professor, University of Amsterdam, 1957–58; professor emeritus, City University of New York, 1965–; lecturer in various university locations, including the University of Amsterdam, the University of Hawaii, the University of Reading, the University of Manchester, and Oxford University, 1965–

Field of Work organization of guidance services, counseling procedures, and foundations of guidance

Affiliations Fellow, American Psychological Association, Divisions of Educational Psychology and Counseling Psychology; American Personnel and Guidance Association; Association for Counselor Education and Supervision; National Vocational Guidance Association; Phi Delta Kappa

SUMMATION OF CONCEPTS:

From Mathewson's writings it appears that he believes that appraisal, adjustment, orientation, development, and coordination are the basic functions of a guidance counselor. He also introduces the concept that a two-year program of graduate work is most appropriate for a graduate degree in guidance, with the first year of study devoted to psychology and sociology and the second year focused on guidance techniques. In essence, much of what Mathewson expressed in his early philosophy became a guideline for what has been done in the area of guidance.

ANNOTATED BIBLIOGRAPHY:

Mathewson, Robert Hendry. "Educational Problems of Veterans and Other Civilians." *Journal of the American Association of College Registrars*, 21 (July, 1946), 462–74.

From a sampling of the opinions of deans, veterans counselors, and other university officials, it is concluded that the veteran is a serious, better-than-average student, who is "vocational-minded." The educational problems he has seem to reflect a need for additional information regarding such points of interest as the selection process, the purpose of education, the distribution of students in various curricula, the need for guidance and counseling, and the kinds of curricula offered by colleges. Continued investigation seems to indicate that these problems affect nonveterans as well.

———. *Guidance Policy and Practice*. New York: Harper and Brothers, Publishers, 1949. 294 pp.

This reflects an early attempt by Mathewson to publish his concepts of guidance. Strangely enough, much of what he introduces has already transpired. Most interesting to the reader would probably be his outline of a frame of reference from which the guidance counselor might work and from which the very future of guidance might be projected. Seldom if ever has an author had so profound a knowledge of a subject, and seldom if ever has an author set forth guidelines that have served so well and so long in the development of guidance. For those who want to acquire a knowledgeable background in guidance, this book covers four main areas of thought. Part 1, "Fundamental Factors in Guidance Practices," is a presentation of psychological philosophical concepts, the needs of individuals and groups, the institutional setting, the social setting, and the costs of guidance. Part 2, "Guidance Policy and Its Implementation," covers such areas as guidance services in the community and school and guidance as educative and democratic. Part 3 deals with such basic issues as the scope of guidance and educational responsibility for personal development. Part 4, "The Future of Guidance," discusses trends and sets up a projected national policy for guidance in America.

———. "Provisions of Adult-Guidance Services." *School and Society*, 72 (July, 1950), 5–7.

An early article by Mathewson, this is the result of a study involving 17,000 veterans who were counseled during the period from 1945 through 1949. The data compiled served as a guideline for the organization and administration of other counseling centers.

———. "Graduate Training for School Counselors." *Occupations*, 30 (February, 1952), 335–39.

Mathewson makes an effort to reflect some of the ideas generally practiced in New York graduate training programs for counselors. Importance is placed on defining a set of acceptable characteristics for counselors, with a focus of attention upon academic training in psychology, sociology, testing, and statistics. The author does much to present a variety of new concepts in counselor education.

———. "General Guidance Counselor." *Personnel and Guidance Journal*, 32 (May, 1954), 544–47.

Mathewson discusses the training needs of counselors. His main emphasis seems to be on the counselor as an appraiser of emotionally normal individuals and as a builder of positive dispositions. His responsibility to the student is met through his work with parents, teachers, administrators, and community members, as well as with the student and his peers.

———, and Jeanne L. Noble. "Evaluating a Program of Counselor Training Through Group Conferences." *Personnel and Guidance Journal*, 34 (January, 1956), 285–88.

This study reflects an attempt by Mathewson to evaluate graduates of the counselor education program through the use of group techniques. His ideas are worthy of consideration.

———. "Analysis of Unstructured Self-Appraisal: A Technique in Counselor Education." *Journal of Counseling Psychology*, 3 (1956), 32–36.

This is the presentation of a most interesting approach designed to assist the counselor-trainee in understanding the client's perception of the world. The technique involves closely structured analyses of recorded initial interviews.

KARL A. MENNINGER

————. *Strategy for American Education.* New York: Harper and Brothers, Publishers, 1957. 296 pp.

This is an inquiry into the feasibility of education for individual and social development. The book's four main parts cover a new strategy of education, foundations for an individual-social theory of education, education for individual and social development, and ways of working toward an educative society. The major theme introduces the necessity for education in a democratic society and the significance of guidance in developing more adequate educational programs.

————. "Manpower or Persons." *Personnel and Guidance Journal,* 43 (October, 1964), 338-42.

Mathewson criticizes the manpower utilization orientation instituted in guidance programs and suggests the emphasis should be on individual development. This emphasis is more consistent, he maintains, with the long-range goals of developmental progress and eliminates the mundane practices of troubleshooting and direction pointing so characteristic of many guidance programs.

Menninger, Karl A.

BIRTH: July 22, 1893, Topeka, Kansas

PRESENT STATUS: dean, Menninger School of Psychiatry; staff, Stormont-Vail Hospital; chairman of the board, Menninger Foundation, Topeka, Kansas

BACKGROUND: *Educational* A.B., University of Wisconsin, 1914; B.S., University of Wisconsin, 1915; M.D., Harvard Medical School, 1917; honorary doctorates from Washburn University, Park College, Parsons College, Kansas State University, Jefferson Medical College of Philadelphia, Benedict's College, the University of Wisconsin, Baker University, Depaul University, and Pepperdine University

Professional assistant physician, Boston Psychopathic Hospital, 1918-20; assistant in neurology, Tufts Medical School, 1918-19; assistant in neuropathology, Harvard Medical School, 1918-20; established with his father and brother the Menninger Clinic, 1919; staff member, Stormont-Vail Hospital, Topeka, Kansas, 1919-; chief of staff, Menninger Clinic, 1925-46; associate in psychology and currently professor-at-large, Graduate School, University of Kansas, 1946-; dean, Menninger School of Psychiatry, 1946-; chairman of the board, Menninger Foundation, 1954-

Field of Work psychiatry, neurology, psychoanalysis, and mental health

Affiliations Life Fellow, American Psychiatric Association; Fellow, American Medical Association; life member, American Psychoanalytic Association (president, 1941-43); American Psychological Association; charter member,

KARL A. MENNINGER

American Orthopsychiatric Association; charter member, Topeka Institute for Psychoanalysis; founder member, World Medical Association, U.S. Committee; American Academy for Child Psychiatry; Group for the Advancement of Psychiatry

SUMMATION OF CONCEPTS:

Menninger is concerned with individual needs, and he is equally mindful of the masses of people who need but do not have the benefit of psychological services. His experiences have convinced him that psychiatric treatment is more successful when a team effort is utilized. This principle led him to develop the Menninger Foundation, where psychologists, psychiatrists, psychoanalysts, psychiatric social workers, clergymen, neurosurgeons, child-care nurses, and internists work together to help patients in their recovery. Although a psychoanalyst, Menninger sees the tendency of the practitioner to treat a few wealthy patients while thousands suffer. Annoyed by this trend, he has attempted to arouse within psychiatrists a greater sense of social responsibility. A key to understanding Menninger is that he is a starter of projects. He believes that many people can finish things, but the job is to find someone to initiate them. To Menninger, discipline, sacrifice, and training that result in service to humanity is what life is all about.

ANNOTATED BIBLIOGRAPHY:

Menninger, Karl A. *Man Against Himself.* New York: Harcourt, Brace, and World, 1938. 483 pp.

Menninger analyzes the destructive forces that seem to exist in man's nature, especially his self-destructiveness. Although very little concrete research is available on suicide, an attempt is made to evaluate the motives and situations leading to one's wish to die or to be killed. The book focuses on the idea that the student of human behavior cannot escape the conclusion that man is potentially his own greatest enemy. This idea is based on Freud's death-instinct theory, which proposes that existing in man are strong dispositions toward self-destruction. These inclinations may result in suicide when the death instinct becomes greater than the life instinct.

―――――. *Love Against Hate.* Harcourt, Brace, and World, 1942. 310 pp.

This book is dedicated to the memory of Sigmund Freud, who stimulated Menninger's interest in *thanatos*, the death instinct, and *eros*, the life instinct, the two opponents waging battle within man. Love and hate are presented as the emotional representatives of the destructive and constructive forces. Whereas *thanatos* is man against himself, *eros* is man's hope and/or his life instinct. When asked to name the saddest word in the English language, Menninger's reply was, "Unloved." Love, presented as more than a sentimental, romantic precept, is viewed as a transforming means of making sick people well and strong people stronger. It has power over the destructive forces within man's personality, which he is incapable of fully understanding. The accompanying action for hate is destructiveness.

———. *The Human Mind*. 3rd rev. ed. New York: Alfred A. Knopf, 1945. 517 pp.

This is one of the most widely distributed publications on psychiatry for the general public. It was written by Menninger to fulfill his need for an appropriate textbook while teaching a course on mental health at Washburn University. Quite readable, the book deals with the principles, personalities, symptoms, motives, treatments, and applications of the human mind as it relates to mental health. Menninger suggests that mental health is "the adjustment of human beings to the world and to each other with a maximum of effectiveness and happiness." All persons, he believes, are subject to weaknesses and faults, for these are characteristics of the human mind. The greatest enemy of mental health is one's compulsion to believe that he is exempt from all failure and abnormal tendencies.

———. *A Psychiatrist's World: The Selected Papers of Karl Menninger*. New York: Viking Press, 1959. 931 pp.

This is a representative sample of Menninger's writings, selected by a professional committee to commemorate his sixty-fifth birthday. One cannot help but be impressed by this man's major contributions to psychiatry and mental health. For the student interested in the aims, goals, history, and growth of psychiatry and mental health, these selected papers present the ideas of one who has been a forerunner in the movement to make America the "healthiest" as well as the wealthiest country in the world.

———. *The Vital Balance: The Life Process in Mental Health and Illness*. New York: Viking Press, 1963. 531 pp.

ADOLF MEYER

Menninger reflects a positive view of man, emphasizing that where there is life there is hope. He views life as a composite of many conflicts that require attention and presents a theory of human behavior that stresses the holistic concept of personality as an incorporation of physical, chemical, psychological, and social elements. The vital balance suggests that equilibrium, self-regulation, organismic integrity, and homeostasis are necessary in the long-range adjustment processes of life if mental health is to be achieved.

Meyer, Adolf

BIRTH: September 13, 1866, Niederweningen-Zurich, Switzerland
PRESENT STATUS: deceased; March 17, 1950, Baltimore, Maryland
BACKGROUND: *Educational* Swiss state examination to practice medicine, 1890; postgraduate studies at Paris, London, Edinburgh, Zurich, Vienna, and Berlin, 1890–92; M.D., University of Zurich, 1892; honorary LL.D., Glasgow University, 1901, Clark University, 1909; honorary Sc.D., Yale University, 1934, Harvard University, 1942
Professional honorary Fellow, then lecturer, in neurology, University of Chicago, 1892–95; pathologist, Illinois Eastern Hospital for the Insane, Kankakee, 1893–95; pathologist and later director of clinical and laboratory work, Worcester (Mass.) Insane Hospital, and lecturer in psychiatry, Clark University, 1895–1902; director, Psychiatric Institute, New York State Hospitals, 1902–10; professor of psychiatry, Cornell University Medical College, 1904–09; professor of psychiatry, Johns Hopkins University Medical School, and director of the Henry Phipps Psychiatric Clinic, Johns Hopkins Hospital, 1910–41; guest lecturer, Academy of Neurology and Psychiatry, Kharkov, U.S.S.R., 1933; professor emeritus, Johns Hopkins University Medical School, 1941–50
Field of Work notable contributions in psychiatry, pathology, neurology, and mental hygiene; credited with suggesting the term "mental hygiene" for the new movement pioneered by Clifford Beers in the early twentieth century
Affiliations American Psychiatric Association (president, 1927), American Neurological Association (president, 1922), American Psychopathological Association (president, 1912, 1916), American Association for the Advancement of Science, American Psychological Association, American Orthopsychiatric Association, New York Psychiatric Society (president, 1905–07), National Committee for Mental Hygiene (honorary president), International Conference for Mental Hygiene (president), Thomas Salmon Medal for distinguished service in psychiatry, 1942

SUMMATION OF CONCEPTS:

One of the outstanding influences in the development of psychiatry in America, Meyer referred to himself as a pragmatist, a pluralist, and a naturalist. He sought opportunities to make improvements, always believing that the individual should realistically do his best rather than striving for perfection. Meyer rejected determinism, fatalism, and dogmatism, insisting that life itself, and not the Freudian doctrine of the unconscious, should serve as psychiatry's major point of reference. He placed emphasis on the whole range of factors and suggested that the gastrointestinal body function could influence personality as readily as the unconscious processes. By using common sense and an open mind, Meyer made a significant contribution in actual service to mankind instead of developing a theoretical system, which tends to place one's name in textbooks. He did not offer his followers "the Truth"; rather he offered ways of finding truth, which keep the channels of thought open for fresh discovery, struggle, and growth.

ANNOTATED BIBLIOGRAPHY:

Lief, Alfred, ed. *The Commonsense Psychiatry of Dr. Adolf Meyer: Fifty-two Selected Papers.* New York: McGraw-Hill Book Co., 1948. 677 pp.

Adolf Meyer wrote nearly two hundred papers during his lifetime and received honorary doctorates from both Harvard and Yale, yet he never published a book. Students may find this strange, especially after reading the works of such men as Karl Menninger, Carl Jung, and Sigmund Freud. Yet, as one begins to understand Meyer and his apparent desire to avoid finality, his actions seem less strange. Obviously he had little need for closure—probably less than the average researcher. As a result, he found no real need to write a book. His compilation of papers is, in itself, a real tribute to his profession. Perhaps of all of these papers, the fifty-two here are among the most important. They were carefully selected for this volume and are accompanied by Lief's progressive, biographical narrative. This book presents a clear, evolutionary picture of the thought and contributions of a man whose life reflects the unfolding history of early American psychiatry.

Mowrer, O. Hobart
  BIRTH: January 23, 1907, Unionville, Missouri
  PRESENT STATUS: professor emeritus, Department of Psychology, University of Illinois

O. HOBART MOWRER

BACKGROUND: *Educational* A.B., University of Missouri, 1929; Ph.D., Johns Hopkins University, 1932
Professional Fellow, National Research Council, Northwestern University, 1932–33; Princeton University, 1933–34; Sterling Research Fellow, Yale University, 1934–36; instructor, Department of Psychology, and member of research staff, Institute of Human Relations, Yale University, 1936–40; assistant professor of psychology, 1940–43, associate professor, 1943–48, Harvard University; clinical psychologist, Office of Strategic Services, 1944–45; research professor, Department of Psychology, University of Illinois, 1948–75; professor emeritus, Department of Psychology, University of Illinois, 1975–
Field of Work personality dynamics, group therapy, and learning theory
Affiliations Fellow, American Psychological Association (president, 1954), Divisions of Personality and Social Psychology (president, 1953) and Clinical Psychology (president, 1953); American Academy of Psychotherapists; American Association of University Professors; American Psychological Foundation (president, 1959–60)

SUMMATION OF CONCEPTS:

After some years of experience in psychoanalysis, Mowrer conceptualized a new direction in psychotherapy, known as the new group therapy and/or integrity therapy. According to this concept, neuroses are forms of what is theologically classified as a state of sin. Mowrer believes that, if therapy is to be effective, the concepts of guilt, confession, penance, expiation, and moral responsibility must be taken seriously. Using the stimulus-response model of learning, Mowrer indicates that personal responsibility must intervene between the stimulus and the response. If man's ethics (what he says) and his morals (what he does) are in conflict, then he is basically dishonest and inauthentic. In his approach to group therapy, individuals confess their moral failures to "significant others" and accept the shame and punishment that result. Confession is believed to relieve guilt, but one must continue to remain open, make restitution, and assume personal responsibility for his behavior. Mowrer suggests that this experience reverses one's life pattern and provides a new sense of direction. Thus, a new avenue of approach is utilized in dealing with the theological problem of sin and the psychological problem of neurosis.

ANNOTATED BIBLIOGRAPHY:

Mowrer, O. Hobart. *Learning Theory and Personality Dynamics.* New York: Ronald Press Co., 1950. 776 pp.

These selected papers attempt to define the bridge existing between learning theory and personality theory. Mowrer suggests that both learning and personality refer to the same set of realities, which are the principles and processes by which human nature functions. An interesting development is Mowrer's rejection of various Freudian doctrines and the emergence of some new ideas, which later become tenets of the new group therapy.

———. *Psychotherapy Theory and Research*. New York: Ronald Press Co., 1953. 700 pp.

Representing the research and thought of Mowrer and twenty-one outstanding contributors, including Rollo May, Carl Rogers, Julius Seeman, and Edward J. Shoben, Jr., this book is, in fact, a well-organized presentation of research in the area of psychotherapy. Mowrer reports that findings in animal and comparative psychology have given man a useful lead in understanding his own behavior. This is, of course, an indication of the author's behavioral position.

———. *The New Group Therapy*. New York: D. Van Nostrand Co., 1964. 262 pp.

This volume, a sequel to Mowrer's *The Crisis in Psychiatry and Religion*, is a collection of published articles and lectures depicting a new kind of interpersonal therapy. Tracing a brief history of the Christian church, Mowrer interprets early Christianity as a small-groups movement that provided sinful ("neurotic") people with opportunities for confession and penance. These encounter groups or congregations found these sharing experiences to be redemptive, practical, and rehabilitative. The twentieth-century local church is viewed as having become too large, rigid, legalistic, and sophisticated, emphasizing the vertical rather than the horizontal dimension of sin and alienation. Mowrer thinks that the modern church has become ineffective in its effort to create vitality in religion. The new group therapy does not claim magical powers, but it focuses on the following principles as the means of dealing with neuroses: all persons have a value system of conscience that, if violated, produces guilt; open confession of past mistakes, sins, and secrets to "significant others" is the first step back to emotional health; concealment of good works provides a sense of stored inner strength; openness about weaknesses is encouraged, as is making restitution for past failures.

GARDNER MURPHY

———, ed. *Morality and Mental Health.* Chicago: Rand McNally and Co., 1967. 669 pp.
An edited collection of readings from psychiatry, psychology, social science, theology, literature, and biography as they relate to the place of morality and responsibility in mental health, this is probably the best source book on that subject. This work is the result of Mowrer's conviction that an abundant life, which people consciously or unconsciously desire, is vitally dependent on moral integration and integrity.

Murphy, Gardner

BIRTH: July 8, 1895, Chillicothe, Ohio
PRESENT STATUS: visiting professor of psychology, George Washington University, Washington, D.C.
BACKGROUND: *Educational* B.A., Yale University, 1916; A.M., Harvard University, 1917; Ph.D., Columbia University, 1923
Professional United States Army, 1917–19; lecturer, 1921–25, instructor, 1925–29, assistant professor, 1929–40, Columbia University; professor and chairman, Department of Psychology, City College of New York, 1940–52; UNESCO consultant to India to investigate the causes of social tension, 1950; director of research, Menninger Foundation in Topeka, Kansas, 1952–67; visiting professor of psychology, George Washington University, 1967–
Field of Work psychology of personality, social psychology, and parapsychology
Affiliations American Association for the Advancement of Science; Eastern Psychological Association (president, 1941–42); American Psychological Association (president, 1943–44), Divisions of Personality and Social Psychology, Philosophical Psychology, History of Psychology, and the Society for the Psychological Study of Social Issues (chairman, 1938); awarded the Butler Medal by Columbia University for his studies in experimental social psychology

SUMMATION OF CONCEPTS:

As one major proponent of the biosocial theory of personality, Murphy in his writings explores the concepts, principles, assumptions, and various components of this theory. The one term that best characterizes him seems to be "eclectic," primarily because he has never limited his study of human behavior to any one discipline. Evidence of his flexibility is apparent as he draws from the contributions in biology, psychology, and sociology. To Murphy, man is both a biological and a social animal. For this reason he refuses to look only at one part of man's makeup without looking at the total unification of man. In simple terms, explaining man's behavior from one dimension (*e.g.*, the unconscious processes) is good, but it is not good enough to provide a meaningful perspective. Man cannot be understood through compartmentalization. Murphy's eclectic viewpoint encompasses and identifies with field theory, is strongly holistic in structure, and also emphasizes the tenets of functionalism. Positive psychological growth, he believes, is reflected through integration, interaction, and interdependence of all of man's basic forces.

ANNOTATED BIBLIOGRAPHY:

Murphy, Gardner, and Lois Barclay Murphy. *Experimental Social Psychology*. New York: Harper and Brothers, Publishers, 1931. 709 pp.

Although Murphy's major writing on personality did not appear until 1947, this early work served as a springboard for later research and as a strong indication of the trend he was later to take in developing understandings of the structure and dynamics of personality. One segment of this book discusses the development and measurement of our social and moral attitudes. The six categories, designed to measure the moral basis for behavior, are the law of God, public opinion, civic law, parental law, the greatest good of the greatest number, and the spirit in which the act is done.

_____. *Personality: A Biosocial Approach to Origins and Structure*. New York: Harper and Brothers, Publishers, 1947. 999 pp.

Murphy's exposition of personality is many sided. He conceptualizes the study of personality as an art, an engineering enterprise, and a science and boldly states that these three must remain undivided and in harmony. He emphasizes the wholeness of man, the fundamental tenet upon which field theory rests. Murphy presents his thoughts on personality and cleverly combines his own research with that of others. Since he perceives personality theory as synonymous with motivation theory, one key to understanding him is to recognize that personality is defined in terms of motives.

_____. *Historical Introduction to Modern Psychology*. Rev. ed. New York: Harcourt, Brace, and World, 1949. 466 pp.

This volume, Murphy's first published book, surveys the history of psychology. Even today, although it is outdated, it is a respected source of the early study of psychology. Covered is a wide range of subject matter, including the antecedent of modern psychology, the rise of the research spirit, and the contemporary psychological systems of 1928. An indication of Murphy's interest is noted by the five specific areas he chose to consider. It is not surprising to find that this writing was comprehensive and did in fact cover personality, social psychology, child psychology, physiological psychology, and the measurement of intelligence.

———. *Human Potentialities.* New York: Basic Books, 1958. 340 pp.

This is Murphy's contribution to what a person needs to know if he is to realize his potential as a human being. He organizes the book around the concept of three kinds of human nature and tends to trichotomize his ideas. The reader may approach this book from the perspective of examining those things one should know. Ultimately, to know becomes an antecedent to one's potential to actualize.

———, and Herbert E. Spohn. *Encounter with Reality: New Forms for an Old Quest.* Boston: Houghton Mifflin Co., 1968. 162 pp.

Similar to Murphy's other writings, this work is philosophically and ethically oriented. The subtitle provides a clue to its underlying purpose. Man is viewed as a mystery, although he is perceived as the highest form of animal. The authors suggest that man's understanding of his physical world has increased vastly in our scientific age but that his "inner" or psychological understanding has progressed slowly, in spite of serious behavioral research. This book is an effort to seek clues in solving the riddle of man's nature.

Murray, Henry Alexander

BIRTH: May 13, 1893, New York City

PRESENT STATUS: professor emeritus, Department of Psychology, Harvard University

BACKGROUND: *Educational* A.B., Harvard University, 1915; M.D., Columbia University, 1919; M. A., Columbia University, 1920; Ph.D. (biochemistry), Cambridge University, England, 1927; completed training in psychoanalysis under Han Sachs and Franz Alexander, 1935; honorary L.H.D., Lawrence University, 1964; doctor of psychology, Louvain University, Belgium, 1966

Professional instructor of physiology, Harvard University, 1920; surgical intern, Presbyterian Hospital, New York City, 1920–22; assistant, Rockefeller

HENRY ALEXANDER MURRAY

Institute of Medical Research, 1922-24; research in biochemistry, Cambridge University, 1924-25; associate, Rockefeller Institute of Medical Research, 1925-26; instructor of psychology, 1926-28, assistant professor, 1928-37, associate professor, 1937-46, lecturer, 1946-50, professor of clinical psychology, 1950-62, Harvard University; director, Harvard Psychological Clinic, 1928-43; lieutenant colonel, Medical Corps, Office of Strategic Services, U.S. Army, 1943-48 (received leave of absence from Harvard); professor emeritus, Harvard University, 1962–

Field of Work psychological research in personality assessment, primarily in the development of personology as a holistic theory of personality

Affiliations Fellow, American Academy of Arts and Sciences; Fellow, American Medical Association; Fellow, Psychoanalytic Society; Fellow, American Psychological Association, Divisions of Personality and Social Psychology, the Society for the Psychological Study of Social Issues, Clinical Psychology, and Maturity and Old Age (awarded the Distinguished Scientific Contribution Award, 1961); received the Legion of Merit Award for his work with the Office of Strategic Services during World War II in the screening and selecting of men to do counterespionage work; patron, Jung Institute of Zurich

SUMMATION OF CONCEPTS:

Because Murray introduces the concept of personology as a theory of personality based on needs and/or motivational dispositions, most of his writings are directed toward the definition and expansion of these ideas. Extremely sophisticated in his approach, he leans heavily on his experiences in academic psychology, clinical practice, literature (the humanities), and the biological sciences to formulate his system. He consistently supports the organic quality of behavior, stressing that a single expression of behavior is understood only as it relates to the rest of the functioning person. Personality is viewed as the mediator between environmental demands and individual needs. *Need* is the key word in gaining insight into Murray's explanation of behavior. Much like Abraham Maslow, Murray believes that a person's behavior is motivated by primary and secondary needs, which he also calls basic motivational dispositions. Man is viewed as possessing a "divine discontent" and is motivated to go beyond his present state of existence. Murray's taxonomy of needs is discussed fully in his major work, *Explorations in Personality*. Unlike Maslow, his classification of needs is quite extensive, noted by the twenty categories he uses. Some indication of the influence of Murray's theory is the Edwards Personal Preference Schedule, which was designed to measure the strength of fifteen of Murray's twenty basic motivational dispositions or needs.

HENRY ALEXANDER MURRAY

ANNOTATED BIBLIOGRAPHY:

Murray, H. A., et al. *Explorations in Personality.* New York: Oxford University Press, 1938. 761 pp.

This book reports on the clinical and experimental study of fifty college-age men at the Harvard Psychological Clinic, in which the researchers attempted to identify the most fundamental human needs. These are classified into twenty groupings and then divided into two types, viscerogenic and psychogenic. Viscerogenic needs are the primary needs that arise from organic processes and lead to physical satisfaction. Psychogenic needs, such as achievement, dominance, recognition, aggression, and affiliation, are the secondary needs that are not associated with specific organic processes. This is Murray's major work, and it introduces "personology," defined by the author as the science of men. It encompasses the use of psychoanalysis, analytical psychology, individual psychology, and more than twenty other methods of psychological assessments as means of inquiry rather than realms of knowledge. This approach stresses the uniqueness of the individual, because it is thought that each person expresses his needs and develops his patterns in his own way. Based on this assumption, attention is focused on the in-depth study of individuals rather than a statistical investigation of a large population. Murray concludes his intensive investigations of single individuals using this wide variety of techniques, approaches, and observers. In the end the diagnosis is made up of a synthesis of many factors, including physical, social, and psychological, which reflect a total picture of the person in opposition to a picture of only one dimension of personality.

_____. *Manual of Thematic Apperception Test.* Cambridge: Harvard University Press, 1943. 20 pp.

This manual introduces one of the most noted projective techniques being utilized today in America. This instrument reveals the attitudes, feelings, and personality characteristics of an individual in the process of making up stories about a standard series of pictures. The TAT, introduced at the Harvard Psychological Clinic in 1938, was used as a new and innovative way of assessing feelings along with the twenty-five other techniques that had been in use for some time. It is a test of the imagination that seeks to elicit responses that reveal fantasies, basic emotional reactions, attitudes toward authority, feelings about sex, and the use of adjustment mechanisms. The chief value of this clinical instrument is its ability to detect emotional disturbances. Along with the Rorschach, it is one of the most sophisticated projective techniques being used by the clinical psychologist.

———. *Assessment of Men.* New York: Holt, Rinehart, and Winston, 1948. 761 pp.

This book is a summary of Murray's establishment and direction of an assessment service for the Office of Strategic Services. His major task involved screening candidates for secret and dangerous missions. As an army officer in the Medical Corps, Murray and his fellow workers attempted to devise successful methods of selecting men for counterespionage missions. The program was relatively successful, and Murray received the Legion of Merit Award in recognition of his outstanding service.

Norris, Willa

BIRTH: July 14, 1911, Inavale, Nebraska

PRESENT STATUS: professor of education, Michigan State University, East Lansing

BACKGROUND: *Educational* B.S., University of Nebraska, 1934; M.A., Columbia University, 1943; Ed.D., George Washington University, 1954

Professional teacher in three Nebraska high schools, 1934–42; personal counselor, YWCA, Omaha, Nebraska, 1942–45; personal counselor, YWCA, Washington, D.C., 1945–46; director and counselor, Kendall House YWCA, Washington, D.C., 1946–47; vocational counselor, George Washington University, 1947–49; assistant executive secretary, National Vocational Guidance Association, 1949–52; acting executive secretary, American Personnel and Guidance Association, 1952; assistant professor, associate professor, and professor of education, Michigan State University, 1952–

Field of Work vocational and educational counseling, counselor training techniques, and group procedures

Affiliations American Personnel and Guidance Association; National Vocational Guidance Association; American School Counselor Association; Association for Counselor Education and Supervision; American Psychological Association, Division of Counseling Psychology

SUMMATION OF CONCEPTS:

Norris places a great deal of emphasis on organizing guidance services for maximum efficiency. She stresses the significance of proper vocational and educational counseling and the necessity for properly using the information service in the school.

ANNOTATED BIBLIOGRAPHY:

Norris, Willa, Franklin R. Zeran, and Raymond Hatch. *The Information Service in Guidance.* Chicago: Rand McNally and Co., 1960. 598 pp.

The authors organized the content after a careful study of the recommended training programs for counselors developed by professional organizations and the United States Office of Education. The book is designed to serve as a textbook to help the counselor-trainee develop competence in providing occupational and educational information. It is also intended as a resource book for teachers, administrators, or anyone else who might seek information of this nature. Much emphasis is placed on present conditions and future changes within the areas of educational, occupational, and social information.

―――. *Occupational Information in the Elementary School.* Chicago: Science Research Associates, 1963. 243 pp.

This is a unique book in the area of guidance, for it was written specifically to assist teachers and counselors to facilitate the vocational maturation of elementary school children. The approach seems most interesting in that Norris calls for self-understanding and a realistic awareness of the world through the proper use of occupational information and other resources. The book is also unique in that it provides the classroom teacher with some help in the dissemination of information and lists for the teacher various films, books, and other materials that can introduce occupational information into the traditional classroom.

North, Robert Davidson

BIRTH: July 23, 1918, Pascagoula, Mississippi

PRESENT STATUS: associate director, Professional Examination Division, the Psychological Corporation

BACKGROUND: *Educational* A.B., New York University, 1941; M.A., Columbia University, 1947; Ph.D., Columbia University, 1949

Professional psychological assistant, United States Army Air Force, 1942–43; instructor, Long Island University, 1946–49; lecturer in psychology, Columbia University, 1949–50; assistant professor of psychology, assistant director of personnel, and assistant director of the Cooperative Counseling and Testing Service, University of Kentucky, 1950–54; associate director, Educational Records Bureau, New York, 1954–64; vice-president, Educational Records Bureau, New York, 1964–65; associate director, Professional Examination Division, the Psychological Corporation, New York, 1965–

Field of Work research in the development of intellectual aptitude, achievement, and personality tests

Affiliations American Psychological Association, Division of Evaluation and Measurement; American Educational Research Association; National Council on Measurements in Education; American Personnel and Guidance Association

SUMMATION OF CONCEPTS:

North stresses the need for a more effective utilization of guidance services in the school. He seems to recognize the problems confronting guidance counselors and emphasizes the need for research and evaluation to assist in making guidance a more integral part of the total educational program. Much of his work has been done in the area of testing, and many of his articles on testing are reported in the *Educational Records Bulletin* from 1955 through 1961.

ANNOTATED BIBLIOGRAPHY:

North, Robert D. "Tests for the Accounting Profession." *Educational and Psychological Measurement*, 18 (Winter, 1958), 691–714.

This article is devoted to the results of a study subsidized by the American Institute of Certified Public Accountants. The purpose of the study was to produce a battery of tests that might logically be used by guidance counselors in high schools and colleges to select students who seem to have some potential in the accounting field. It is implied that such a battery of tests might further serve as an objective basis for the selection and promotion of personnel already in the area of accounting.

———, Anthony J. Humphreys, and Arthur E. Traxler. *Guidance Services.* Chicago: Science Research Associates, 1960. 414 pp.

Designed to present the guidance student with basic principles, concepts, and procedures relative to the area, this book will give him some insight into guidance services at all educational levels. The book once served as an introduction to the field of guidance and would probably have value today as a historical example of how early in-service training programs were directed toward assisting faculty members to develop a better understanding of guidance services. Much emphasis is placed on the need for and utilization of tools and techniques that assisted counselors to better understand clients.

Oates, Wayne E.

BIRTH: June 24, 1917, Greenville, South Carolina

PRESENT STATUS: professor of psychiatry and behavioral sciences, University of Louisville School of Medicine

BACKGROUND: *Educational* B.A., Wake Forest College, 1940; B.D., Southern Baptist Theological Seminary, 1945; Th.D., Southern Baptist Theological Seminary, 1947; sabbatical study, Union Theological Seminary, New York City, 1952, 1960-61; sabbatical study, University of Louisville Medical School, 1968-69

Professional instructor, philosophy and psychology, Wake Forest College, 1940-42; chaplain, general and mental hospitals in Kentucky, 1944-46; interim pastor, Broadway Baptist Church, Louisville, 1947-48; assistant professor, associate professor, and professor of psychology of religion, Southern Baptist Theological Seminary, 1948-74; theological consultant, Norton Psychiatric Clinic, 1949-; visiting professor of pastoral counseling, Union Theological Seminary, ten summers, 1952-70; visiting professor, Princeton Theological Seminary, 1960; professor of psychiatry and behavioral sciences, University of Louisville School of Medicine, 1974-

Field of Work pastoral counseling and psychology of religion

Affiliations American Association of Pastoral Counselors, National Association of Clinical Pastoral Education, American Association of University Professors, and member of the editorial boards for *Pastoral Psychology* and the *Journal of Pastoral Care*

SUMMATION OF CONCEPTS:

Most of Oates's work is concentrated on understanding the impact of religious faith on the total development of personality. He supports the biblical concept of man as a whole being created in the *imago dei*. His work attempts to explain the complexity of man's wholeness as he relates to himself, to his fellowman, and to God. Oates concerns himself with developing understandings about man. He emphasizes man's need to develop a faith that serves him as he faces critical experiences. For Oates, this type of faith is in opposition to neurotic faith based on unrealistic dependency.

WAYNE E. OATES

ANNOTATED BIBLIOGRAPHY:

Oates, Wayne E. *Religious Factors in Mental Illness*. New York: Association Press, 1955. 239 pp.

Although Oates does not agree that neuroses are caused by religion, as some psychologists imply, he admits that some religious persons are neurotic and psychotic. He writes of the "hindering" and "helping" powers of religion. Unhealthy religion is viewed as the attempt of man to "use" God rather than to function through God. The author notes that mental patients often feel they have committed the unpardonable sin, have flesh-spirit conflicts, are unforgiving legalists, are confused about the end of time, or possess a messiah complex. These are examples of how certain forms of religion have ultimately resulted in disintegration rather than integration of personality. Focusing on specific groups that give context to some of the ideals held by the mentally ill, Oates includes perfectionistic groups, "second-coming" groups, ascetic groups, and leader-deification groups.

———. *Where to Go for Help*. Philadelphia: Westminster Press, 1957. 115 pp.

This book serves as a resource guide for persons in the helping professions. It deals with special concerns and referral sources for such problems as marital conflicts, sexual difficulties, unwanted pregnancies, adoption, alcoholism, and mental illness. For example, the volume contains information about homes for unwed mothers, problems related to adoption, and a listing of agencies designed to assist with such problems.

———. *The Religious Dimensions of Personality*. New York: Association Press, 1957. 320 pp.

This is an interdisciplinary approach to the psychology of religion as it relates to human personality. Rejecting dualism, Oates makes a Christian interpretation of the psychological understandings of personality. He discusses the theories associated with the conception of religion, including religion as an instinct, a derived reality, an illusion, and an encounter with the Infinite. This book, ranging historically from Plato to Carl R. Rogers, may well be one of the clearest presentations of the structure of personality. Also, the process of human development is explained in theological terms, using the work of outstanding writers such as Augustine, Sören Kierkegaard, Horace Bushnell, and William James.

Paterson, Donald Gildersleeve

BIRTH: January 18, 1892, Columbus, Ohio
PRESENT STATUS: deceased; October 4, 1961, Minneapolis, Minnesota
BACKGROUND: *Educational* Olivet College, 1910–12; B.A., Ohio State University, 1914; M.A., Ohio State University, 1916; honorary LL.D., Ohio State University, 1952
Professional assistant in psychology, Ohio State University, 1914–16; instructor, University of Kansas, 1916–17; chief of psychological examinations, Surgeon General's Office, U.S. Army, 1917–19; consulting psychologist, the Scott Company of Philadelphia, 1919–21; associate professor of psychology, University of Minnesota, 1921–23; professor of psychology, University of Minnesota, 1923–60; Walter V. Bingham Lecturer, Ohio State University, 1956; professor emeritus, University of Minnesota, 1960–61
Field of Work prediction and guidance in occupational adjustment
Affiliations Fellow, American Psychological Association, Divisions of Industrial Psychology and Counseling Psychology; American Association of Applied Psychology (president, 1938–39); American Association for the Advancement of Science; Phi Delta Kappa; Sigma Xi

SUMMATION OF CONCEPTS:

Paterson's basic concepts concern the theory of unique traits. That is to say, whatever a person possesses in structure characteristics correlates only slightly with such factors as intelligence.

ANNOTATED BIBLIOGRAPHY:

Paterson, Donald G. "Use of New Type Examination Questions in Psychology." *School and Sociology*, 28 (1928), 369.
This is a presentation of information regarding the collection and use of 2,261 examination questions recognized by the author as "new type," which were designed to determine the emphasis given to various topics in an introductory course in psychology and the degree to which various types of questions can successfully differentiate levels of student ability.
―――. *Physique and Intellect*. New York: Century, 1930. 304 pp.
This text presents some of Paterson's early concepts regarding his examination of physical traits and measures of mental development. In many respects the book is a presentation of conflicting concepts when

viewed in terms of the challenging ideas introduced by such eminent researchers as Rostan, Viola, Kretschmer, and Sheldon. Paterson indicates that he found only slight evidence of a correlation between structure characteristics and intelligence.

———, et al. *The Measurement of Man*. Minneapolis: University of Minnesota Press, 1930. 586 pp.

Paterson presents a summary of his work on correlations between physical characteristics and intelligence.

———, G. G. Schneidler, and E. G. Williamson. *Student Guidance Techniques*. New York: McGraw-Hill Book Co., 1938. 316 pp.

This is a handbook for counselors who are working in the high school or college. Much of the text is devoted to diagnostic techniques with special emphasis upon methods used for collecting and treating data and interpreting test results. Stress is also placed on the summarization of tests with a focus on major areas of interest, such as description of test, test design, norms, reliability, validity, and cost. Some attention is also given to the application of test results in educational, vocational, and personal-social areas of interest.

———. "The Conservation of Human Talent." *American Psychologist*, 12 (1957), 134-44.

Paterson deals with data on social status as reflected by various occupations, occupational choice, and job dissatisfaction. He attempts to apply psychological findings of the past to the presently existing problems in educational, vocational and personal-social areas of adjustment. Paterson also introduces the idea that much needs to be done to assist the physically handicapped and to utilize the abilities and experiences of the older people in our society.

Patterson, Cecil Holden

BIRTH: June 22, 1912, Lynn, Massachusetts
PRESENT STATUS: professor of educational psychology, University of Illinois
BACKGROUND: *Educational* A.B., University of Chicago, 1938; M.A., University of Minnesota, 1945; Ph.D., University of Minnesota, 1955
Professional research assistant, Fels Research Institute at Antioch College, 1938-41; senior teaching assistant, Institute of Child Welfare, University of Minnesota, 1941-42; United States Air Force, 1942-45; clinical psychologist,

CECIL HOLDEN PATTERSON

Veterans Administration Hospital, Canandigua, New York, 1946-47; counseling psychologist, Veterans Administration Regional Office, St. Paul, 1947-56; associate professor of education, University of Illinois, 1956-60; professor of education, University of Illinois, 1960-63; professor of educational psychology, University of Illinois, 1963-; chairman, Division of Guidance and Counseling, University of Illinois, 1965-69

Field of Work research in the area of counseling and psychotherapy, counselor education, and rehabilitation counseling

Affiliations Fellow, American Psychological Association, Divisions of Counseling Psychology, Educational Psychology, Psychotherapy, and the Psychological Aspects of Disability; American Personnel and Guidance Association; National Rehabilitation Association; American Rehabilitation Counseling Association (president, 1961-62)

SUMMATION OF CONCEPTS:

Patterson stresses the client-centered and group-centered approach as a means of assisting the client who seeks rehabilitation counseling to become capable of managing his life. He feels that the emphasis in rehabilitation counseling should be placed on developing a good understanding of human relations from both practical and theoretical learning experiences and that less emphasis should be placed on the counselor-coordinator approach currently popular among some leaders. The understanding that he refers to is not necessarily a by-product of testing but rather a resultant factor of client- and/or group-centered functions. Patterson feels that, before tests can be effective, considerable refinement must take place. He concludes that, in the present state of development, projective techniques have little to offer to vocational guidance and concurs with the concept that much research remains to be done before the Rorschach interpretations can be regarded as trustworthy.

ANNOTATED BIBLIOGRAPHY:

Patterson, Cecil H. *A Guide for Counselors.* Springfield, Ill.: Charles C. Thomas, Publisher, 1953. 146 pp.

This supplements information prepared for the Veterans Administration in 1948. The content is designed to show vocational counselors how to utilize information gained on the Wechsler scale.

———. *Counseling the Emotionally Disturbed.* New York: Harper Brothers, 1958. 458 pp.

This book is designed to serve the counselor who works with emotionally disturbed clients seeking vocational rehabilitation. Patterson points out that vocational rehabilitation is only one part of the total rehabilitation process and that psychotherapy and medical treatments are other parts.

──────. *Counseling and Psychotherapy: Theory and Practice.* New York: Harper and Brothers, Publishers, 1959. 322 pp.

Patterson gives a vivid description of his concept of phenomenological psychology and client-centered therapy with the greatest focus of attention upon theory and philosophy rather than technique.

──────. "Methodological Problems in Education." *Personnel and Guidance Journal,* 39 (December, 1960), 270-74.

Emphasis is upon the various stages of research in education and the need for more attention to preliminary stages of research.

──────. "Methods of Assessing the Vocational Adjustment Potential of the Mentally Handicapped." *Training School Bulletin,* 61 (November, 1964), 129-53.

The increasing attention being directed toward the vocational rehabilitation of the mentally handicapped has led to the study of methods of evaluating their vocational potential. In addition to the use of standardized tests of aptitudes, the work sample has been applied in a number of studies. The general attitude is that standardized tests are inadequate and that the work-sample approach is a better method of assessing aptitudes.

──────. "Counseling: Vocational or Therapeutic?" *Vocational Guidance Quarterly,* 15 (September, 1966), 61-65.

A feeling that counseling should divorce itself from the affective and seek the cognitive is expressed as counselors should not view themselves as engaging in clinical psychology or intensive psychotherapy. Counseling is becoming more restrictive, more and more limited to cognitive problems, rather than being concerned with affective problems.

──────. "We Must Communicate Better with Our Guidance Colleagues." *Business Education World,* 47 (January, 1967), 24-25.

The article concerns itself with the idea that too often high school business education classes become the dumping grounds for the unmotivated student. The accusing finger is pointed at the guidance counselor who schedules the misfit by virtue of test scores or the lack of some other place to put him. Better communication between teacher and counselor is suggested to remedy this problem through reeducation of the potential and application of business preparation.

_____. *Relationship Counseling and Psychotherapy*. New York: Harper and Row, 1974. 207 pp.

In his well-tempered, completely enlightened, and totally philosophical way, Patterson presents his own approach to counseling. He has been recognized as a leader in the area of psychotherapy for many years, and both his students and colleagues will welcome this new contribution to the area of counseling. Patterson discusses the conditions of a therapeutic relationship and how to incorporate such conditions. He feels that schools of thought seem to be drawing closer together, but cautions that therapy may nurture variables not yet recognized. Perhaps his greatest contribution is the idea of a relationship therapy—something that is not difficult to live with no matter what school of thought the reader belongs to.

Pepinsky, Harold Brenner

BIRTH: September 16, 1917, St. Paul, Minnesota

PRESENT STATUS: professor of psychology and computer and information science, Ohio State University

BACKGROUND: *Educational* B.A., University of Minnesota, 1938; M.S., University of Minnesota, 1940; Ph.D., University of Minnesota, 1946

Professional counseling and teaching assistant, University of Minnesota, 1939–42; administrative Fellow, Dean of Students' Office, University of Minnesota, 1942–44; assistant professor and assistant director of the Guidance Bureau, University of Kansas, 1944–45; assistant professor, Michigan State University, 1945–48; director of the Student Counseling Center and associate professor of psychology, Washington State University, 1948–51; associate professor of psychology, Ohio State University, 1951–56; director of Research, Counseling, and Testing Center, Ohio State University, 1951–62; Fulbright Research Scholar and Guggenheim Fellow, Tech University of Norway, 1961–62; professor of psychology, 1956–, and professor of computer and information science, 1967–, Ohio State University

Field of Work research in the field of clinical counseling with college students and in the area of student personnel work, measurement, and evaluation

Affiliations Fellow, American Psychological Association, Divisions of the Teaching of Psychology, Evaluation and Measurement, Personality and Social Psychology, Clinical Psychology, and Counseling Psychology; American Personnel and Guidance Association; American College Personnel Association; American Association of University Professors; American Educational Research Association

SUMMATION OF CONCEPTS:

Pepinsky has for many years concerned himself with new approaches to research in the behavioral sciences. It appears that much of what he reflects in his work is directly related to the self-centered approach, which is concerned with an emerging, developing, perceiving, and knowing self that directs the client's activities; the social-psychological approach, which centers on the interaction between counselor and client; the psychoanalytic approach, which centers on personality dynamics and utilizes "depth interviews" to uncover "hidden motives"; and the neobehavioral approach, which is based on the notion that current models for the explanation of human learning can be adapted to organize and account for the learning of clients.

ANNOTATED BIBLIOGRAPHY:

Pepinsky, Harold Brenner, and Pauline Nichols Pepinsky. *Counseling Theory and Practice.* New York: Ronald Press Co., 1954. 307 pp.

A close parallel with his basic concepts, this book presents the argument for the reconciliation of counseling and research. The Pepinskys do not attempt to promote a specific approach, but urge that those who practice counseling, regardless of their personal philosophy of counseling theory, make explicit their own assumptions in making verifiable predictions about the observable behavior of clients. The text is devoted to a considerable amount of material illustrating ways in which present theoretical positions can be used to set up hypotheses concerning behavioral changes within clients.

————. "Research on the Student in His Educational Setting." *Personnel Services in Education.* The National Society for the Study of Education's 58th Yearbook. Chicago: University of Chicago Press, 1959. Pp. 231–47.

It is Pepinsky's position that research dealing with college students has, in the past, been more concerned with the personnel services provided for students rather than with the process of student development. His recommendations include taking a look at what the individual student is like during successive stages of his educational progress and utilizing this information to establish a more meaningful student personnel program.

Porter, Elias Hull, Jr.

BIRTH: January 29, 1914, Medford, Oregon
PRESENT STATUS: senior systems analyst, Technomics, Inc., Santa Monica, California
BACKGROUND: *Educational* B.A., University of Oregon, 1935; M.A., University of Oregon, 1936; M.S., University of Oregon, 1938; Ph.D., Ohio State University, 1941
Professional director, Merit System Council, Oregon State Public Welfare Commission, 1941–43; classifications officer, United States Navy, 1943–46; head of instructional staff, Counselor Training Program for Veterans Administration, University of Chicago, 1946–47; research associate in psychology, University of Chicago, 1947–53; director of Psychological Services, Science Research Associates, 1953–55; assistant head, Training Department, System Development Division, the Rand Corporation, Santa Monica, California, 1956–57; assistant head, Human Factors Department, System Development Corporation, Santa Monica, 1957–60; senior human factors scientist, System Development Corporation, 1960–64; private practice, 1964–66; senior systems analyst, Technomics, Inc., Santa Monica, 1960–
Field of Work major contributions in the nature and course of nondirective therapy, training in man-machine system design, and system-training development
Affiliations Fellow, American Psychological Association, Divisions of Clinical Psychology and Consulting Psychology

SUMMATION OF CONCEPTS:

Porter appears to favor a client-centered point of view and believes that the reorganization of the disturbed personality will take place more readily when external intervention is at a minimum and self-exploration is at a maximum. He believes that a counselor is better prepared to work with clients when his background of experiences and training permits him to observe what happens as he interacts with the client. In essence, the counselor is confronted with two major challenges. First, his attitude will play an important part in the counselor-client relationship. Second, his skill or lack of it will become instrumental as he tries to help the client. The attitudes that the counselor holds will, in effect, be an expression of his feelings and values, thus making his approach one that reflects his own personal value system. Porter discusses techniques and emphasizes the fact that the usefulness of a technique is determined by whether it aids the therapeutic process—this is to say, the process of change that takes place when the client has reorganized the meaning of events in his life and developed new attitudes toward himself and his environment.

ANNOTATED BIBLIOGRAPHY:

Porter, Elias Hull, Jr. *An Introduction to Therapeutic Counseling.* Boston: Houghton Mifflin Co., 1950. 223 pp.

The major contribution here is from the establishment of exercises to assist the novice counselor in gaining insight into his attitudes and skills. Scoring these exercises provides the counselor with a picture of the psychological climate in which he is working. The book introduces some interesting concepts that might lend themselves well to research.

——. "On the Nature of Psychotherapeutic Interpretation." *Journal of Consulting Psychology,* 16 (1952), 343–46.

This article reflects the point of view that the therapist interprets the expressions of his client as indicative of a certain kind of meaning or a certain kind of significance. The therapist expresses to the client that which he feels will best assist the client.

——. "Clients: Evaluations of Services at the University of Chicago Counseling Center." *Journal of Counseling Psychology,* 4 (1957), 274–82.

This is a study designed to evaluate counseling services on the basis of attitudes expressed toward these services.

Raimy, Victor Charles

BIRTH: March 17, 1913, Buffalo, New York

PRESENT STATUS: professor of psychology, University of Colorado

BACKGROUND: *Educational* B.A., Antioch College, 1935; Ph.D., Ohio State University, 1943

Professional assistant to director, Ohio State Bureau of Juvenile Research, 1936–37; clinical psychologist, Juvenile Court, Toledo, Ohio, 1937–38; assistant psychologist, Ohio State University, 1938–40; instructor in psychology, Antioch College, 1940–41; instructor of psychology and assistant to the dean of College of Arts and Science, 1941–43; officer, United States Navy, 1943–46; assistant professor, University of Pittsburgh, 1946; associate professor, Ohio

State University, 1946–48; from associate professor to professor, University of Colorado, 1948–; consultant, National Institute of Mental Health, 1952–; chairman, Department of Psychology, University of Colorado, 1954–62; consultant, Vocational Rehabilitation Division, 1960–
   Field of Work   major interest in personality, psychotherapy, and the definition of standards for clinical psychologists
   Affiliations   Fellow, American Psychological Association, Divisions of Clinical Psychology (president, 1962–63), Counseling Psychology, and Psychotherapy

SUMMATION OF CONCEPTS:

It appears that most of what Raimy does is designed to improve present standards in the area of clinical psychology. It is difficult to focus upon any specific philosophy that he reflects, other than to say that he seems to pursue the belief that the self-concept is a basis for understanding the process of counseling.

ANNOTATED BIBLIOGRAPHY:

Raimy, Victor Charles. *Training in Clinical Psychology.* Englewood Cliffs, N.J.: Prentice-Hall, 1950. 253 pp.
   Most of the content of this book is devoted to clinical psychology. A great deal of emphasis is placed on the problems involved with training students to become clinical psychologists. Much of the text resulted from a conference held at Boulder, Colorado, in August, 1949. This conference, supported by the National Institute of Mental Health, was designed to consider problems connected with the training of clinical psychologists.
   ———, and H. K. Heppell. "Projective Pictures as Interview Devices." *Journal of Consulting Psychology,* 15 (1951), 405–11.
   This is a study in which projective pictures were used during interviews in an attempt to elicit some response from clients. The approach was used on thirty institutionalized boys. Fifteen pictures were ranked in order of usefulness, with statistically significant differences in ratings appearing between the eight top-ranking pictures and the seven low-ranking pictures. Conclusions are that similar sets of tested pictures used by clinicians for specific topics are now investigated through standard techniques.
   ———. *Misunderstandings of the Self.* San Francisco: Jossey-Bass Publishers, 1975. 214 pp.

In this, his most recent book, Raimy supports the idea that man is influenced by his environment. This influence, he feels, can then result in misconceptions. The four psychotherapeutic methods recommended by Raimy for dealing with such misconceptions involve: (a) self-evaluation, (b) explanation, (c) self-demonstration, and (d) vicariation or modeling. Correcting misconceptions through psychotherapy paves the way for building a more stable foundation of behavior from which the person can work.

Rank, Otto

BIRTH: April 22, 1884, Vienna, Austria
PRESENT STATUS: deceased; October 31, 1939, New York City
BACKGROUND: *Educational* Ph.D., University of Vienna, 1912
Professional editor of *Imago* and *International Zietschrift für Psychoanalyse*, the first European journals of psychoanalysis, 1912–24; founder and director, the International Psychoanalytische Verlag, 1919–24; rejected orthodox psychoanalysis and broke all ties with Freud, 1926; lived in Paris and made frequent lecture tours to America, where his views were found to be very stimulating by leading social workers, especially in New York and Philadelphia, 1926–34; moved to America, where he emphasized birth trauma as a source of neurosis and studied the influence of myths and folklore on human behavior, 1934
Field of Work major contribution centered on his effort to modify Freudian theory and adapt it to the contemporary needs of an industrial society
Affiliations Viennese Psychoanalytic Society, International Psychoanalytische Verlag

SUMMATION OF CONCEPTS:

Rank recognized the positive, creative, directional nature of man's striving. He spoke of "will" and rejected the notion of man as pulled or pushed by impersonal forces. Rank saw the therapist as an "ego helper," who was concerned not so much with the past as with the present and not so much with content as with the patient's immediate experience. He felt that the therapist was in no position to educate, since this would intensify the neurotic conflict, and that he must avoid giving love, since this would create dependency. Rank recognized the main objectives of therapy as the constructive change of negative to "positive will assertion," the change from a passive to an active, creative existence, and the change from dependency to autonomy. A point of interest that he introduced regarding the first objective is that the neurotic is not "weak willed" but "strong willed" like the creative person and that, to have positive will assertion occur in the neurotic, one must introduce a subgoal that will permit him to assert his will rather than project it onto other people. With regard to the second objective, Rank indicated that the neurotic cannot express his strong will through sex or creativity, thus making his problem quite serious. Concerning the third objective, the neurotic is seen as dependent because of fear and guilt. Yet this very dependency is what creates within the neurotic a feeling of guilt.

With the therapist keeping these objectives in mind, the ultimate goal is the verbalization of the problem and its ultimate solution by the patient. Since the neurotic is an "all-or-nothing" person, it becomes the responsibility of the therapist to help the patient to give only partially. Rank saw neurotics categorically as of two types—the compulsive type who knows himself well and the hysterical type who does not know himself at all. The goal of the therapist is to increase self-acceptance, with a focus of attention in the case of hysteria upon introspection or self-seeking.

To reach these objectives, Rank saw no universal technique that can be applied in therapy. He felt that each person is unique and must be treated accordingly. Perhaps his recognition of an approach that recognizes uniqueness is, in itself, a technique that could be applied universally.

According to Rank, an understanding of the individual is derived from verbal reflections of the patient as he interacts with the therapist. Rank saw some indications of success if the patient expresses himself more freely within and beyond the therapeutic situation as therapy progresses. The keynote of success seems to be reflected in the individual's change from feelings of dependency to those of autonomy and from rejection to self-acceptance. There is some indication of failure if the patient expresses a feeling of indifference to therapy or if he attempts to buy himself free. An example of the latter would be the attempt by a female patient to surrender herself bodily to the therapist.

ANNOTATED BIBLIOGRAPHY:

Rank, Otto. *Art and Artist: Creative Urge and Personality.* New York: Agathon Press, 1908. 431 pp.

OTTO RANK

Although this is not Rank's most popular book among American readers, it is highly significant because Freud helped him revise and publish the first German edition in 1907. This was the period in which Rank served as secretary for Freud's psychoanalytic group. The 1907 edition had the title *Der Kunstler*, but Rank expanded and rewrote it under its current title. The book is primarily an application of psychoanalytic theory to literature, myth, and art.

———. *Trauma of Birth*. New York: Harcourt, Brace, and World, 1929. 224 pp.

The basic distinguishing teachings of Rank emerged in this book. It is of interest that he dedicated this work to Freud, although it caused a controversy stemming from the accusation that he had deviated from Freudian principles. This led Rank to break all ties with Freud. Essentially, Rank believed that the emotions experienced during the birth process affect the later course of life development and may establish the potential for neuroses. He said that all persons are drawn to return to the womb, as seen in the tendency to grow toward the parent and in the satisfaction achieved through sexual intercourse. We also have an instinct, according to Rank, to break away and develop into independent beings. Rank viewed these two impulses, "life fear" and "death fear," as contradictory and concluded that human existence is a struggle between them.

———. *Beyond Psychology*. New York: Dover Publications, 1941. 291 pp.

Rank's last work and the only one written in English, this book was published after his death. It does not include a statement of his contribution to psychology. Rather, it presents his ultimate philosophy and world view, bringing to a conclusion some of his hypotheses in *Psychology of the Soul*.

———. *Will Therapy and Truth and Reality*. New York: Alfred A. Knopf, 1945. 307 pp.

Will Therapy and *Truth and Reality* were first published separately and translated into English by Jessie Taft in 1936. The former work is intended as a presentation of Rank's unique contribution to modern psychology in its application of therapeutic techniques. It represents a criticism of the Freudian teachings and method as Rank arrived at his own conclusions, resulting in his inevitable break with Freudianism. Conceiving the will as a hitherto unrecognized force in the analytic situation, he ascribed positive value to the patient's resistance to treatment and utilized the frustrated creativity of the neurotic in a therapeutic sense. *Truth and Reality*, with the subtitle *An Outline of a Philosophy of the Psychic*, presents Rank's unique contribution to psychology and philosophy, which did not come into full consciousness until this book was published.

————. *Psychology and the Soul*. New York: A. S. Barnes and Co., 1950. 195 pp.

The writing of this book marked Rank's deepening interest in the history of civilization and his beginning criticism of modern depth psychology. His central idea is that intellectual psychology cannot give man the immortal soul he wants but instills in man a spirit of doubt that tends to destroy the soul he does have.

Robinson, Francis Pleasant

BIRTH: December 21, 1906, Danville, Indiana

PRESENT STATUS: professor emeritus of psychology, Ohio State University

BACKGROUND: *Educational* B.A., University of Oregon, 1929; M.A., State University of Iowa, 1930; Ph.D., State University of Iowa, 1932

Professional director of Reading Clinic, State University of Iowa, 1929-33; instructor in psychology, State University of Iowa, 1932-33; professor of psychology and education, Stout Institute, 1933-37; head of the Department of Psychology, Stout Institute, 1934-37; assistant professor of psychology, Ohio State University, 1937-41; associate professor of psychology, Ohio State University, 1941-44; professor of psychology, Ohio State University, 1944-72; professor emeritus of psychology, Ohio State University, 1972-

Field of Work notable contribution in the area of counseling concepts with emphasis on the dimensions of counseling, sometimes called the communications approach

Affiliations Fellow, American Psychological Association, Divisions of Counseling Psychology and Educational Psychology; American Personnel and Guidance Association; American College Personnel Association; American Educational Research Association

SUMMATION OF CONCEPTS:

Much of what Robinson considers important in the area of personnel work is directly related to counseling. He places considerable emphasis on principles and procedures that he feels are applicable to a counseling relationship. An interesting point of view that he expresses is that, in helping someone to achieve more effective study habits, the counselor must realize that effective study habits are not brought about by studying more or by concentrating more intensely but rather by changing the quality of the method of study. Throughout this work, he reiterates that the process of counseling takes place within the client himself and that for a counselor to be effective he must be sensitive to the context of the complete situation and reflect his understanding of the situation in his actions. Robinson's emphasis on the various dimensions of counseling suggests categorizing client problems at different levels. Because the counselor deals with a variety of problems and concerns, he should use a wide variety of techniques.

ANNOTATED BIBLIOGRAPHY:

Robinson, Francis Pleasant. *Effective Study.* New York: Harper and Brothers, Publishers, 1946. 262 pp.

Robinson considers this book a working aid for the student and counselor that will increase the efficiency of classroom and counseling sessions. He developed the text from materials gathered from fifteen years of experience in the how-to-study program at Ohio State University. One of the most frequently listed student problems is study habits. As a result, Robinson introduces a three-step plan on how to study. The first step is to evaluate how well a student does in a skill or trait. The second step is to have the student read how he can improve these abilities and skills. The third step is to have the student practice.

————. *Principles and Procedures in Student Counseling.* New York: Harper and Brothers, Publishers, 1950. 321 pp.

Extremely helpful to the personnel worker who wants to develop a more sophisticated understanding of counseling, this book introduces extensive research designed to stimulate an ever-growing interest in counseling. Robinson presents an analysis of the techniques employed by the novice counselor and the academic and experiential deficiencies of these people as they conduct interviews.

————, Sidney L. Pressey, and John E. Horrpeks. *Psychology in Education.* New York: Harper and Brothers, Publishers, 1959. 658 pp.

The authors introduce four major contributions that psychology has made to education. Most of Robinson's material is concerned with personal counseling.

Roe, Anne (Mrs. George Gaylord Simpson)

BIRTH: August 20, 1904, Denver, Colorado

PRESENT STATUS: professor emeritus of education, Graduate School of Education, Harvard University; lecturer, University of Arizona

BACKGROUND: *Educational* B.A., University of Denver, 1923; M.A., University of Denver, 1925; Ph.D., Columbia University, 1933; honorary M.A., Harvard University, 1963; honorary L.H.D., Lesley College, 1965

Professional graduate assistant, University of Denver, 1923-25; graduate studies, Columbia University, 1925-27; research psychologist, Commonwealth Fund Grant to T. H. Weisenberg for research in aphasia, 1931-33; assistant psychologist, Worcester State Hospital, 1933-34; research psychologist, WPA project, New York Infirmary for Women and Children, 1935-36; private consulting psychologist, 1936-38; assistant editor for Research Council on Problems of Alcohol, 1940-41; consultant, foster child study, Carnegie Grant under Social Science Research Council, 1941-42; director, study of alcohol in the U.S., Yale School of Alcohol Studies and Research Council on Problems of Alcohol, 1941-42; research assistant professor, Laboratory of Applied Psychology, Yale University, 1943-46; chief clinical psychologist in charge of research, Veterans Administration, 1946-47; research grant recipient, U.S. Public Health Service, 1947-51; Guggenheim Fellow, 1952-53; chief psychologist, Montrose, New York, VA Training Unit, 1953-57; adjunct professor, New York University, 1957-59; lecturer in education and research associate, Harvard University Graduate School of Education, 1959-63; professor of education, Harvard University, 1963-67; director, Center Research on Careers, 1963-66; professor emeritus of education, Harvard University, 1967-; lecturer, University of Arizona, 1967-72; lecturer, honorary, University of Arizona, 1972-

Field of Work major concern in the interrelationship between vocational and personality interviewing techniques; interest in the personality characteristics of preeminent scientists

Affiliations Fellow, American Psychological Association, Divisions of the Teaching of Psychology, Personality and Social Psychology, Clinical Psychology (president, 1957-58), and Counseling Psychology; American Personnel and Guidance Association; National Vocational Guidance Association (Lifetime Career Award, 1967)

SUMMATION OF CONCEPTS:

Most of what Roe has done reflects her effort to understand personality patterns. Much of her research is directed toward identifying the characteristics of people who reflect a uniqueness, such as a proclivity for alcoholism. After studying the children of alcoholic parents and contrasting them with children of apparently normal parents, she concluded that all children need the same basic things emotionally, physically, and socially, regardless of home environment.

ANNOTATED BIBLIOGRAPHY:

Roe, Anne. "A Rorschach Study of a Group of Scientists and Technicians." *Journal of Consulting Psychology*, 10 (1946), 317–27.

The data used to support this article were compiled from a small group of individuals engaged in a highly specialized vocation. As a group, certain well-defined characteristics of personality seemed to emerge. Although these individuals did well on problems involving abstractions, they did little to project themselves into a situation. From the standpoint of fraternity, it might be said that individuals within the group showed little empathy for other people. Another finding was that those who could project, to a small degree, appeared to produce work that was of theoretical value and more widely significant. Whatever the findings, one must remember that the sampling was quite limited and that a continued need for research seems to be the major theme.

_____. "New Light on Heredity: Adult Adjustment of Foster Home Children." *Child Study*, 23 (Summer, 1946), 119–20.

This study involved twenty-five children from normal parents, thirty-six children from alcoholic parents, and six children from psychotic parents. The study seems to indicate that there are at least two things that play a large part in life adjustment. The first is a need for a form of biological integration that produces an emotional-social-physical balance. The second concerns the acceptance of an individual and seems to indicate a need for group recognition and feelings of security. Roe does much to introduce many new concepts regarding the child and the society in which he lives.

_____. "Psychological Examinations of Eminent Biologists." *Journal of Consulting Psychology*, 13 (August, 1949), 225–46.

Roe reports the results of tests administered as part of a project to study the lives, personalities, and work of eminent biologists. It was her intent to isolate any features of personality structure that would reflect a uniqueness common only to eminent biologists. Through a comprehensive investigation of such characteristics, she thought that some pattern might be established between vocational choice and personality. Three tests, *i.e.*, the Rorschach, the thematic apperception, and a verbal-spatial-mathematical test, were given to twenty research biologists. Data indicated wide individual differences and revealed that geneticists and biochemists appear, without exception, to be better at both the spatial and mathematical tests than they were at the verbal test.

———. "A Psychological Study of Physical Scientists." *Genetic Psychology Monograph*, 18 (February, 1952), 18–22.

This study involved nine theoretical physicists, nine experimental physicists, three physical chemists primarily engaged in theoretical research, and one physical chemist primarily engaged in experimental research. There were many individual differences among the scientists. Although the study reveals that in specific areas theorists and experimentalists appear to be poorly adjusted socially, it also reveals parental attitudes and the effect of such attitudes, if any, upon the child.

———. "Group Rorschachs of University Faculties." *Journal of Consulting Psychology*, 16 (April, 1952), 18–22.

This article concerns itself with faculty members from the biological, physical, and social sciences. The Rorschach was administered to a representative sample of 347 males and 35 females who ranged in age from twenty-five to thirty-seven. A previous study indicated that sex was not a determinant when working in this specific research area. The results of this study bring forth many concepts for future research.

———. *The Psychology of Occupations*. New York: John Wiley and Sons, 1956. 340 pp.

This book reflects an interest in the fields of vocational guidance, personnel selection, and industrial psychology, with emphasis placed upon the relationship of personality to vocational choice. Much attention is given to the differences in occupations, the differences in people, and the implications of such differences. Roe suggests that some effort be made to study the various types of work and the people who are engaged in these types of work. It is her contention that occupational choice might be closely related to the way an individual sees himself.

———. *Graduate Education in Psychology*. Washington, D.C.: American Psychological Association, 1958. 97 pp.

This is a discussion of major issues introduced at the Conference on Graduate Education in Psychology held at Miami Beach, Florida, in 1958. Issues of concern seem to gravitate toward the following three questions: For what roles, as perceived by society, should we educate psychologists; what is the function of subdoctoral training, and what should be its components; and how may graduate education be facilitated or hampered by controls? Roe emphasizes the nondoctoral training program that would help train teachers of psychology for junior colleges and small four-year institutions. A program of this type would be different from a doctoral program in that it would preclude the area of research, which is considered so essential to doctoral candidates.

Roeber, Edward Charles

BIRTH: April 14, 1913, Rhinelander, Wisconsin
PRESENT STATUS: deceased; February 8, 1969
BACKGROUND: *Educational* B.A., Lawrence College, 1935; M.A., Northwestern University, 1938; Ph.D., Northwestern University, 1942

Professional public schoolteacher in Wisconsin, 1935–43; associate professor of educational psychology and director of placement, Hamline University, 1943–45; director of guidance and counseling, Kansas State Teachers College, 1945–47; associate professor of education, University of Missouri, 1947–53; from associate professor to professor of education, University of Michigan, 1953–66; W. R. Holmstedt Distinguished Professor of Education, Indiana State University, 1966–69

Field of Work vocational and educational counseling, with emphasis on occupational choice and vocational theory

Affiliations American Psychological Association, Division of Counseling Psychology; American Personnel and Guidance Association (president, 1961–62); National Vocational Guidance Association (president, 1958–59); American College Personnel Association; Association of Counselor Education and Supervision; American Educational Research Association

SUMMATION OF CONCEPTS:

Roeber's writing is in the areas of counseling and occupational information. In his work on counseling, it appears that he attempted to give the reader some knowledge of the characteristics of good counseling, the characteristics of a good counselor, and the position of the counselor relative to other school personnel. Recognized as a foremost authority in the area of occupational information, he did much to describe how such information should be organized and introduced within the school.

ANNOTATED BIBLIOGRAPHY:

Roeber, Edward C., Glenn E. Smith, and Clifford E. Erickson. *Organization and Administration of Guidance Services.* New York: McGraw-Hill Book Co., 1955. 294 pp.

The authors do much to define and clarify the relationship of school personnel to the guidance services program. Much emphasis is placed on the descriptive presentation of materials that provide a sophisticated look at how the guidance services within a school might logically be organized to obtain maximum benefits. This information might serve in a variety of situations, such as for the training of counselors, the revision of a guidance program, the establishment of a new program, or the in-service training of faculty members.

———, and Max F. Baer. *Occupational Information*. Chicago: Science Research Associates, 1958. 495 pp.

This book seems to cover the area of occupational information quite thoroughly. The authors stress such aspects as the collection, filing, and dissemination of occupational information. The book seems to have a potential for serving a variety of needs. A most interesting feature is the ability of the authors to relate occupational information to group work, interviews, curriculum planning, and job selection.

———, et al. "Guidance and Counseling." *Review of Educational Research*, 30 (April, 1960), 93–179.

A reflection of work done through the American Personnel and Guidance Association and the American Educational Research Association, the articles included represent a review of the major research findings in the area of guidance over a three-year period. The effort to assimilate such findings in a meaningful way was done by a joint committee whose chairman was Roeber. An evaluation of such articles indicates an increase in the quality of research now being done in guidance. The articles cover eight chapters and deal with such pertinent areas of interest as the philosophical foundations of guidance, organization of guidance services, preparation of personnel in guidance, counseling as a service, appraising guidance, the information service, group procedures, and evaluation of guidance services.

———. *The School Counselor*. Washington, D.C.: Center for Applied Research in Education, 1963. 107 pp.

Roeber introduces some of the critical issues confronting the counselor today. He attempts to show the present status of counseling and to provide guidelines for the selection and certification of counselors.

Rogers, Carl Ransom

BIRTH: January 8, 1902, Oak Park, Illinois

PRESENT STATUS: Resident Fellow, Center for Studies of the Person, La Jolla, California

BACKGROUND: *Educational* B.A., University of Wisconsin, 1924; student at Union Theological Seminary, 1924-26; M.A., Columbia University, 1928; Ph.D., Columbia University, 1931; honorary L.H.D., Lawrence College, 1956; honorary Litt.D., Gonzaga University, 1968

Professional Fellow, New York Institute of Child Guidance, 1927-28; psychologist, Child Study Department, Society for the Prevention of Cruelty to Children, Rochester, New York, 1928-30; director of the Child Study Department, 1930-39; director, Rochester Guidance Center, 1939-40; professor of clinical psychology, Ohio State University, 1940-45; professor of psychology and executive secretary of the Counseling Center, University of Chicago, 1945-57; Professor of Psychology and Psychiatry, University of Wisconsin, 1957-63; Resident Fellow, Western Behavioral Sciences Institute, La Jolla, California, 1964-68; Resident Fellow, Center for Studies of the Person, La Jolla, California, 1968-; visiting professor at various institutions of higher education, including Columbia University, University of Rochester, UCLA, Harvard University, Occidental College, University of California at Berkeley, and Brandeis University

Field of Work major contribution is his conceptualization and development of the client-centered, nondirective approach to therapy

Affiliations Fellow, American Psychological Association (president, 1946-47), Divisions of Clinical Psychology, Personality and Social Psychology, Philosophical Psychology, and Psychotherapy; American Academy of Psychotherapists (president, 1956-58); American Association of Applied Psychology (president, 1944-45); American Orthopsychiatric Association (vice-president, 1944-45); Phi Beta Kappa

SUMMATION OF CONCEPTS:

For many years, Rogers has emphasized the importance of combating serious adjustment problems through the use of preventive measures in homes, schools, colleges, and institutions. He does not see these measures as treatment but rather as an approach that might have the same effect in this circumstance as preventive medicine has in the field of health. To Rogers it appears more important to take steps to prevent adjustment problems than to treat the problem after it occurs. His approach to counseling seems to center on the belief that the constructive forces that alter perception reside primarily within the client and probably cannot come from the outside. Therefore, if diagnosis is done, it must be done by the client, since he is the only one capable of understanding his own problem completely.

ANNOTATED BIBLIOGRAPHY:

Rogers, Carl Ransom. *Measuring Personality Adjustment in Children Nine to Thirteen Years of Age.* New York: Columbia University Press, 1931. 107 pp.

Rogers' dissertation, this study concerns itself with fifty-two children from the Institute for Child Guidance and two groups of children from private and public schools. Most of the material presented is devoted to the results obtained from a test of personality adjustment.

———. "The Processes of Therapy." *Journal of Consulting Psychology*, 4 (1940), 161–64.

Rogers lists the following basic conditions for successful therapy: the client's awareness of dissatisfaction with his current adjustment, the awareness that adverse social factors will be manipulated, and the assistance of a skilled therapist whose purpose is to strengthen the individual. The steps necessary for successful therapy are the establishment of rapport with a delicate balance between identification and objectivity, a freedom of expression of thoughts and feelings by the client, the client's recognition and acceptance of his spontaneous self, the development of autonomy to the extent that the client can assume responsibility for making his own choice, a gain in insight by the client through assimilated interpretation, and the continued growth of the client's independence.

———. "Electrically Recorded Interviews in Improving Psychotherapeutic Techniques." *American Journal of Orthopsychiatry*, 12 (1942), 429–35.

The usefulness of recorded interviews is discussed in terms of teaching psychotherapeutic concepts, teaching counseling techniques, and research.

———. "Therapy in Guidance Clinics." *Journal of Abnormal Social Psychology*, 3 (1943), 284–89.

From this article it appears that Rogers' concept is that the skilled therapist no longer tries to reform his client but merely tries to reveal the client to himself, encouraging catharsis. This is followed by the development of self-understanding, from which comes the choice of more appropriate goals and the decisions and actions that guide the client toward those goals. The therapist should not suggest goals or actions. Rogers also states that the ultimate responsibility for destiny resides within the client and not the therapist.

———. "The Development of Insight in a Counseling Relationship." *Journal of Consulting Psychology*, 8 (1944), 331–41.

Rogers promotes the idea that counseling of a nondirective nature— that is, an approach that subscribes to the development of insight and an understanding of the self-concept—develops spontaneously. It follows free expression of negative emotion and is likely to develop if the counselor uses responses that are accepting and clarifying. Procedures that make defensiveness by the client completely unnecessary and that make the client feel that he is deeply understood are most successful.

———, and V. M. Axline. "A Teacher-Therapist Deals with a Handicapped Child." *Journal of Abnormal Social Psychology*, 40 (1945), 119–42.

Rogers covers a detailed case history that reveals how a skillful teacher-therapist treated a maladjusted six-year-old boy whose problems included a throat constriction that prevented eating, infantile and antisocial behavior, rejection by his mother and first foster mother, and several severe illnesses. Nondirective therapy was adhered to, with apparent acceptance of the child just as he was. Signs of transference appeared because of the obvious interest of the teacher, but no dependence remained after therapy was discontinued. The therapist helped the boy to recognize his underlying feelings and conflicting desires by interpreting his statements and actions. Projected play situations were quite revealing.

———. "Recent Research in Non-Directive Therapy and Its Implications." *American Journal of Orthopsychiatry*, 16 (1946), 581–88.

Evidence is cited by Rogers to show that client-centered, catalytic, nondirective therapy achieves a predictable and measurable process of release, insight, integration, and choice in the client. Evidence indicates that such therapy, differing sharply in technique from directive therapy and psychoanalysis, does produce measurable alterations in the attitude, self-concept, behavior, and personality structure of the client. Rogers stresses the need for a more scientific approach to psychotherapy and predicts an end for psychotherapy as an art and a beginning for psychotherapy as a science.

———. "Significant Aspects of Client-Centered Therapy." *American Psychologist*, 1 (1946), 415–22.

Here Rogers discusses the difference between nondirected therapy and other therapeutic procedures. He feels that the one condition necessary for the forces of the client to be released is the proper psychological atmosphere between client and therapist. The factors promoting a proper atmosphere are listed.

———. "Some Observations on the Organization of Personality." *American Psychologist*, 2 (1947), 358–68.

Nondirective therapy provides an opportunity to observe the inner dynamics of personality as they proceed with a minimum of interference from the therapist. It appears that the perception of self is a basic factor influencing the behavior and adjustment of the individual. Under certain conditions the client can reorganize his field of perception, including the way he perceives himself. Successful therapy does not solve problems. It gives a feeling of freedom and contentment, which follows from an accurate and realistic perception of the self. The conditions necessary for this reorganization are an atmosphere of permissiveness and understanding and some assistance in focusing upon the perception of self. The advantages of tape recording interviews are discussed.

———. "Some Implications of Client-Centered Counseling for College Personnel Work." *Journal of Educational and Psychological Measurement*, 8 (1948), 540–49.

The current trend of accumulating a large body of information about individual students is protested by the author, who feels that this approach places the center of organization on the counselor or dean of students and not within the student himself. One of the primary principles of client-centered counseling is that it is the student who should and can best integrate this information and take responsibility for planning and action. Rogers also points out specific ways in which the attitudes basic to client-centered counseling can be applied to group situations, classroom teaching, and administrative and organizational relationships. The author states that the application of client-centered principles to administration holds the possibility of discovering basic scientific truth about interpersonal organization relationships, truths that may enrich and deepen our concept of democracy.

_____, Bill L. Kell, and Helen McNeil. "The Role of Self Understanding in the Prediction of Behavior." *Journal of Consulting Psychology*, 12 (1948), 174–86.

This article resulted from a study of a group of delinquents, eight to eighteen years of age, who were rated on a seven-point scale for favorableness of heredity, physical condition, mental ability, family environment, socioeconomic status, social experience, and self-insight. Correlating each of these ratings with later adjustment over a two-year period, the authors found that self-insight gave the best prediction of good adjustment even when the individual returned to a bad home environment. Such findings seemed to support Rogers' contention that self-perception is more important than situational factors in determining adjustment.

_____. "The Attitude and Orientation of the Counselor in Client-Centered Therapy." *Journal of Consulting Psychology*, 13 (1949), 82–94.

Here Rogers promulgates the concept that the basic operational philosophy of an individual, which may or may not resemble his expressed philosophy, largely determines the time it will take him to become a skillful counselor. It appears that persons who have maintained an orientation stressing individual significance and worth can learn the client-centered approach more readily than those who do not hold the worth of a person in high esteem. The counselor's role is to assume, as best he can, the internal frame of reference of the client—to see the world as the client sees it, to see the client himself as he is seen by himself, and to put aside all perceptions from the external frame of reference while doing so.

_____, and R. Becker. "A Basic Orientation for Counseling." *Pastoral Psychology*, 1 (1950), 26–34.

The authors present the idea that the client-centered counselor acts on the hypothesis that each person is of unique worth and has the capacity for self-understanding and self-direction. They further maintain that the counselor adopts, insofar as possible, the internal reference of the client, creating an atmosphere of understanding and acceptance, and that the client, by an exploration of self, comes to a deeper understanding and acceptance of himself. The authors feel that at this point the client begins to reorganize the self on a new perceptual basis, behaviorally moving in a new direction, independent of the counselor.

———. *Client-Centered Therapy.* Boston: Houghton Mifflin Co., 1951. 560 pp.

The main conceptual components of Rogers' theory of personality are: (1) the *self*, which is a differentiated portion of the phenomenal field and which consists of a pattern of conscious perceptions and values of the "I" or "me"; (2) the *organism*, which is the total individual; and (3) the *phenomenal field*, which is the totality of experience. The organism is felt to function in the following ways: it reacts as an organized whole to the phenomenal field in order to satisfy its needs; it has one basic motive, namely, to actualize, maintain, and enhance itself; and it may symbolize its experiences so that they remain unconscious, or it may ignore its experiences. The self functions in the following ways: it develops out of the organism's interactions with the environment; it may introject the values of other people and perceive them in a distorted fashion; it strives for consistency; the organism behaves in ways that are consistent with the self; experiences that are not consistent with the self-structure are perceived as threats; and the self may change as a result of maturation and learning. Rogers formulates nineteen propositions to explain the nature of these concepts and their interrelations.

———. "Communication: Its Blocking and Facilitation." *Etc.: Review of General Semantics,* 9 (1952), 83–88.

Rogers sees the task of psychotherapy as dealing with a failure in communication between or within men. He feels that stating another's viewpoint, attitude, or idea, in a manner that is acceptable to him, requires and develops insight. As the client enters another frame of reference with regard to a specific value, he may feel threatened, since it suggests the possibility of changing his own viewpoints. The difficulty is aggravated by the fact that blocked communication often accompanies or generates emotions that are easier to cope with if a defensive or hostile attitude can be taken toward the other person. The author feels that experience demonstrates, however, that in a face-to-face situation the results repay the effort and confirm the hope. The solution to noncommunication is provided for Rogers by creating a situation in which each of the different parties comes to understand the other from the other's point of view.

———. "Personality Change in Psychotherapy." *International Journal of Social Psychiatry,* 1 (1955), 31–41.

This is an illustration of how controlled studies of the outcome of psychotherapy might be made by testing detailed hypotheses based on the dynamics of psychotherapy. The study indicates that methodological progress made in recent years has thrown open the whole therapeutic process to research investigations. Illustrated designs using Stephenson's Q technique to measure progress made in therapy are included.

———. "The Necessary and Sufficient Conditions of Therapeutic Personality Change." *Journal of Consulting Psychology*, 21 (1957), 95–103.

The six conditions necessary and sufficient for constructive personality changes to occur are (it is necessary that these conditions exist and continue over a period of time): (1) two persons are in psychological contact; (2) the first, termed the client, is in a state of incongruence, being vulnerable or anxious; (3) the second person, termed the therapist, is congruent or integrated in the relationship; (4) the therapist experiences an unconditional positive regard for the client; (5) the therapist experiences an empathic understanding of the client's internal frame of reference and endeavors to communicate this experience to the client; and (6) the communication to the client of the therapist's empathic understanding and unconditional positive regard is achieved to a minimal degree. No other conditions are necessary. Rogers feels that if these six conditions exist and continue over a period of time, then the process of constructive personality change will follow. The remainder of the article is devoted to explaining, qualifying, and illustrating the six conditions.

———. *On Becoming a Person*. Boston: Houghton Mifflin Co., 1961. 420 pp.

Rogers recapitulates, bringing forth materials previously presented in lectures, articles, and books. The book is both interesting and refreshing and gives an insight to the life of Carl Rogers, his research, and his philosophy, with some attention on those people who have made significant contributions to his present point of view.

Sanderson, Herbert Z.
 BIRTH: May 4, 1910, Rostov, Russia
 PRESENT STATUS: professor of education, San Francisco State College

HERBERT Z. SANDERSON

BACKGROUND: *Educational* B.S., City College of New York, 1939; M.A., New York University, 1941; Ph.D., New York University, 1948

Professional junior psychologist, New York City Department of Corrections, 1936–40; psychologist, Federal Employment Service of New York, 1940–41; psychologist, New York State Department of Corrections, 1941–43; counseling psychologist, Community Vocational Service of Newark, 1943–45; director, Jewish Community Services of Buffalo, 1945–53; counseling psychologist, University of Buffalo, 1953–55; director, Jewish Vocational Service of Miami, 1955–57; professor of education, San Francisco State College, 1957–

Field of Work major contribution in vocational guidance, counseling, and rehabilitation; high interest in the use of projectives

Affiliations Fellow, American Psychological Association, Division of Counseling Psychology; American Association for the Advancement of Science

SUMMATION OF CONCEPTS:

Sanderson focuses on the area of vocational counseling, with specific attention to theory concerning the practical application of effective vocational counseling techniques. Much of what he does in the area of research and counseling seems to lend itself well to projective techniques.

ANNOTATED BIBLIOGRAPHY:

Sanderson, Herbert Z. "Norms for 'Shock' in the Rorschach." *Journal of Consulting Psychology,* 15 (1951), 127–29.

In this study, the author touches on the development of statistically significant criteria for "shock" through the measurement of the reaction time to each Rorschach card. Sanderson maintains that the application of norms developed for this purpose will bring greater objectivity to the meaning of increased reaction time, specifically as it applies "shock" as a basic concept.

———. "Card Titles in Testing the Limits in Rorschach." *Journal of Counseling Psychology,* 33 (1952), 27–29.

This article reflects the results of a study in which the Rorschach test was administered to twenty-five adults who were asked, upon completion of the test, to go through the Rorschach cards again and give each one a name or title. It was presumed that such a technique might logically be employed to obtain whole responses rather than meaningless or superficial responses to cards. It also enables the test administrator to test client flexibility in shifting from an unstructured to a structured position.

VERNON GEORGE SCHAEFER

———. *Basic Concepts in Vocational Guidance.* New York: McGraw-Hill Book Co., 1954. 327 pp.

Here, in a most readable way, Sanderson attempts to present a theoretical and functional guide to vocational counseling. It is with great concern that he emphasizes the fact that theoretical principles are best illustrated through the presentation of actual cases. For the serious student of vocational counseling, this book offers many interesting hours of study.

Schaefer, Vernon George

BIRTH: January 1, 1904, Tonica, Illinois
PRESENT STATUS: deceased; 1965, Naperville, Illinois
BACKGROUND: *Educational* B.A., North Central College, 1926; M.A., University of Chicago, 1931; Ph.D., Northwestern University, 1937

Professional high school teacher in Batavia, Illinois, 1926–28; teacher, Chicago Board of Education, 1928–37; associate professor, Pennsylvania State College, 1937–43; personnel manager, RCA Victor, 1943–44; director of supervisory training, Westinghouse Electric Corporation, East Pittsburgh, Pennsylvania, 1944–46; professor, Iowa State College, 1946–49; staff psychologist, George Fry Associates, 1949–56; professor and head of the Department of Psychology, North Central College, 1950–59; consultant in private industry, 1959–65

Field of Work industrial psychology, with emphasis on supervision, leadership, and human relations in industry

Affiliations Fellow, American Psychological Association, Division of Industrial and Business Psychology

SUMMATION OF CONCEPTS:

Schaefer concerned himself with concepts relating to industrial psychology. His attention, for the most part, was centered upon the selection of supervisors for industrial positions and upon selective testing for more effective industrial performance. It appears that his basic concept was that greater effectiveness in industry becomes possible only after some efforts have been made through selective testing and special job instruction.

ANNOTATED BIBLIOGRAPHY:

Schaefer, Vernon G., and W. Wissler. *Industrial Organization.* New York: McGraw-Hill Book Co., 1941. 267 pp.

Most of what Schaefer says here is focused upon the human side of supervision, with emphasis upon human nature, interesting the worker, building morale, reducing turnover, promoting safety, labor relations, and leadership. This book appears to be designed to cover many aspects of the selection and training of individuals for industry, as well as the organization and supervision of effective industrial settings.

———. *Job Instruction.* New York: McGraw-Hill Book Co., 1941. 316 pp.

This book attempts to outline and discuss the fundamental principles of job instruction in terms of language adapted to the practical situations encountered in teaching adults how to do industrial jobs effectively.

———. *Safety Supervision.* New York: McGraw-Hill Book Co., 1942. 357 pp.

This is a book directed toward assisting supervisors who must train workers to follow safety practices. Emphasis is placed on specific methods to be used in various situations as individuals are brought to a new level of thinking regarding safety and safety practices.

Shartle, Carroll Leonard

BIRTH: June 26, 1903, Ruthven, Iowa

PRESENT STATUS: professor emeritus of psychology, Ohio State University

BACKGROUND: *Educational* B.A., Iowa State Teachers College, 1927; M.A., Columbia University, 1932; Ph.D., Ohio State University, 1933

Professional assistant psychologist, Milwaukee Electric Railroad and Light Company, 1927-31; lecturer, Ohio State University, 1931-33; instructor in psychology, Michigan State College, 1933-35; chief of Occupational Analysis Section, Social Security Board, United States Employment Service, 1939-42; chief of Division of Occupational Analysis and Manning Tables, War Manpower Commission, 1942-44; professor of psychology, Ohio State University, 1944-61; executive director and later chairman, Personnel Research Board, Ohio State University, 1944-61; director of research, Human Resources Research Institute, United States Air Force, 1952-53; staff adviser for behavior sciences, Office of the Director of Defense Research and Engineering, Office of the Secretary of Defense, 1961-64; director of Research Division, Ohio State University, 1964-68; professor emeritus of psychology, Ohio State University, 1968-

Field of Work research in areas of occupational classification, executive performance and leadership, and job analysis

Affiliations Fellow, American Psychological Association, Divisions of Industrial Psychology and Military Psychology; National Vocational Guidance Association; American Association for the Advancement of Science, International Association for Applied Psychology; Sigma Xi; Phi Beta Kappa

SUMMATION OF CONCEPTS:

Shartle has done much to improve the reader's understanding of occupational information and the problems involved in job selection. Perhaps the basic concept most frequently reflected in his writing is the need for counselors to revise, modify, and update information, as well as to improve their methods of disseminating and filing information.

ANNOTATED BIBLIOGRAPHY:

Shartle, Carroll L. "A Clinical Approach to Foremanship." *Personnel and Guidance Journal*, 13 (1934), 135-39.

This study involved a group of successful foremen and a group of workers with job skills equal to those of the foremen but with little or no skill in supervising other workers. These two groups were studied in a clinical setting in which interviews and questionnaires were used to detect elements that would differentiate the groups. After careful study, it was determined that the foremen showed from early childhood a development that involved less withdrawal from others and less indifference to the actions of others. In many cases there was a close relationship between childhood behavior and present job behavior.

———. "Fitting Workers to Jobs." *Personnel and Guidance Journal*, 20 (1942), 328-32.

This article introduces findings by the Occupational Analysis Section of the U.S. Employment Service. It provides information concerning the types of jobs in a particular industry and the specific abilities necessary to carry out such responsibilities. Shartle stresses the importance of testing in industry and presents the specific ways in which tests are being used to select workers for various jobs.

———. "Developments in Occupational Classification." *Journal of Consulting Psychology*, 10 (1946), 83-84.

Shartle points out that there have been few developments in occupational classification. Rather, it appears that what has already been provided in the area of classification has simply been expanded. Since the techniques involved in classification now appear to be limited, it seems necessary to work toward developing a more satisfactory system of occupational information. One method, introduced by psychologists, that appears quite promising is a classification system emphasizing worker traits involved rather than duties performed.

──────. *Executive Performance and Leadership.* Englewood Cliffs, N.J.: Prentice-Hall, 1956. 295 pp.

Shartle feels that executive leadership takes on a role that is, at least in part, dictated by the responsibilities involved and the types of people performing. In essence, it appears that each executive leadership role is relative to the specific situation in which it functions. Thus, for many executives it may appear that what is done by other executives in other organizations is wrong. In an effort to curb unwarranted criticism of one executive by another, Shartle presents some examples of executive leadership in government, industry, and education.

──────. *Occupational Information.* 2nd ed. Englewood Cliffs, N.J.: Prentice-Hall, 1957. 391 pp.

Shartle illustrates the many and varied types of occupational information and the use of such information. Further, some attention is given to the significance of updating materials on occupations, employment, and training opportunities. Of interest to the counselor as well as to the student is the fact that this second edition includes a list of sources of occupational information, a complete job analysis to serve as a format for the preparation of job analyses, and a presentation of practical methods for filing information materials.

Shertzer, Bruce E.

BIRTH: January 11, 1928, Bloomington, Indiana

PRESENT STATUS: professor of education and chairman, Counseling and Personnel Services, Purdue University

BACKGROUND: *Educational* B.S., Indiana University, 1952; M.S., Indiana University, 1953; Ed.D., Indiana University, 1958

Professional teacher counselor and director of guidance, Martinsville, Indiana, Metropolitan School District, 1952–56; state director of guidance, Indiana State Department of Public Instruction, 1956–58; associate director, Project on Guidance of Superior Students, North Central Association of Colleges and Universities, 1958–60; assistant professor, 1960–62, associate professor, 1962–66, professor, 1966–, Purdue University; visiting professor of education psychology, University of Hawaii, summer, 1967; director, various NDEA coun-

BRUCE E. SHERTZER

seling and guidance institutes; Fulbright Senior Lecturer Award, University of Reading, England, 1967-68; Counselor-Educator of the Year Award, Indiana Personnel and Guidance Association, 1969

Field of Work notable contributions in guidance and counseling, with emphasis on counselor education

Affiliations American Personnel and Guidance Association (president, 1972-73), Indiana Personnel and Guidance Association (president, 1963), Association for Counselor Education and Supervision (president, 1970), North Central Association for Counselor Education and Supervision (chairman, 1968)

SUMMATION OF CONCEPTS:

Shertzer's primary concern is with counselor education, not counseling theory. He seems to be more interested in clarifying various points of view than in dictating a specific viewpoint. Many of his writings give the impression that he is an observer rather than a participant, an attitude that seemingly permits him to assume the role of a reporter rather than a crusader. He denies that a person can operate without theoretical assumptions and seems to believe that the best educational preparation for the counselor-trainee in developing theoretical foundations is to gain as much knowledge and practical experience as possible. From this personal struggle to integrate the theoretical and the practical, the individual discovers a position that works best in his own particular situation.

ANNOTATED BIBLIOGRAPHY:

Shertzer, Bruce E., and Herman J. Peters. *Guidance: Techniques for Individual Appraisal and Development.* New York: Macmillan Co., 1965. 390 pp.

The authors introduce material that lends itself well to a developmental approach to guidance. Much emphasis is placed on the tools used in the analysis of the individual, including both psychometric and nontesting techniques utilized in a complete guidance inventory. The authors also introduce what they consider are appropriate practices in the presentation and interpretation of test data.

―――, and Shelly C. Stone. *Fundamentals of Counseling.* Boston: Houghton Mifflin Co., 1968. 637 pp.

This book is designed for use as a textbook in the basic graduate course in counseling. The purpose is not to present a new theory or to introduce revolutionary practices. Rather, the emphasis is on the treatment of factual material and on the way it relates to a wide scope of counseling theories and practices. The book is well documented, and much of the coverage is directed toward seven counseling theories, which are discussed in terms of cognitively and affectively oriented approaches.

———, and Shelley C. Stone. *Fundamentals of Guidance.* 2nd ed. Boston: Houghton Mifflin Co., 1971. 575 pp.

This is one of the best examples of contemporary textbook writing in the entire field of guidance. Although the authors are modest in their claims, this work represents a thorough and scholarly presentation of the concepts and practices associated with the daily functions of the counselor. Included are a brief history of developments in guidance, a concise introduction to the guidance services, and a comprehensive discussion of the contemporary issues and trends in guidance.

———, and Shelly C. Stone. *Careers in Guidance and Counseling.* Boston: Houghton Mifflin Co., 1972. 168 pp.

In a practical, simple, and straightforward approach, the authors identify and describe many settings in which the counseling process occurs. These descriptions include the work of the elementary counselor, the secondary counselor, the vocational counselor, the college counselor, the rehabilitation counselor, the Veterans Administration counselor, the community–mental health counselor, the marriage counselor, the pastoral counselor, and the counselor in private practice. Relevant information is presented concerning these various work situations, with special consideration given to supply and demand, preparation required, working conditions, salaries, career patterns, and the occupational outlook.

Shoben, Edward Joseph, Jr.

BIRTH: October 3, 1918, Oberlin, Ohio

PRESENT STATUS: executive vice-president, Evergreen State College, Olympia, Washington

BACKGROUND: *Educational* A.B., University of Southern California, 1939; M.A., University of Southern California, 1945; Ph.D., University of Southern California, 1947

Professional teacher of mathematics, social science, English, and jour-

EDWARD JOSEPH SHOBEN, JR.

nalism, California public schools, 1940-42; personnel director, Southern California Motor Freight, 1942-45; clinical psychologist, Psychological Guidance Center, Los Angeles, 1945-46; junior counselor, USC Veterans Guidance Center, 1946; teaching and clinical assistant in psychology, University of Southern California, 1946-47; assistant professor of psychology and counselor in Student Counseling Office, University of Iowa, 1947-50; director, Student Counseling Office, University of Iowa, 1949-50; from associate professor to professor of psychology and education, Columbia University Teachers College, 1950-65; editor, *Teachers College Record*, 1960-65; director of clinical training, Department of Psychology, Columbia University, 1962-64; coordinator of college relations, Columbia University, 1964-65; professor of higher education and psychology and director of the Center for Research and Training in Higher Education, University of Cincinnati, 1965-66; director of the Commission on Academic Affairs and editor of the *Educational Record*, American Council on Education, 1966-68; chairman, Council on Higher Education Studies, State University of New York at Buffalo, 1968-69; executive vice-president, Evergreen State College, 1969-

Field of Work dynamics of human development as related to mental health, counseling, and the learning process

Affiliations Fellow, American Psychological Association, Divisions of the Teaching of Psychology, Educational Psychology, Counseling Psychology, Philosophical Psychology, and Community Psychology; Fellow, American Association for the Advancement of Science; American Law and Psychological Society (president, 1971-72); Sigma Xi; Psi Chi

SUMMATION OF CONCEPTS:

Shoben seems to feel that the primary function of counseling is to provide a situation in which the client has an opportunity to learn new patterns of response that, in effect, will help him live more harmoniously with other people. For the client, therapy provides a world in which he can learn and from which he can generalize his learnings to the larger world outside.

ANNOTATED BIBLIOGRAPHY:

Shoben, Edward Joseph, Jr., and L. F. Shaffer. *The Psychology of Adjustment*. Boston: Houghton Mifflin Co., 1956. 672 pp.

This appears to be an attempt to synthesize many of the concepts introduced by the great psychological advances during the twentieth century, with some emphasis on the experimental study of behavior and the psychoanalytic approach to psychopathology. There are four major sections, a set of discussion questions, and a comprehensive bibliography.

---. "Viewpoints from Related Disciplines: Learning Theory." *Teachers College Record*, 60 (1959), 272-82.

Much that is done in the area of learning theory seems to focus on the "how" and the "what" of learning. Shoben feels that the development of a systematic pattern of understanding relative to learning is possible when one makes an effort to define problems, gather evidence, make inferences, and apply generalizations.

Simpson, Mrs. George Gaylord. *See* Roe, Anne

Skinner, Burrhus Frederic

BIRTH: March 20, 1904, Susquehanna, Pennsylvania

PRESENT STATUS: professor emeritus, Harvard University, Department of Psychology and Social Relations

BACKGROUND: *Educational* A.B., Hamilton College, 1926; M.A., Harvard University, 1930; Ph.D., Harvard University, 1931; honorary Sc.D., Hamilton College, 1951, North Carolina State College, 1960, University of Chicago, 1967, and University of Missouri, 1968; honorary Litt.D., Ripon College, 1961

Professional Research Fellow, National Research Council, Harvard University, 1931-33; Junior Fellow, Harvard Society of Fellows, 1933-36; instructor in psychology, 1936-37, assistant professor, 1937-39, associate professor, 1939-45, University of Minnesota; conducted war research, 1942-43; received Guggenheim research grant, 1944-45; professor of psychology and department chairman, University of Indiana, 1945-48; William James Lecturer, Harvard University, 1947; professor of psychology, Harvard University, 1948-57; Edgar Pierce Professor of Psychology, Harvard, 1958-74; professor emeritus, Harvard University, Department of Psychology and Social Relations, 1974-

Field of Work most notable contributions in analysis of behavior, operant conditioning, and learning theory; also developed the Skinner box, devised for the study of animal learning and used during World War II in training pigeons to keep guided missiles on target

Affiliations Phi Beta Kappa; American Association for the Advancement of Science; National Academy of Sciences; American Academy of Arts and Sciences; American Philosophical Society; Society of Experimental Psychologists; Swedish Psychological Society; Sigma Xi; Fellow, American Psychological Association, Divisions of General Psychology, Experimental Psychology, Educational Psychology, Experimental Analysis of Behavior, and Psychopharmacology

BURRHUS FREDERIC SKINNER

SUMMATION OF CONCEPTS:

Based on a sampling of the members of the American Psychological Association, it seems most appropriate to introduce B. F. Skinner as one of the most influential and controversial American psychologists of the twentieth century. His greatest contribution to behavioral science is his refinement of Pavlovian classical conditioning, which he calls operant conditioning. Learning, he believes, comes about through activity. For learning to occur, Skinner suggests that you bring about the response you want made and then reinforce it positively. The principle is that organisms tend to repeat behavior that is followed by pleasant consequences and avoid behavior that is followed by unpleasant consequences. Skinner challenges our society to take this approach beyond the laboratory and to use it to shape and control the foundations from which our society emerges. It was this argument in *Beyond Freedom and Dignity* that gained him the reputation of being an iconoclast. His major critics fear that Skinner's technique of shaping behavior will dehumanize the individual and threaten his freedom and dignity. The Skinnerian view, according to his critics, perceives man as little more than protein controlled by reflexes and instincts. Skinner, however, avows that his concern is for a better man in a better world. Hypothesizing that a person is determined by his situation, Skinner believes man's potential to become a better man is implemented by changing the world in which he lives. Skinner seems to welcome the opportunity to clarify his position while challenging the validity of his critics' arguments.

ANNOTATED BIBLIOGRAPHY:

Skinner, B. F. *The Behavior of Organisms: An Experimental Analysis.* New York: Appleton-Century-Crofts, 1938. 457 pp.

This book is a classic for students of the behavioral sciences. It reflects Skinnerian thinking in terms of the laboratory before his writings turned toward coping with the critical problems of mankind. The emphasis is on operant conditioning as a means of learning. A distinction is established between two kinds of behavior, one called respondent and the other operant. According to Skinner, one has little or no control over respondent behavior, *e.g.*, the pupillary reflex when the pupil of the eye contracts in a bright light. On the other hand, operant behavior is controlled by the events that follow the response. Some of his experiments with operant behavior and his use of Skinner conditioning boxes are discussed.

———. *Walden Two*. New York: Macmillan Co., 1948. 320 pp.

If an unknowing person held *The Behavior of Organisms* and *Walden Two* in his hands and quickly glanced through the contents of each, perhaps he would never realize that the same author had written both books. Over the years, Skinner moved from the confinement of the scientific laboratory to the core of his society. In *Walden Two* he attempts to fashion a utopia based on a planned order. He conceptualizes an effective and more productive society predicated on his experiments in behavior modification. Skinner describes various procedures designed to produce desirable adult characteristics. For example, in the utopia he visualizes for the future, babies are isolated from any destructive influences such as germs, frustrating influences, or physical discomforts, and children learn to build up a tolerance for annoying situations through scientific control of the environment, *e.g.*, learning to tolerate artificially through the use of shocks that become increasingly more painful. In a discussion with Richard Evans, Skinner stated that he honestly believes that the utopian community in *Walden Two* is a possibility for a group of well-meaning people.

———. *Science and Human Behavior*. New York: Macmillan Co., 1953. 461 pp.

This book is a blend of Skinner's two earlier works. It is philosophical as well as experimental in nature. He discusses the misuse of science and suggests that science is a search for order among the events in nature that deal with facts rather than with what someone says about them. Skinner deals with the analysis of behavior, reviewing his earlier ideas. Then he delineates the behavior of people in groups, an interest depicted in *Walden Two*, and considers the five societal agencies designed to control groups through the power to reinforce or punish; *i.e.*, he discusses government and law, religion, psychotherapy, economics, and education as the major influences of group behavior. A concluding section reviews the problem of who will, rather than who should, control the group that does survive in our world order.

———. *Verbal Behavior*. New York: Appleton-Century-Crofts, 1957. 478 pp.

In 1947, the year before Skinner returned to Harvard as a professor of psychology, he delivered the William James Lectures there and presented much of the information available in this book, which is an experimental analysis of verbal behavior. Discussions focus on controlling variables, multiple variables, the manipulation of verbal behavior, and the production of verbal behavior.

———. *Beyond Freedom and Dignity.* New York: Alfred A. Knopf, 1972. 225 pp.

Skinner declares that our traditional concepts of freedom and dignity must be sharply revised. His arguments are based on his pioneering work in the experimental analysis of behavior, in which he rejects explanations of behavior in terms of states of mind, feelings, and other mental attributes. Skinner argues that our attention should be directed to the physical and social environments in which people live. This argument rests on the idea that if the goals of the struggle for freedom and dignity are to be reached, then the environment must be changed rather than man himself. Skinner denies that the evolution of a culture will leave man in a hopeless state. Instead, man may go beyond his present state and achieve goals thought impossible.

Snygg, Donald

BIRTH: September 24, 1904, Magnet, Nebraska
PRESENT STATUS: deceased; February 1, 1967, Oswego, New York
BACKGROUND: *Educational* A.B., Nebraska State Teachers College, 1924; M.A., University of Iowa, 1931; Ph.D., University of Toronto, 1935
Professional secondary science and athletics teacher, Dakota City, Nebraska, 1922–23; secondary science and athletics teacher, Randolph, Nebraska, 1924–25; principal, Randolph High School, 1925–30; superintendent of schools, Verdigre, Nebraska, 1930–33; psychologist, Toronto, Canada, Juvenile Court, 1934–35; director of the Mental Hygiene Clinic, Toronto Infants Home, 1935–37; professor of psychology, State University of New York at Oswego, 1937–67
Field of Work phenomenological psychology
Affiliations Fellow, American Psychological Association, Divisions of Educational Psychology and the Society for the Psychological Study of Social Issues

SUMMATION OF CONCEPTS:

Snygg believed that behavior is governed by each individual's respective perception of the personal experience he is having at the time of perception.

ANNOTATED BIBLIOGRAPHY:

Snygg, Donald, and Arthur Combs. *Individual Behavior: A Perceptual Approach to Behavior.* Rev. ed. New York: Harper and Brothers, Publishers, 1959. 522 pp.

The authors introduce an understanding of man that is phenomenological in nature. They see man as an emerging entity who interacts with his fellow human beings not on the basis of the way *they* see the facts, but on the way *he* sees the facts. Each person is governed by his own perceptions at the particular moment that the experience takes place. The authors cover such areas as the interdependence of man, the perceptual view of behavior, the development of the phenomenal self, and the approach to treatment. The key to understanding this approach is to realize that those things that exist for each individual may exist for him alone and only at that moment. It is necessary for the individual to see those things that fulfill his needs. An interesting chapter in the book focuses upon how a person can help himself. According to the authors, the essential parts of self-improvement are a positive regard for self, a capacity for acceptance of self and others, and an ability to identify with others.

Stoops, Emory

BIRTH: December 13, 1902, Pratt, Kansas

PRESENT STATUS: professor emeritus of educational administration and supervision, University of Southern California

BACKGROUND: *Educational* B.A., University of Colorado, 1930; M.A., University of Southern California, 1934; Ed.D., University of Southern California, 1941

Professional assistant instructor of general and educational psychology, University of Colorado, 1929-30; superintendent, Richfield, Kansas, public schools, 1932-33; Research Fellow, University of Southern California, 1933-34; teacher of English and speech, California public schools, 1934-38; training teacher, University of California Training School, Los Angeles, 1938-42; assistant supervisor of the Personnel Division, Los Angeles City Schools, 1942; principal of the Adult School, University High School, Los Angeles, 1942-44; vice-principal of Bancroft Junior High School, 1944-45; coordinator of research and guidance, Los Angeles County schools, 1945-47; administrative assistant, Los Angeles County schools, 1947-53; professor of educational administration and supervision, University of Southern California, 1953-70; professor emeritus, University of Southern California, 1970-

EDWARD KELLOGG STRONG, JR.

Field of Work   educational administration, supervision, and guidance
Affiliations   American Educational Research Association, National Vocational Guidance Association, National Association of Secondary School Principals, American Association of School Administrators, National Education Association

SUMMATION OF CONCEPTS:

Stoops directs his writings toward the organization and administration of guidance services. He stresses the significance of administrative support in the implementation of guidance services and does much to present a sophisticated picture of guidance through proper school administration.

ANNOTATED BIBLIOGRAPHY:

Stoops, Emory. *Principles and Practices in Guidance.* New York: McGraw-Hill Book Co., 1958. 367 pp.
   Stoops designed this book to meet three purposes. First, he felt that a text such as this could serve those interested in learning more about guidance. Second, he felt it necessary to present guidance as a systematically organized pattern of services that help the youngster from the moment he enters school until he enters the world of work. Third, he felt it necessary to emphasize present practices. Stoops covers each major guidance service with care and provides much information that might well assist the novice counselor in making guidance a reality within the school.
   ———. *Guidance Services: Organization and Administration.* New York: McGraw-Hill Book Co., 1959. 302 pp.
   For many years Stoops has emphasized the significance of the administrator in the development of the guidance program. In this book he outlines in detail the relationship of the school administrator to guidance and points out the administrator's role in making guidance an effective part of the total school setting. He emphasizes the importance of a guidance point of view if guidance is to be successful and the need for good public relations techniques if guidance is to grow.

Strong, Edward Kellogg, Jr.
BIRTH: August 18, 1884, Syracuse, New York
PRESENT STATUS: deceased; December 4, 1963, Menlo Park, California

EDWARD KELLOGG STRONG, JR.

BACKGROUND: *Educational* B.S., University of California, 1906; M.S., University of California, 1909; Ph.D., Columbia University, 1911
Professional assistant in psychology, Columbia University (Barnard College), 1909–10; Fellow in Psychology, Columbia University, 1910–11; Research Fellow in Advertising for the Men's League, New York City, 1911–12; Research Fellow, Association of National Advertisers, 1912–15; lecturer in Extension Department, Columbia University, 1911–14; professor of psychology and education, George Peabody College, 1914–17; served in U.S. Army, 1918–19; professor and head of the Department of Vocational Education, Carnegie Institute of Technology, 1919–21; head of the Bureau of Educational Research, Carnegie Institute of Technology, 1921–23; published the Strong vocational interest blank, developed by Strong and his associates at the Carnegie Institute, 1927; professor of psychology, Graduate School of Business, Stanford University, 1923–49; professor emeritus, Stanford University, 1949–63
Field of Work outstanding contributions in vocational interest research, resulting in the Strong vocational interest blank (SVIB), the earliest standardized inventory of this type
Affiliations Fellow, American Psychological Association, Divisions of Clinical Psychology and Industrial Psychology; American Association for the Advancement of Science; Sigma Xi; Phi Delta Kappa

SUMMATION OF CONCEPTS:

Strong believed that occupational interest areas could be determined through the utilization of properly designed inventories. He contributed to the design of such inventories and continued throughout his lifetime to modify and revise this design.

ANNOTATED BIBLIOGRAPHY:

Strong, Edward K., Jr. *Introductory Psychology for Teachers*. Baltimore: Warwick and York, 1922. 255 pp.

In this book Strong presents his views on psychology. He was drawn to the functional approach, and one of his objectives was to train students by having them experience that thing that they were attempting to learn. According to Strong, experience would go beyond the scope of memorization and would call for placing into effect one's experiences. Much of this material serves as a guideline for teachers of introductory courses in psychology.

―――. *Vocational Interest Blank Manual*. Stanford: Stanford University Press, 1935. 40 pp.

This is the result of Strong's attempt to measure vocational interest.

The inventory manual contains information on administration, norms, test reliability, validity, and many other items of importance to those concerned with tests and measurements.

———. *Vocational Interests of Men and Women.* Stanford: Stanford University Press, 1943. 746 pp.

Strong stresses the significance of vocational guidance for young and old people. The book is divided into seven parts, and research done by the author is included as a point of reference. Strong devotes the entire book to vocational guidance and to those factors that have been instrumental in its sustenance.

———. "Weighted Versus Unit Scales." *Journal of Educational Psychology,* 36 (April, 1945), 193–216.

This is a comparison of unit and weighted scales using six measures. Correlations by J. W. Dunlap and his associates between scores on the two scales yielded a coefficient of .961. Strong indicates that, although shortcuts are recommended for scoring test blanks, such modifications appear to lead to distinctly less valid methods.

———, and Anthony C. Tucker. "Ten-Year Follow-up of Vocational Interest Scores of 1950 Medical College Seniors." *Journal of Applied Psychology,* 46 (April, 1962), 81–86.

For those readers interested in follow-up studies and research, this article offers some pertinent information. The article reflects the results of a ten-year study initiated in 1950 in which 783 seniors in fifteen medical schools were given the Strong vocational interest blank and the medical specialists preference blank. In 1960, 87 percent of this group responded to questionnaires designed to collect data for the follow-up study.

Sullivan, Harry Stack

BIRTH: February 21, 1892, Norwick, New York
PRESENT STATUS: deceased; January 14, 1949, Paris, France
BACKGROUND: *Educational* M.D., Chicago College of Medicine and Surgery, 1917
Professional served on U.S. Army Medical Examining Board, 1917–19; medical officer, Federal Board for Vocational Education, and executive officer, Public Health Service, 1919–22; associated with the University of Maryland Medical School and with the Enoch Pratt Hospital in Towson, Maryland,

where he conducted research on schizophrenia, 1923–30; president, William Alanson White Foundation, 1933–43; director, Washington School of Psychiatry, the training institution of the William Alanson White Foundation, 1936–49; co-editor and editor of the professional journal *Psychiatry*, which promoted his theory of interpersonal relations and advanced his public recognition, 1938–49; consultant in psychiatry, Selective Service System, 1940–41

Field of Work   research in the science of psychiatry, resulting in the creation of a new viewpoint known as the interpersonal theory of psychiatry

Affiliations   American Psychiatric Association, World Federation for Mental Health

SUMMATION OF CONCEPTS:

Sullivan's basic concept relates to a working definition of psychiatry. For Sullivan, psychiatry was viewed as the study of processes that involve or go on between people. He maintained that psychiatry is a field of interpersonal relations under any and all circumstances in which there is a relationship.

ANNOTATED BIBLIOGRAPHY:

Sullivan, Harry Stack. *Conception of Modern Psychiatry*. Washington, D.C.: William Alanson White Foundation, 1947. 147 pp.

A counselor may find this material of some consequence since Sullivan places considerable emphasis on a discussion of the initial interview. Here, in this theoretical idiom of thought, he introduces what he refers to as five preconceptions.

———. *The Interpersonal Theory of Psychiatry*. New York: W. W. Norton and Co., 1953. 393 pp.

Much like Karen Horney and Erich Fromm, Sullivan introduces the idea that the motivating force in the formation of personality is the avoidance of anxiety. He believes anxiety to be an interpersonal phenomenon occurring when an individual is placed in a derogative situation in which his self-esteem seems to be threatened. It appears to Sullivan that the individual is rarely, if ever, free from interpersonal tension and that the motivating principle of behavior must therefore be the reduction of anxiety. He feels that, to understand a person, one must have some idea of the interpersonal techniques that the person employs in an effort to avoid or immunize anxiety.

———. *The Psychiatric Interview*. New York: W. W. Norton and Co., 1954. 246 pp.

This is a profound source of knowledge based on Sullivan's view regarding the methods and objectives involved in the therapeutic interview. Sullivan does much to introduce the importance of the syntaxic mode. The mode is defined by the extent that observation, analysis, and the education of relations are subjected to a consensual validation with others. By consensual validation he means the degree of approximate agreement with a significant other person or persons, which permits fairly exact communication by speech or otherwise, and the drawing of a generally useful inference about the action and thought of the other. Thus it is that, when two people consensually agree upon the basic premise formulating a relationship as they enter into a situation requiring interaction and when they concur regarding their perceptions of self and each other, then they are communicating in the syntaxic mode. He goes on to define the interview as a situation of primarily vocal communication in a two-group setting that is more or less voluntarily integrated on a progressively unfolding expert-client basis. The purpose of this setting is to help the client elucidate characteristic patterns of understanding from which he can benefit. Interestingly enough, Sullivan also introduces what he refers to as an initial interview, which would precede the treatment proper and might logically afford the therapist the opportunity to begin preparing a chronology of the client's life. Although Sullivan outlines what appears to be a rigid format of procedure, it is essential to note that he feels that the therapist must not be rigid in his relationship with his client. In essence, it might be said that the rigidity of the procedure serves as a frame of reference within which there is great flexibility.

His therapeutic process is divided into four categories: (1) the *inception*, the period during which the client introduces his problem and the therapist gives him the opportunity to correct any information that the therapist has received prior to the interview; (2) the *reconnaissance*, the time when the client is asked conventional questions, thus providing responses that will be utilized as a background of understanding until a more detailed inquiry is possible; (3) the *detailed inquiry*, the period during which the client is confronted by the therapist with detailed questioning on many different topics; and (4) the *termination or interruption*, the time when a summary statement is made or, in the case of interruption, when the therapist gives the patient a prescription for the interval.

Perhaps of greatest importance to the counselor is Sullivan's theory of anxiety reduction. Whether or not one agrees with this theory, it certainly seems worthy of consideration when attempting to develop a sophisticated knowledge and background of understanding in the area of counseling.

Super, Donald Edwin

BIRTH: July 10, 1910, Honolulu, Hawaii

PRESENT STATUS: director of the Division of Psychology and Education, Columbia University Teachers College, and research associate at the Horace Mann–Lincoln Institute at Columbia University

BACKGROUND: *Educational* B.A., Oxford University, 1932; M.A., Oxford University, 1936; Ph.D., Columbia University, 1940

Professional assistant employment secretary, Cleveland YMCA, 1932–35; instructor, Fenn College, 1932–35; director, Cleveland Guidance Service, 1935–36; research assistant, Columbia University Teachers College, 1936–38; associate professor of psychology, Clark University, 1938–42; aviation psychologist, United States Army Air Force, 1942–45; from associate professor to professor of psychology and education, Columbia University, 1945–; director, Division of Psychology and Education, Columbia University, 1965–; Fulbright lecturer in psychology, University of Paris, 1958–59; research associate, Horace Mann–Lincoln Institute, Columbia University, 1945–

Field of Work research in career development, vocational counseling, and the self-concept theory

Affiliations Fellow, American Psychological Association, Divisions of Clinical Psychology, Industrial Psychology, Educational Psychology, and Counseling Psychology; American Personnel and Guidance Association (president, 1953); National Vocational Guidance Association (president, 1969–70); International Association of Education and Vocational Guidance; International Association for Applied Psychology

SUMMATION OF CONCEPTS:

The focus in Super's writings is on theories of vocational choice. He appears to feel that much of the unhappiness and dissatisfaction experienced by people is caused by their employment. The main themes of his writings are vocational counseling and vocational adjustment. Super feels that all members of the community have a direct and important stake in vocational guidance and promotes the idea that the public school must take the initiative for guidance in the choice of, the preparation for, and to some extent the entry into an occupation. It is therefore imperative that a teacher know how his subject matter relates to occupational fields and how best to disseminate such information in the classroom.

ANNOTATED BIBLIOGRAPHY:

Super, Donald E. *The Dynamics of Vocational Adjustment.* New York: Harper and Brothers, Publishers, 1942. 286 pp.

Super presents an interesting picture of the world of work and the many challenges facing those who are active in this world. He discusses personality characteristics and job satisfaction with a comprehensiveness seldom found in literature and suggests that modern life poses three challenges: finding ways of modifying attitudes toward occupations, working out methods of assisting individuals to understand their own abilities and to relate these abilities to the world in which they live and work, and organizing materials, services, and resources so that they will be available to those who seek assistance.

————. *The Psychology of Careers.* New York: Harper and Brothers, Publishers, 1957. 362 pp.

Among other things, this book introduces some areas that appear to lend themselves well to research. Perhaps the greatest attention is given to theories of vocational choice and to the knowledge that has led researchers to believe that such theories are logical approaches to vocational counseling. Super shows a sophisticated understanding of career patterns and their significance for vocational counseling. He seems to feel that personal adjustment in the world of everyday living is a key to vocational adjustment.

————, and John O. Crites. *Appraising Vocational Fitness.* New York: Harper and Brothers, Publishers, 1962. 688 pp.

Crites and Super present a most comprehensive picture of vocational appraisal and the utilization of tests in vocational counseling. They cover such pertinent areas as testing and appraisal in vocational guidance, testing and prediction in vocational selection, methods of test construction, test administration, aptitude tests, intelligence tests, and the use of test results. In addition, the authors present a sophisticated review of tests and test batteries that seem to have some value for those interested in vocational counseling. Particular attention is directed toward the proper use of tests, with the realization that some users of tests are prone to neglect other methods of appraisal.

_____. "Goal Specificity in the Vocational Counseling of Future College Students." *Personnel and Guidance Journal*, 43 (October, 1964), 127-34.

Super comments on the inbred nature of choices to be made by college-bound youths. The choices are two-fold, of either an exploratory nature or a specific existence. Overriding this concept is the necessity of declaring an academic preparation along occupational lines. Usually little consideration is given to the ways in which the specific resources of the college are to be used in exploration, and little provision is made for the continuity of counseling implied in using a block of time for exploratory purposes. Institutions should assume responsibility for providing this exploratory behavior by adjusting curricula, systematizing educational information, and giving information on occupation exploration. Two types of students seem likely to find specific vocational preparation suitable; they have in common a need for a relatively high degree of structure. Those who do not, and perhaps should not, specialize are the multiple talented and the untalented. For many college-bound students, and for some even after college, vocational goals are emergent rather than existent.

Symonds, Percival Mallon

BIRTH: April 18, 1893, Newtonville, Massachusetts

PRESENT STATUS: deceased; August 6, 1960, Salem, Massachusetts

BACKGROUND: *Educational* A.B., Harvard University, 1915; A.M., Columbia University, 1920; Ph.D., Columbia University, 1923

Professional teacher in Andover, Massachusetts, 1915-17; teacher at the Worcester Academy in Massachusetts, 1917-18; assistant in the Institute of Educational Research, Columbia University Teachers College, 1921-22; professor of education and psychology, University of Hawaii, 1922-24; assistant professor, associate professor, and professor, Columbia University, 1924-58; chairman, Division of Theory and Techniques of Measurement and Research, Columbia University, 1933-37; head, Department of Research Methods, Columbia University, 1937-42; professor emeritus of education, Columbia University, 1958-60

Field of Work research in psychodynamics, psychotherapy, projective techniques, and the psychology of teaching

Affiliations Fellow, American Psychological Association, Divisions of Educational Psychology (president, 1947-48), Developmental Psychology, Personality and Social Psychology, the Society for the Psychological Study of

Social Issues, Clinical Psychology, and School Psychology; American Educational Research Association (president, 1956-57); Fellow, American Orthopsychiatric Association; Society for Projective Techniques; Society for Research in Child Development; New York Society of Clinical Psychologists; Phi Beta Kappa; Phi Delta Kappa; Sigma Xi

SUMMATION OF CONCEPTS:

Symonds subscribed to the belief that the adjustment of the individual and of society is based on fundamental psychological principles. Even though many problems could be solved through reasoning and the use of intellectual ability, the large part of adjustment is carried on through impulses and emotions and by various psychological mechanisms. The psychoanalytic approach is obvious in Symonds' thinking when he states that, although the foundations of personality are inherited, the learnings of the first six years of life determine the development of personality.

ANNOTATED BIBLIOGRAPHY:

Symonds, Percival M. *The Dynamics of Human Adjustment*. New York: Appleton-Century-Crofts, 1946. 666 pp.

The author identifies his work as "largely an exposition of man's reaction to frustration." He seeks to uncover the psychological needs for which the individual seeks satisfaction from his physical and social environment and to explain human behavior in terms of the mechanisms that develop as frustration is met. Frustration is not pictured as bad, yet severe frustration or frustration poorly handled can cause neurosis. One might judge the quality of adjustment in terms of ability to work, play, love, feel happy and content, accept reality, express one's emotions freely, and exhibit normal inhibitions, rather than to pattern one's behavior according to any set formula or standards. Of help in the study of this and related fields are the 883 bibliographical references.

―――――. *Adolescent Fantasy: An Investigation of the Picture-Story Method of Personality Study*. New York: Columbia University Press, 1949. 379 pp.

Here the author seeks to capture the meaning of adolescent daydreams, stray thoughts, images, and more constructed mental processes through the use of H. A. Murray's thematic apperception test. He hypothesizes that projective responses are prone to reveal the direction of personality, its motivational tendencies, and the seemingly dynamic forces that appear to guide behavior. From responses to the test, it seems that aggression and love are the universal themes of the adolescent. Variations of these themes or feelings, such as depression, happiness, anxiety, and moral conflict, are readily recognized by educators. Identification of such themes, if they do exist, seems essential if one is to assist the adolescent in gaining a more meaningful school experience.

———. *The Ego and the Self.* New York: Appleton-Century-Crofts, 1951. 229 pp.

Symonds maintains that philosophers and social psychologists have been aware of the "self," but that only recently have psychologists become aware of the ego-self problem. He refers to the ego as the "I" perceiving, thinking, and acting. The self seems to be the "me" in a social milieu. A mature person can be said to have developed both ego and self satisfactorily. Imbalance between the ego and application of the ego-self in psychotherapy is also discussed. The approach to the subject is eclectic but predominantly Freudian in orientation. However, the author's view of human nature appears to be more optimistic than Freud's. At the end of the book, the reader will find a listing and evaluation of 211 books in the field.

Thorne, Frederick Charles

BIRTH: May 30, 1909, New York City

PRESENT STATUS: private practice in psychiatry and editor and publisher of the *Journal of Clinical Psychology*

BACKGROUND: *Educational* A.B., Columbia University, 1930; A.M., Columbia University, 1931; Ph.D., Columbia University, 1934; M.D., Cornell University, 1938

Professional laboratory assistant, Columbia University, 1931–34; instructor, Long Island University, 1932–36; instructor, Hunter College, 1936–39; director, Brandon State School of Vermont, 1939–47; instructor, assistant professor of psychiatry, University of Vermont, 1939–54; editor and publisher, *Journal of Clinical Psychology*, 1945–; private practice in psychiatry, 1947–; adjunct professor of psychology, University of Miami, 1965

Field of Work major advocate of an eclectic clinical approach to counseling and psychotherapy

Affiliations Fellow, American Psychological Association, Division of Clinical Psychology; American Psychiatric Association

FREDERICK CHARLES THORNE

SUMMATION OF CONCEPTS:

Thorne's writings seem to stress the importance of maintaining objective and practical perspectives regarding all forms of therapeutic or behavioral adjustment services. He has for years maintained a philosophy that is sometimes recognized as quite directive. His writings appear to indicate that he recognizes an absolute, rather than a relative, right and wrong. His writings seem to reflect the belief that none of the behavioral sciences should manipulate for personal self-gratification and that the sciences should avoid all forms of opportunism in order to serve man. Since much of what he has written seems to imply a desire to find merit in many different techniques, it seems axiomatic that he favors the eclectic approach to counseling. As a matter of fact, E. L. Tolbert states in his *Introduction to Counseling* that Thorne has probably contributed more to the systematic development of the eclectic point of view than has anyone else.

ANNOTATED BIBLIOGRAPHY:

Thorne, Frederick C. "Critique of Recent Developments in Personality Counseling Theory." *Journal of Clinical Psychology*, 13 (July, 1957), 234-44.

Thorne places some emphasis on the importance of semantics and talks about the strengths and weaknesses of psychotherapy, client-centered counseling, eclectic counseling, and disciplinary counseling. His purpose appears to be to introduce new concepts of personality counseling theory. He maintains that it is the responsibility of leaders in the field of counseling and psychotherapy to issue periodic statements concerning modifications in their theories.

———. "An Operational Approach to the Diagnosis of Levels of Personality Integration or Psychopathology." *Journal of Clinical Psychology*, 15 (July, 1959), 255-59.

This article defines the nature of personality integration, theory of personality integration, and levels of behavior integration.

———. "If Clinical Psychology Should Come of Age." *Journal of Clinical Psychology*, 19 (January, 1963), 136.

Thorne holds that unidimensional systems of psychotherapy—*i.e.*, the nutritional deficiency theory, stressing cure through the restoration of nutritional balance; the self-infection theory, holding that the cure of chronic body infection is the key to curing psychological disorders; Freudian psychoanalysis, stressing removal of unconscious conflicts; Rogerian therapy, emphasizing growth through the development of realistic self-concepts—all may be of value but each is inadequate by itself.

Tiedeman, David Valentine

BIRTH: August 12, 1919, Americus, Georgia
PRESENT STATUS: professor of education, Northern Illinois University
BACKGROUND: *Educational* A.B., Union College, 1941; A.M., University of Rochester, 1943; Ed.M., Harvard University, 1948; Sheldon Traveling Fellow, Cambridge and Princeton, 1948-49; Ed.D., Harvard University, 1949
Professional staff member, Naval Reserve Corps Committee on Selection and Training of Aircraft Pilots, University of Rochester, 1941-43; member to head of the Test Construction Department, College Entrance Examination Board, 1943-44; associate director of the Statistics Division, Manhattan Project, School of Medicine and Dentistry, University of Rochester, 1944-46; Teaching Fellow, Harvard University, 1946-48; instructor, assistant professor, lecturer, associate professor, and professor, Harvard University 1949-70; associate director, Center for Research in Careers, Harvard University, 1962-67; chairman of Executive Committee, Newton Information System for Vocational Decisions, Harvard University, 1966-70; professor of education, Northern Illinois University, 1970-
Field of Work research in career development, occupational theory, and computer-based counseling systems
Affiliations Fellow, American Psychological Association, Divisions of Evaluation and Measurement and Counseling Psychology; American Personnel and Guidance Association; National Vocational Guidance Association (president, 1965-66); American Educational Research Association; Phi Beta Kappa; Phi Delta Kappa; Sigma Xi

SUMMATION OF CONCEPTS:

Tiedeman appears most interested in the area of vocational choice. His writings reflect a comprehensive knowledge of this area and a desire to forge ahead in career development theory. He emphasizes computer-assisted instruction in testing and guidance and has expressed a strong interest in decision-making processes.

ANNOTATED BIBLIOGRAPHY:

Tiedeman, David V., ed. *Teacher Competence and Its Relation to Salary.* Cambridge, Mass.: Spaulding House, 1956. 110 pp.

This is the result of a nine-year study conducted by the Merit-Salary Committee of the New England School Development Council to determine teacher competence relative to salary. Much of the study is devoted to techniques for evaluating teachers. Selections from the writings of W. I. Ackerman and others are included.

―――, and Frank L. Field. "Guidance: The Science of Purposeful Action Applied Through Education." *Harvard Educational Review*, 32 (Fall, 1962), 483–501.

The authors do a most comprehensive analysis of guidance, evaluating it in terms of a profession, efforts that have been made to make it a profession, and its deficiencies. The article has a philosophical slant and, for some readers, will present a most stimulating point of view.

Tolman, Edward Chase

BIRTH: April 14, 1886, West Newton, Massachusetts
PRESENT STATUS: deceased; November 19, 1959, Berkeley, California
BACKGROUND: *Educational* S.B., Massachusetts Institute of Technology, 1911; A.M., Harvard University, 1912; Ph.D., Harvard University, 1915; honorary Sc.D., Yale University, 1951; honorary Sc.D., McGill University, 1954; honorary LL.D., University of California, 1959

Professional instructor, Northwestern University, 1915–18; instructor in psychology, University of California, 1918–20; assistant professor, University of California, 1920–23; associate professor, University of California, 1923–28; professor of psychology, University of California, 1928–54; contributed scientific articles to psychological periodicals and served as associate editor of the *Journal of Comparative Psychology*; professor emeritus, University of California, 1954–59

Field of Work experimental psychology

Affiliations Fellow, American Psychological Association (president, 1937), Divisions of General Psychology, Experimental Psychology, and the Society for the Psychological Study of Social Issues (chairman, 1940, and recipient of the Kurt Lewin Award, 1949); Fellow, American Academy of Arts and Sciences; National Academy of Sciences; American Philosophical Society; Phi Beta Kappa; Sigma Xi

SUMMATION OF CONCEPTS:

When reading Tolman, one usually feels his open-minded attitude toward all schools of psychology. He apparently felt that he could find basic concepts in all of these schools and that from these concepts he could, through synthesizing these many and varied ideas, bring about a better understanding of behavior. Tolman believed that understanding was of primary concern if people were to advance and that it could not be restricted to any one field, but rather that it had to be a broad and all-enveloping approach to life.

ANNOTATED BIBLIOGRAPHY:

Tolman, Edward Chase. *Purposive Behavior in Animals and Men*. Berkeley and Los Angeles: University of California Press, 1951. 463 pp.

Here Tolman presents behaviorism as mental processes to be conceived of as determinants of behavior. These determinants are actually functional variables that intermediate in the causal equation between environmental stimuli and the initiation of physiological states on one side and final overt behavior on the other. He states that, although behaviorism exerts an emotional appeal because it appears radical, modern, and simple, it is nevertheless much more challenging than first appearances lead one to believe. Tolman uses graphs and illustrations to explain the mechanics of the learning process as he sees it.

_____. *Collected Papers in Psychology*. Berkeley and Los Angeles: University of California Press, 1951. 269 pp.

A collection of papers by a group of Tolman's colleagues given to him in commemoration for more than thirty years at the University of California, the publication traces the history and development of Tolman's original concepts.

Traxler, Arthur Edwin

BIRTH: February 19, 1900, Irving, Kansas

PRESENT STATUS: president emeritus, Educational Records Bureau, and adjunct lecturer in education, University of Miami, Florida

BACKGROUND: *Educational* B.S., Kansas State Teachers College, 1920; M.A., University of Chicago, 1924; Ph.D., University of Chicago, 1932

Professional superintendent of public schools in Kansas, 1918-24; principal, Wakefield, Kansas, Rural High School, 1924-28; psychologist, University of Chicago High School, 1931-36; research associate, Educational Records Bureau (ERB) of New York City, 1936-38; assistant director of ERB, 1938-41; associate director of ERB, 1941-50; executive director of ERB, 1950-65; adjunct lecturer in education, University of Miami, 1965-; president emeritus, Educational Records Bureau, 1965-

Field of Work extensive research in the improvement of reading, educational and psychological measurement, and guidance services

ARTHUR EDWIN TRAXLER

Affiliations Fellow, American Psychological Association, Divisions of Evaluation and Measurement and Educational Psychology; National Council of Measurement in Education (president, 1959–60); American Educational Research Association (president, 1950–51); American Association for the Advancement of Science (vice-president, 1957); American Personnel and Guidance Association; International Reading Association; Phi Delta Kappa; Kappa Delta Pi

SUMMATION OF CONCEPTS:

Traxler believes that guidance lends itself well to a scientific approach and that, even though there is a certain element of error in this approach, it is possible to formulate a hypothesis, gather data, test the hypothesis, and evaluate the results. He maintains that the success of guidance in the school depends on making personnel work a kind of science. Through this science we first assemble the facts about our students and then add those overtones of personal understanding that provide a more complete look at each individual.

ANNOTATED BIBLIOGRAPHY:

Traxler, Arthur Edwin. *Guidance in Public Secondary Schools*. Lancaster, Pa.: Lancaster Press, 1939. 54 pp.

This book presents the results of a study directed toward enabling the Educational Records Bureau to continue to expand its work in the public schools. The study was confined to junior and senior high schools because the need for a better understanding of measurement and record keeping seemed to be greatest at this level. Each school was permitted to work out its own pattern of guidance services, thus creating a situation in which certain confirmatory indications of practical importance have served as the focus of attention: first, the success of a school system in developing *adequate* guidance services and the relationship of this success to the effectiveness of the teacher reeducation program; second, the care and maintenance of cumulative records. In essence, this study seems to confirm some need for further investigation into the educational needs of pupils.

_____. *Case Study Procedures in Guidance*. Educational Records Supplementary Bulletin B, 1946. 54 pp.

This interesting bulletin reveals a step-by-step procedure involved in organizing material relative to initiating a case study. Traxler illustrates his ideas through the use of outlines and actual case studies.

———. *Techniques of Guidance*. New York: Harper and Brothers, Publishers, 1957. 374 pp.

Of the many gaps that could be filled by such a book, perhaps the area to which it lends itself most readily is that of instituting guidance services. Traxler sets up a systematic pattern of introductory guidance services through a series of nine questions designed to alert faculty members to existing conditions. A listing of information regarding tests, the use of tests, and test evaluation is included as part of the text, with some attention devoted to numerous samples of records that could be used in developing a better understanding of guidance.

Tyler, Leona Elizabeth

BIRTH: May 10, 1906, Chetek, Wisconsin
PRESENT STATUS: retired
BACKGROUND: *Educational* B.S., University of Minnesota, 1925; M.S., University of Minnesota, 1939; Ph.D., University of Minnesota, 1941

Professional high school teacher, 1925–38; graduate assistant, University of Minnesota, 1938–40; instructor, 1940–42, assistant professor, 1942–47, associate professor, 1947–55, professor of psychology, 1955–71, University of Oregon; dean, Graduate School, University of Oregon, 1965–71; research study, Institute of Psychiatry, University of London, 1951–52; visiting professor of psychology, University of California in Berkeley, 1957–58; Fulbright visiting professorship, University of Amsterdam, 1962–63

Field of Work individual differences, psychological measurement, and counseling

Affiliations Fellow, American Psychological Association (president, 1972–73), Divisions of Evaluation and Measurement, Counseling Psychology, and the Society for the Psychological Study of Social Issues; Oregon Psychological Association (president, 1956–57); Western Psychological Association (president, 1957–58); American Association for the Advancement of Science

SUMMATION OF CONCEPTS:

Tyler has written in three general areas that relate directly to human behavior, *i.e.*, individual differences, psychological measurement, and counseling. Seemingly she has interrelated these ideas throughout her work. She acknowledges unique traits in each person, always believing that these individual differences represent a common good. Further, she believes that, because of a person's uniqueness, each counseling interview has both common and diverse characteristics. She thus cautions against standardizing counseling techniques and concluding that "this is *the way* to counsel." Her logic is based on the idea that there is a unity of organization in goal orientation but a diversity of action as one reaches out toward that goal. This suggests that a counselor may propose the same or similar results for two or more of his clients yet approach his counseling interviews with a uniqueness engendered by his sensitivity to each client.

ANNOTATED BIBLIOGRAPHY:

Tyler, Leona E. *Test and Measurements*. Englewood Cliffs, N.J.: Prentice-Hall, 1963. 116 pp.

This is one of fourteen paperbacks in the Foundations of Modern Psychology Series, which was designed as a new approach to understanding general psychology. Each book in the series is a contribution by a noted authority in a particular area. Because of her research experience, Tyler seems to be a logical choice for the area of psychological testing. Her stated purpose is to teach the basic principles of psychological testing for students who have little interest in becoming mathematical statisticians. She seems to have accomplished this goal through her presentation of basic statistics and her review of major types of tests.

_____. *The Psychology of Human Differences*. New York: Appleton-Century-Crofts, 1965. 572 pp.

Tyler begins by emphasizing that human uniqueness is a basic fact of life. To convey her message she has divided the book into four parts: "The Field of Differential Psychology," "Major Dimensions of Individual Differences," "Varieties of Group Differences," and "Factors Producing Differences." This book has also been designed to introduce students to various methods and tools used in measuring individual differences. An extensive bibliography of forty-seven pages is included.

_____. *The Work of the Counselor*. 3rd ed. New York: Appleton-Century-Crofts, 1969. 274 pp.

Originally published in 1953, this work introduces concepts based on Tyler's many experiences in the counseling field. Attention is focused on specific dimensions of counseling, which include the nature of counseling, the counseling encounter, the uses of information, decision making, and the counselor as a person. Tyler, like Adrian Van Kaam, shares many of her own feelings about counseling. Unlike Van Kaam, however, she includes research summaries at the end of each chapter. She seems to view counseling primarily as a service provided for normal individuals seeking assistance in their personal development. Her attention is always on a growth curve rather than a normal bell-shaped curve, *i.e.*, on idiographic growth rather than normative growth.

Van Kaam, Adrian Leo

BIRTH: April 19, 1920, the Netherlands

PRESENT STATUS: director, Institute of Man, and professor of psychology, Duquesne University

BACKGROUND: *Educational* M.O., Dutch Study Center, 1954; Ph.D., Case Western Reserve University, 1958

Professional professor, Major Seminary, Gemert, Holland, 1947-50; counselor, Government Observation Center, Delin, Holland, 1951-52; psychological consultant, Spiritus Publishing Company, 1952-54; counselor, University of Chicago, 1956-57; instructor of psychology, Duquesne University, 1957-62; professor of psychology, Duquesne University, 1962-; director, Institute of Man, Duquesne University, 1963-; editor, *Review of Existential Psychology and Psychiatry*, 1961-; editor, *Humanitas and Envoy*, 1964-

Field of Work personality theory, phenomenological and existential psychology, and religious anthropology

Affiliations Fellow, American Psychological Association, Division of Philosophical Psychology

SUMMATION OF CONCEPTS:

Most of Van Kaam's writings seem to reflect a desire to interpret counseling and psychotherapy in existential and philosophical terms. He appears to believe that growth is more dependent on the counseling relationship than on the techniques employed within that relationship. Emphasis is placed on authentic encounter, which Van Kaam suggests is therapeutic in itself. Effective counseling presupposes that the therapist is willing to leave his own self-centered world and authentically be *with* and *for* the client. Counselor attitudes such as acceptance, flexibility, gentleness, openness, and sincerity are viewed as necessary to such an encounter. Van Kaam does not negate the importance of personality and counseling theories, but he warns that preoccupation with theory may turn the counseling session into a classroom situation rather than being a unique human encounter.

ANNOTATED BIBLIOGRAPHY:

Van Kaam, Adrian. *The Art of Existential Counseling*. Wilkes-Barre, Pa.: Dimension Books, 1966. 205 pp.

This is not a textbook for counseling theory and practice, but rather a series of discussions on some of the vital questions related to the counseling process. Van Kaam seems more interested in provoking thought than presenting factual data. The book reads like an essay, because the author deals with his own feelings about counseling. Existential psychology is defined as an attitude or a point of view seemingly represented by the therapist. Ultimately, therefore, it can appear in any school of thought in the area of psychotherapy.

―――――, and Kathleen Healy. *The Demon and the Dove: Personality Growth Through Literature*. Pittsburgh: Duquesne University Press, 1967. 308 pp.

This book introduces a parallel between psychology and literature. The authors do not believe it is an accident that the works of great writers such as Henry James, Leo Tolstoi, Albert Camus, William Faulkner, and Fedor Dostoevski have been studies in human personality. According to Van Kaam, these writers are all existential psychologists.

―――――, Bert Van Croonerburg, and Susan A. Muto. *The Emergent Self*. 4 vols. Wilkes-Barre, Pa.: Dimension Books, 1968. 367 pp.

According to the authors, these four volumes represent a compilation of questions about the meaning of life in relation to the self, the self and others, the self and community, and the self and reality. Each volume deals with one of these specific areas. Included are discussions concerning openness to others, distrust of others, respect for others, and personal relationships.

Willey, Roy DeVerl
BIRTH: July 31, 1910, Bryon, Wyoming
PRESENT STATUS: professor of education and chairman of the Department of Elementary Education, University of Nevada

ROY DEVERL WILLEY

BACKGROUND: *Educational* B.A., University of Wyoming, 1929; M.A., Brigham Young University, 1936; Ph.D., Stanford University, 1942
Professional instructor in elementary education, San Jose State College, 1938–42; United States Naval Reserve, 1942–46; professor of psychology, University of Utah, 1947–55; chairman, Department of Educational Psychology, University of Utah, 1953–55; visiting professor of education, University of Redlands, 1952, San Francisco State College, 1953, and University of North Dakota, 1955; professor of elementary education and department chairman, University of Nevada, 1955–
Field of Work organization of guidance services, with a special interest in elementary guidance
Affiliations American Psychological Association, Association for Childhood Education, Phi Kappa Phi, Phi Delta Kappa

SUMMATION OF CONCEPTS:

Willey has written in varied fields, but in the area of guidance he gives evidence of being organization conscious. He stresses the need for a systematized method of introducing guidance services and for a clarification of responsibility for those participating in such services.

ANNOTATED BIBLIOGRAPHY:

Willey, Roy DeVerl, and D. C. Andrew. *Modern Methods and Techniques in Guidance.* New York: Harper and Brothers, Publishers, 1955. 635 pp.

The authors touch upon such significant aspects of guidance as semantics, characteristics of good counselors, counseling theories, and the genesis of guidance. Although the concepts of guidance presented here vary somewhat from present-day concepts, the book seems of value in understanding some of the problems encountered by guidance as it grew to the position it now enjoys.

―――, and D. C. Andrew. *Administration and Organization of the Guidance Program.* New York: Harper and Brothers, Publishers, 1958. 330 pp.

Here the authors set up guidelines for a systematic pattern of introducing and maintaining guidance services within the total school setting. They outline those services that they feel most appropriately fit into a guidance program and discuss in some detail the delegation of responsibility and the effective initiation and implementation of such services.

―――. *Guidance in Elementary Education.* New York: Harper and Brothers, Publishers, 1960. 426 pp.

This book is an attempt by Willey to bring the elementary school teacher and the guidance worker closer together. He stresses the need for better coordination of school personnel and the significance of the classroom teacher in guidance. Willey also emphasizes the need for a better relationship between guidance and community referral agencies as one means of making guidance a more effective part of the total school program.

Williamson, Edmund Griffith

BIRTH: August 14, 1900, Rossville, Illinois

PRESENT STATUS: dean of students and professor of psychology, emeritus, University of Minnesota

BACKGROUND: *Educational* A.B., University of Illinois, 1925; Ph.D., University of Minnesota, 1931

Professional assistant in psychology, 1926-31, assistant professor of psychology, 1931-38, director of the Testing Bureau, 1931-38, associate professor and coordinator of Student Personnel Services, 1938-41, University of Minnesota; chairman, American Education Committee on Student Personnel Work, 1943-52; Fulbright lecturer to Tokyo, 1955; Asia Foundation lecturer to the Japan Vocational Guidance Association, 1967; dean of students and professor of psychology, University of Minnesota, 1941-69; dean of students and professor of psychology, emeritus, University of Minnesota, 1969-

Field of Work noted for his development of the clinical approach to counseling and for his contributions to student personnel work

Affiliations Fellow, American Psychological Association, Divisions of Educational Psychology and Counseling Psychology; American Personnel and Guidance Association (president, 1967); Sigma Xi; Phi Delta Kappa; Alpha Kappa Lambda

SUMMATION OF CONCEPTS:

Williamson is a leading exponent of the counselor-centered approach. He has for many years supported the concept that counseling can be carried out through the following steps: (1) analysis, or collecting data from many sources; (2) synthesis, or collating and summarizing data by means of case-study techniques and test profiles; (3) diagnosis, or describing outstanding characteristics; (4) prognosis, or judging probable outcomes; (5) counseling, or cooperative advising with students; and (6) follow-up, or helping students to carry out a desirable course of action. He feels that, because the individual does not fully understand himself, data are necessary for the counselor to get a true picture. He further believes that data must be used to form a tentative hypothesis concerning the individual and not to classify him. Williamson feels that counselors can impart values as they work with clients and that these values can be instrumental in steering clients away from inappropriate values and toward appropriate ones.

ANNOTATED BIBLIOGRAPHY:

Williamson, Edmund G. *How to Counsel Students: A Manual of Techniques for Clinical Counselors*. New York: McGraw-Hill Book Co., 1939. 562 pp.

With the exception of Sigmund Freud, few authors had stated a theory of counseling when Williamson published this book describing counseling based on a directive, clinical, and trait approach to the individual. This point of view is closely related to the development of psychological tests and the growth of educational and vocational counseling. A major impact of this book is that it served as a reference point for other theorists to react to, especially Carl R. Rogers in his 1942 publication, *Counseling and Psychotherapy*. From these two authors and their contributions, a legion of counseling theories have grown.

_____, and J. D. Fraley. *Counseling and Discipline*. New York: McGraw-Hill Book Co., 1949. 387 pp.

For many years people have considered counseling and discipline to be at opposite extremes. Here Williamson expresses the view that discipline must first be defined. If one uses the word to mean punishment for violating school policy, then it cannot be regarded as a type of guidance, as the meaning of that word is normally construed. If, on the other hand, one defines discipline as self-adjustive behavior in the face of new experiences, then the object of discipline is not too far removed from that of guidance.

_____. *Counseling Adolescents*. New York: McGraw-Hill Book Co., 1950. 548 pp.

This book covers techniques employed in various counseling situations. It includes data from the files of the Student Counseling Bureau at the University of Minnesota. Much has been done by the author to clarify his technique and to help those novice counselors who are looking for a more sophisticated approach.

_____. "Value Orientation in Counseling." *Personnel and Guidance Journal*, 38 (April, 1958), 520–28.

Williamson points out the significance of a value system in counseling. He feels that the counselor must accept the teaching of values as one of his functions, but must be aware of the risk of imposing a set of values upon a student. It is the counselor's purpose to help the client understand more clearly what his value system is like and how he can guide his behavior in terms of the standards he has chosen.

———, and D. A. Biggs. *Student Personnel Work: A Program of Developmental Relationships*. New York: John Wiley and Sons, 1975. 390 pp.

Major emphasis is on various types of student personnel work and the need for student personnel workers to do research to establish themselves within their academic settings. A great single contribution of the book is its seemingly limitless source of updated references. This, combined with some innovative thoughts on student personnel work—*i.e.*, student activism, disciplinary counseling, and research—should offer professionals in student personnel work some interesting things to think about.

Wrenn, Charles Gilbert

BIRTH: April 2, 1902, New Paris, Ohio

PRESENT STATUS: professor emeritus of educational psychology, Arizona State University

BACKGROUND: *Educational* A.B., Willamette University, 1926; A.M., Stanford University, 1929; Ph.D., Stanford University, 1932; honorary Litt.D., Willamette University, 1952

Professional director of guidance, Raymond High School in Washington, 1926–27; assistant professor and director of the Training Center, Oregon Normal College, 1927–28; director, Vocational Guidance Center, Stanford University, 1929–36; assistant professor of education, Stanford University, 1934–36; assistant dean of the General College, University of Minnesota, 1936–38; from associate professor to professor of education, University of Minnesota, 1936–64; commander, personnel officer, and recipient of the Bronze Star, U.S. Navy, 1942–45; editor, *Journal of Counseling Psychology*, 1954–63; professor of educational psychology, Arizona State University, 1964–68; Fulbright Distinguished Scholar, England, 1965–66; psychological consultant, Edward Glaser and Associates, 1952–; visiting professor, Arizona State University, 1968–72; Distinguished Barclay Acheson Professor in Liberal Arts Education, Macalester College, 1968–71; professor emeritus of educational psychology, Arizona State University, 1972–

Field of Work student personnel services in higher education and the evaluation of counselor procedures and training

CHARLES GILBERT WRENN

Affiliations   Fellow, American Psychological Association, Divisions of Consulting Psychology, Educational Psychology, and Counseling Psychology (president, 1950–51); Academy of Religion and Mental Health; American Personnel and Guidance Association; National Vocational Guidance Association (president); American Educational Research Association; Higher Education Association; Association for Counselor Education and Supervision

SUMMATION OF CONCEPTS:

Wrenn has for many years worked in the area of student personnel services. He stresses the importance of personnel work at all levels within our educational system and of training counselors to focus their primary attention on the developmental and preventive aspects of counseling. He recognizes the significance of the counselor-client relationship and cautions the counselor to be alert for high-ability students.

ANNOTATED BIBLIOGRAPHY:

Wrenn, C. Gilbert. *Student Personnel Work in Colleges.* New York: Ronald Press Co., 1951. 589 pp.

The author sees student personnel work as a broad pattern of services offered to students in addition to the regular academic program. He places great emphasis on the breadth of student personnel services and leaves the distinct impression that the field consists of more than counseling or advising. Wrenn attempts to define student personnel services in terms of their relationship to the total institutional program and relative to the responsibilities involved.

———. *The Counselor in a Changing World.* Washington, D.C.: American Personnel and Guidance Association, 1962. 195 pp.

At the request of the American Personnel and Guidance Association, Wrenn investigated the role of the counselor in our changing society. His report includes his perception of society, education, and the counselor in the years ahead. Some attention is directed toward preparing counselors for the world of tomorrow.

———. *The World of the Contemporary Counselor.* Boston: Houghton Mifflin Co., 1973. 294 pp.

Wrenn focuses on specific values that he feels are in the process of change, *i.e.*, those concerning drugs, sex, leisure, authority, and patriotism. He discusses these value changes in terms of research and literature. Counselors are challenged to examine their attitudes and how they deal with changes in values, within both themselves and their clients. As always, Wrenn stimulates one's thinking. He seems constantly to reach out and touch the future with what one recognizes as his wisdom of the past.

Zeran, Franklin Royalton

BIRTH: December 13, 1906, Chicago, Illinois
PRESENT STATUS: professor emeritus of education, Oregon State University
BACKGROUND: *Educational* B.A., University of Wisconsin, 1930; M.A., University of Wisconsin, 1932; Ph.D., University of Wisconsin, 1937
Professional assistant dean, University of Wisconsin, 1930-32; director of testing and guidance, Manitowoc, Wisconsin, 1932-40; specialist in occupational information and guidance, U.S. Office of Education, Washington, D.C., 1940-47; registrar, director of admissions, and director of the Testing Bureau, University of New Mexico, 1945-46; associate dean, School of Education, Oregon State University, 1947; dean, School of Education, Oregon State University, 1948-68; professor of education, Oregon State University, 1948-72; professor of education emeritus, Oregon State University, 1972-
Field of Work major contribution in occupational, social, and educational information
Affiliations American Psychological Association, Division of Counseling Psychology; American Personnel and Guidance Association; Association for Counselor Education and Supervision; American Vocational Association; Phi Delta Kappa

SUMMATION OF CONCEPTS:

Zeran has directed much of his writing toward concepts that he believes will ultimately result in improved guidance techniques. He has done much to establish guidelines for better guidance programs and continues to present improved techniques for understanding and assisting students.

ANNOTATED BIBLIOGRAPHY:

Zeran, Franklin R., ed. *Life Adjustment Education in Action.* New York: Chartwell House, 1953. 541 pp.

Zeran indicates the need for meaningful learning experiences in the school. He emphasizes the importance of education and attempts to understand how schools with low dropout rates differ from those with high rates.

_____, et al. *Guidance Services in Elementary Schools.* New York: Chartwell House, 1954. 403 pp.

This book is an attempt to supply teachers with the answers to questions they so frequently ask about guidance. Much attention is devoted to the mental hygiene approach, to specific techniques designed to help teachers better understand students, and to the significance of the individual's environmental situation on his growth.

About the Authors:

KENNETH URIAL GUTSCH, an energetic and productive scholar, has been a prolific contributor to scholarly journals and is the co-author of three books, *Guidance in Action* (with John Alcorn), *In Search for Identity* (with Herman Peters), and *Nexus Psychotherapy: Between Humanism and Behaviorism* (with J. V. Ritenour). He has edited a professional newsletter, served as a book reviewer, and developed an original school of psychotherapy known as nexus psychotherapy. Active in both research and teaching, he received the Excellence in Teaching Award from the University of Southern Mississippi (1973–74) and the Mississippi Personnel and Guidance Association Research Award (1974). Before assuming his present position as director of the Program of Counseling Psychology at the University of Southern Mississippi, Dr. Gutsch served as director of the USM Laboratory of Human Development from 1963 to 1971. He is a Fellow in the American Psychological Association (Division 17, Counseling Psychology) and is an active member of the American Personnel and Guidance Association. A number of his former students have made vital contributions to the science and profession of psychology.

LARRY L. THORNTON cites theology, philosophy, counseling, and psychology as his major fields of interest and experience. After receiving a liberal arts undergraduate degree from Mississippi College in 1959, he studied theology at the Baptist seminaries in both New Orleans and Ruschlikon-Zurich, Switzerland. He received his Ph.D. degree in 1969 from the University of Southern Mississippi, with a major in counseling and with minors in both psychology and European history. His dissertation, directed by Kenneth Gutsch, studied the moral and ethical values of a population of graduating university seniors. In 1968 he assumed a position at Delta State University, teaching jointly in the counseling graduate program and the education and psychology undergraduate program. Recently his areas of concentration for the university have been in adolescent psychology and the history of educational thought. He is an

ABOUT THE AUTHORS

active member in Division 17, Counseling Psychology, of the American Psychological Association and the American Personnel and Guidance Association. Additionally, Dr. Thornton is a minister-at-large in the Christian community, serving as a pulpit guest, as a faculty adviser for the Baptist Campus Ministry, and as a retreat and seminar leader.

Chapter One

June 1983

It was never easy to put Lola Sheridan to bed. Two months from her second birthday, she was unwilling to go to sleep before her older sisters, resistant to nap time, and often screaming until Anna finally brought her back to the "real world." When Anna was in a good mood about it, she joked that Lola was her "wild child," the one most apt to take on the world and demand more from it. When Anna was exhausted, it took every bit of inner strength she had not to sob when little Lola refused her crib, when she kicked her legs and shook her fists.

"Come on, Lola." Anna heaved Lola back into her arms and blinked tiredly through the dark shadows of the Sheridan House. Out Lola's window, the Vineyard Sound lapped gently against the dock and their boat, shimmering beneath a hungry, empty moon.

Downstairs, Susan was curled up next to her father, reading a book quietly as Wes watched baseball on television. Susan was seven years old going on fifteen, an old soul in every sense of the word— and often, Anna's saving grace. She helped with chores, with the baby, and with tasks around the Sunrise Cove. Anna often felt guilty about this, as seven was too young for such difficult adult tasks. But Susan constantly pestered Anna about it, demanding more to do, wanting to carry the weight of the family and the Sunrise Cove on her little shoulders.

Now, Susan closed her book. "She still won't sleep?"

Anna shook her head and placed Lola gently on the floor. Christine, who was four years old, was curled up in the corner of the living room, her knees tucked beneath her as she drew on a pad of paper. Christine was her quiet, moody child, apt to spend hours and hours alone in her bedroom. When Christine was upset, she didn't kick and scream and cry as other children did; rather, she isolated herself from the rest of the world and kept herself occupied. Already, Anna envied her ability to sense her own needs and meet them. Then again, being a mother meant that you pushed your own needs to the backburner when necessary, and it would remain that way for the rest of your life. Anna had known this before getting pregnant, of course. But she hadn't known how alienated she would eventually feel from her own body.

On the floor, Lola babbled happily, bouncing on her diaper with her arms raised. Christine, Susan, Anna, and Wes watched her, giving her the attention she so craved, while the Boston Red Sox entered the fourth inning of a game they would eventually lose— casting Wes into a sour mood that would last the next twenty-four hours.

"She'll get tired soon," Wes assured Anna, his eyes hardly twitching from the television.

Anna's shoulders slumped forward with exhaustion.

"Did everything work out with that family? The Hamiltons?"

Wes finally looked away from the screen. "Yes. Thankfully, Jeff dropped off their suitcases this afternoon."

Anna sighed, still reeling from the horrific looks on the Hamilton family's faces when they'd learned the ferry company had lost their baggage. As was common with Sunrise Cove Inn guests, they'd decided to blame this on the Sunrise Cove itself, Wes, Anna or whoever else was in front of them, and they'd threatened to tell all their friends back in Wisconsin never to stay there.

"Did they apologize?" Anna demanded.

"The ferry company?" Wes asked.

"No. The Hamiltons. They were so rude!"

Wes grimaced. "That's just hospitality. People say things they don't mean." He paused for a split-second before he added, "You'll get used to it," which made Anna shimmer with anger. She'd worked with Wes at the Sunrise Cove since the age of eighteen when she'd given birth to Susan. The only difference now, of course, was that Wes' parents, who'd originally operated the Sunrise Cove, had both passed away, leaving the entire workload on Anna and Wes' shoulders. Anna had suggested they hire more help. Wes had said, "We'll see."

Anna tried again to put Lola to bed a half-hour later. But again, Lola just blinked up at her from the crib, her little hands around the bars. Lola looked at Anna as though she could see all the way through her, as though she, in her little toddler mind, could read everything that flitted through Anna's mind. Anna left her bedroom for a while, helping Christine get ready, before Lola let out several high-pitched screams, dragging Anna back.

But this time, when Anna picked Lola back up, Lola was running hot with a fever.

"Oh no! Oh no." Anna groaned and cuddled Lola close, rocking her on the rocking chair Wes' mother had left behind from her own mothering days. "What happened, sweetie? Huh?" She cooed to her youngest, who continued to smile even as her forehead glistened with sweat.

Anna loved Wes. Sometimes, she thought she might love him too much, that she'd given him too much territory in the wide space of her heart. Still, she couldn't help, sometimes, but feel resentful. As he headed to bed, she remained awake with their sick baby, lost in the loneliness of the night, flicking through stations on television until they gave out and left a screen of static. Lola's temperature was manageable, nothing that required a hospital visit— but her cries were consistent when Anna put her in her crib, and Anna wanted to ensure Christine and Susan were able to sleep, even if she and Lola couldn't.

When Wes woke up at five-thirty to get ready for work at the Sunrise Cove, he seemed surprised to find Anna and Lola still awake in the easy chair downstairs. Anna wanted to scream.

"She's slept only about an hour all together," she said, forcing herself to take long breaths to remind herself of her deep, powerful love for Wes. To remember that they'd been through thick and thin together and that one night of his "inconsistent" parenting meant nothing. He took care of them. He managed the inn. He handled the money. They needed him so much.

"Poor baby." To Anna's surprise, Wes bent down to take Lola in his arms, cuddled her against him, and asked, "You want a cup of coffee?"

A Vineyard Tide

Anna could have cried. Still carrying the baby, Wes poured her a mug of coffee and toasted her a slice of bread, which he slathered with peanut butter. Feeling outside of her body, Anna ate the toast and watched as Wes doted on their youngest— who, she knew, he'd wanted to be a boy. They hadn't talked about it, not since the doctor had announced, "It's a girl!" Would they try for another? Anna couldn't imagine having the stamina.

But Wes' "fathering moment" was short-lived, as he was needed at the Sunrise Cove. As he streamed out the door, there was the first foot on the top step as Susan arrived downstairs, followed by Christine. Both were starving and both needed their mother, Anna.

With Wes gone, Lola decided to scream again, and Anna worked herself up, her tongue swollen with sorrow as she made her other girls toast, put out the knife and peanut butter for Susan, then took Lola upstairs to check her fever again. Her temperature had gone down, a relief. Still, she seemed no closer to sleeping than she'd been last night.

Downstairs, Christine's face was slathered with peanut butter, and Susan was doing Christine's hair, braiding it in a long line down her back. Anna's heart hammered with love for them.

"Girls? We're going for a walk," Anna announced, heading for the garage to grab the two-sided stroller— one side for Christine, who was still quite small, and the other side for Lola. Susan hadn't been in a stroller in years. She wouldn't deign to be.

"Is Lola sick?" Susan asked.

"Just a little bit," Anna replied sweetly, tucking Lola into the stroller and buckling her in. "Christine, would you like to pack your drawing supplies? Susan, your book?"

Once Anna was outside, making her way down the edge of the paved road toward downtown Oaks Bluff, she was able to breathe again. It was a gorgeous morning in mid-June, and the trees were plump with green leaves, which shifted gently in the fresh breeze. Where she walked, she could see the ocean, popping through the trees, dramatic and sparkling. And when she reached the outer edge of downtown, she was thrilled to see people again, tourists who'd come to Martha's Vineyard, knowing it to be one of the most beautiful places in the world. Anna, Wes, and their children were natives; they'd never known anything else. They were lucky.

"Mom!" Susan called. "Lola fell asleep!"

Anna's eyes widened with surprise. She stopped the stroller for a moment and whipped around, peering down at her darling third daughter, who'd finally closed her eyes. Softly, Anna touched Lola's forehead to feel that her fever had broken, and she breathed a sigh of relief, nearly falling to her knees with exhaustion.

"Walking always works, doesn't it?" Anna said to Susan, laughing.

Susan nodded, having been through this song and dance before. She'd gotten very good at reading and walking at once, keeping herself on the inside of the stroller so as not to get too close to the edge of the sidewalk. Christine was busy drawing, ignoring all of them.

"Let's keep walking for a while," Anna said quietly. "I don't want Lola to wake up just yet."

Anna walked like a zombie toward the boardwalk, along the carousel, past world-famous restaurants and shops that were now preparing to open, employees sweeping the front stoops and adjusting the collars of their uniforms. Anna waved to several of them, recognizing them from previous summers. Many came from off the island, working seasonally for the influx of tourists before returning to wherever they'd come from for the winter. Winters on the island could be brutal, lonely, and brittle with cold.

Down the dock, leaning against the boardwalk railing was a woman about Anna's age. Just now, she arched her back and her neck and cried out to the sky, her entire body shuddering with her tears. Across her chest was a baby, just a tiny thing, and one of her hands cupped the baby's head as she sobbed.

After an entire night of listening to Lola crying, Anna stopped short, scared of such sharp emotions. But then, she realized that nearly everyone else on the boardwalk that morning was also avoiding the crying woman, as though she had some kind of disease nobody wanted. Anna raised her chin, willing herself to be stronger.

"Why is that woman crying?" Susan whispered, her eyes shining.

"Let's go make sure she's okay," Anna said, hurrying forward. "Excuse me?"

But the woman continued to shake, weeping as though she couldn't hear what Anna said. Tentatively, Anna reached up and touched the woman's shoulder, and the woman whipped around so quickly that she woke up her baby, who immediately started to cry, too. The baby's mouth opened wide like a red gash. And all that crying, of course, woke up Lola— which nearly brought Anna to her knees.

The woman blinked at Anna confusedly, her face

slack. She'd stopped crying so that now, only her baby and Lola wept.

"I'm so sorry," Anna stuttered, hurrying around the stroller to pick Lola back up. "I didn't mean to scare you."

The woman nodded, bobbing her knees to try to calm her baby. "I am sorry," she said, her voice strained and her accent different, maybe European. Anna wasn't sure. Wherever she was from, English wasn't her first language; that was clear.

"Are you okay?" Anna asked, cradling Lola as she calmed down again.

The woman closed her eyes. Bit-by-bit, their babies both quieted, their eyes enormous.

"I don't know," the woman said.

Anna understood the sentiment. "Can I buy you a cup of coffee or something?"

The woman's cheeks twitched as though she was on the verge of crying again. "I don't know. I don't know where to go. I don't know where I am."

Anna furrowed her brow. This was a lot more serious than she'd initially thought. "You know you're in Martha's Vineyard, right?" Maybe the woman was having a sort of mental breakdown?

The woman nodded. "I know. I do. I just don't know what's supposed to come next. Someone was supposed to show me the way. Someone was supposed to meet me." As she grew more and more upset, her accent intensified, and it was sometimes difficult for Anna to understand what she said.

"Who was supposed to meet you?" Anna asked.

The woman's shoulders slumped forward.

"Where are you staying?" Anna asked.

"I don't know," the woman said. "They took my husband away from me. And I have nowhere to go."

Anna's heart shattered. Briefly, she glanced around the boardwalk, sensing that everyone kept an even wider berth around her and this stranger. They were two women, heavy with sorrow, exhausted and in need of sleep.

"Do you need somewhere to sleep tonight?" Anna asked.

The woman bowed her head and cupped her baby. "Yes." She was very embarrassed.

"My husband and I run an inn," Anna explained. "We have a spare room right now. Maybe you'd like to stay there?"

The woman squinted at Anna, sizing her up.

"I know what it's like to be really, really tired," Anna tried. "You can't think about what comes next, or make any kind of plan, because you can hardly put one foot in front of the other."

The woman nodded.

"My name is Anna. Anna Sheridan. My husband, Wes, is at the inn right now. It's ten minutes away from here. You could be asleep in a bed in thirty minutes."

The woman's voice was strained, almost a croak. "My name is Frederika." And just when Anna thought she was going to refuse the help, that she was going to push Anna away, she breathed, "And I would really like that bed. I don't know what to say or how to thank you."

"Just get some sleep," Anna told her, swimming in her own fatigue. "And when you wake up, everything will seem brighter. I promise."

Chapter Two

Present Day

It was Fourth of July in Martha's Vineyard, and the Sheridan Family was ready to celebrate. About a half mile from shore, they floated on sailboats in the glittering turquoise water: three boats in total, with Lola, Tommy, Audrey, Noah, and Max in one, Amanda, Sam, Kellan, Susan, and Scott in another, and Christine, Zach, Wes, and Beatrice in the third. Christine had left baby Mia on shore with a babysitter, which meant that nearly every hour, on the hour, she checked her phone for updates, ensuring that little Mia was safe and happy, that everything was right as rain. Lola wanted to tease her, to tell her to stop being a helicopter parent— but she understood, beyond anything, that Christine's newfound post as a mother was incredibly important to her, that being a "helicopter parent" was a blessing.

"Mom! Let's do our dive!" Audrey was on the edge of the sailboat in a black bikini, her slender arms extended on either side of her.

A Vineyard Tide

Lola laughed, knowing exactly what Audrey was referring to. Back when Audrey had been a teenager in Boston, Lola and Audrey had spent many summer days at the public pool, perfecting their "synchronized diving" techniques. They'd grown fascinated with the sport during the Olympics and tried to imitate them with flips and back dives, telling themselves they would compete in the next Olympics as a mother-daughter team.

"Don't hurt yourselves!" Susan called from her boat, sitting with her legs in the water and a glass of chardonnay in one hand, smiling sleepily and happily. Scott was beside her, his arm slung around her shoulder as they watched.

Lola and Audrey aligned themselves at the edge of the boat with their toes over the side. Quietly, they spoke about which dive they wanted to try, with Audrey reminding Lola that she hadn't done any of this since before she'd had Max, that probably, she wouldn't be able to do a flip.

"Let's just do a simple tuck dive," Lola suggested, flipping her long hair over her shoulders.

Audrey wrinkled her nose. "That's too easy, isn't it?"

"We had that one mastered," Lola reminded her. "If we're going to show off in front of family, it has to be that one."

Audrey set her jaw and nodded. In this moment, her eyes sparkling, Lola was reminded that Audrey was the closest in looks to her mother, Anna— who'd died back in 1996, the result of a freak boat accident. Audrey had never known her— and Lola had been too young to understand how her death would crater through her life and permanently alter it.

"One, two, three," Lola called, and, together, they

sprang from the side of Tommy's boat, tucked their bodies, and dove easily into the turquoise waters, slipping down into the ocean, too far for comfort, until Lola forced herself back up, her legs screaming as she swam. She wasn't in as good of shape as she'd once been.

Back on the surface, the Sheridan family applauded their synchronized dives.

"It looked just like the Olympics!" Wes called, clapping.

"It really did," Beatrice agreed, her arm through Wes', her black swimsuit sensational on her sixty-something frame. Beatrice was Wes' first attempt at romance since Anna's death, a surprise twist in Wes' story, especially after Wes' dementia diagnosis.

"We haven't practiced in years!" Audrey said as she grabbed the ladder and swung herself back into the boat. There, her toddler, Max, cried out for her happily, and she raised him against her, laughing. Noah, her fiancé, grabbed a towel and wrapped it around both Audrey and her toddler— a toddler Noah had, incidentally, decided to raise as his own.

From the water, Lola's heart swelled with happiness at the sight of her family, her gorgeous family, all together beneath the shimmering July sun.

"Who's hungry?" Scott asked, always ready to grill out— his primary purpose at family parties.

"I'm starving," Zach said, jumping up. Within seconds, he flung himself into the water to swim over to Scott's boat to help out.

"I'll join you, Christine!" Lola called, swimming toward her boat and heaving herself up. As she situated herself, Susan slipped into the water, as well, swimming over to join

A Vineyard Tide

her sisters. By the time Susan was onboard, Christine had poured both Susan and Lola glasses of chardonnay, and Lola was half-dry, her hair whipping through a sea breeze. As they sipped, Amanda and Sam jumped into the water, swimming between the boats, laughing. Just last month, they'd been married in a crazy ceremony at the Aquinnah Cliffside Overlook Hotel, and their happiness since then had beamed off of them, making everything else in the world seem half as bright. Meanwhile, Audrey, Max, and Noah had family time on Tommy's boat as Tommy read a book, his head tilted, often looking over at Lola to smile.

"Look at the newlyweds!" Christine whispered to Susan, not wanting Amanda or Sam to hear. "I can't get over how happy they are."

"They're the sweetest," Lola agreed.

"Any word on when Audrey and Noah will tie the knot?" Susan asked.

Lola shook her head. "What's the rush, anyway? Look at how happy they are!"

"I swear, Noah and Max look the same," Christine said. "Nobody will ever know the difference."

"Noah loves that boy to pieces," Lola said. "I can't imagine a better partner for Audrey."

On the other side of the sailboat, Wes and Beatrice sat together, holding hands, the sea breeze toying with the whites and grays of their hair.

"You know," Wes piped up, perhaps having overheard, "Beatrice and I were talking. And we think it might be time to give the house to the kids."

Lola frowned as Susan and Christine turned toward him, mesmerized. Since Amanda's wedding to Sam, the Sheridan Family House was now just Audrey, Noah,

Max, and Grandpa Wes— a funny collection of souls. It stood to reason Wes would feel like a sore thumb.

"I don't think Audrey wants you to leave," Lola remarked.

Wes glanced at Beatrice, who nodded, her eyes focused. It was clear they'd discussed this, probably numerous times.

"Dad, you were raised in that house," Christine reminded him. "Nobody is asking you to leave."

"If you want, I'm sure Audrey, Noah, and Max would find somewhere else to go," Susan piped up. "It's your home. It's always been your home."

But their father was resolute. "I'm an old man," he told them, although this wasn't entirely true; he was only in his seventies with still so much time left. "I've lived an extraordinary life in that house. But my story has changed significantly, especially since my girls came home. The house wants a new chapter. And I want to leave to allow that to happen. Besides, now that she's found a new place, Beatrice has enough space for both of us. I've spent so much time there over the past few months. It's like I've already moved in!"

Beatrice beamed proudly, swimming on a cloud of love. It was true that since his romance with Beatrice began, Wes had had fewer memory problems. Beatrice had helped him create systems and routines that had fine-tuned his mind. He often acted twenty years younger than he was, and when he did have a memory lapse, Beatrice was right there.

"I'll talk to Audrey about it later this week," Wes said gently. "But I really think it's time that we all moved on. And besides. Anna would have wanted the house to stay in the family like this. She would have just fallen apart with love for that little boy, Max."

As the afternoon slowed and cooled, and a soft pink breeze swept across the sands, the Sheridan Family tugged their anchors up and sailed back to the Sheridan Family Home, where they climbed out, took turns in the shower, and set up for the bigger family dinner that night. From the porch of both the Sheridan House and Susan's new place next door, they could see exquisite fireworks over the Vineyard Sound. Always, this firework display brought back memories of Lola's childhood, when she'd sat in someone's lap— perhaps her mother's— and watched the colorful explosions. She'd been in awe, quiet, unable to comprehend such beauty and loudness at once.

For dinner, Zach and Tommy had planned for cheeseburgers and homemade onion rings, and the smell of grilled meat and frying oil joined with the scents of the salty seas and the surrounding forest with its towering oaks. After Lola's shower, she sat on the back porch with Max on her lap, sipping iced tea and listening to Zach and Scott squabble about how many burgers to grill. Tommy soon interjected, giving his opinion, which, surprisingly, both Scott and Zach agreed with. As they spoke, Lola made eye contact with Susan, who stifled laughter. It pleased them to no end that their chosen romantic partners got along so well — well enough that they were able to have small arguments, as though they were really brothers rather than in-laws.

Max was eager to eat everything himself, rejecting Audrey's attempt to cut his meat or bun for him. This resulted in mustard and ketchup all over his cheeks and lips and even his forehead, which was recorded on several cameras that evening, Max's big, doe eyes peering into the lens. Lola sat next to him, a doting and laughing grandmother, as Tommy wrapped his arm around her shoulders and chuckled along with her. It was sometimes sad for Lola, thinking that they would never have children. But other times, she felt that they had enough love to go around, especially with Audrey and Max close by. Their adventurous spirits got them off the island frequently, sailing across the Atlantic, exploring the wide world around them. A baby kept you quiet, kept you close to home. Lola had already been through that— and loved it, despite its trials. She didn't need to do it again.

When the fireworks began that night, Max remained on Lola's lap, awestruck, as the rest of the Sheridan Family spaced out across the back porch and the rest of the yard. Amanda and Sam were on the dock, their feet in the water, as the explosions reflected in the ocean. Max was up way past his bedtime, which everyone would probably pay for tomorrow— but the look on his face was more than worth it.

Before Lola went home that night, she hugged Audrey tightly, then slipped into Tommy's pickup, cracked the windows, and felt the soft breeze trace past her cheeks and through her hair as they whizzed through the black night. Tommy hummed the songs on the radio, Supertramp and Pink Floyd and Bad Company, and Lola slipped her fingers through his between their seats and told him she loved him for perhaps the millionth time.

That night, as Tommy got ready for bed and Lola sat propped up on her pillows, waiting for him, she checked her email on instinct, not expecting anything important. To her surprise, a mysterious email sat waiting for her— one that immediately intrigued her.

Dear Lola Sheridan,

A Vineyard Tide

My name is Claudia Franklin, and I'm a professor of history at Boston University. In my free time, I write historical fiction novels, which merge my love of history with my love of living in other worlds for a little while. As a writer, I'm sure you can understand that.

Recently, however, I made a potentially debilitating mistake. I began to probe into my past, with the idea that I wanted to try to write a memoir. You see, I was raised in the foster system outside of Chicago and never knew my parents— a fascinating place to begin for any historian. But after several months of research, all I've learned so far is that my parents spent some time in Martha's Vineyard after my birth. I'm stuck.

I suppose you could say I'm a relatively new fan of yours. I've been reading your long-form articles for the past few days and am genuinely impressed at your level of expertise as an investigative journalist. Bravo!

I imagine you are a very busy woman. With that said, would you be willing to have a chat so that I can pick your brain on how you would get to the bottom of something like my mysterious past? Of course, if you are at all interested in my story, I would welcome any help you can offer— and would pay whatever your rate is.

Looking forward to speaking soon.
All the best,
Claudia

Tommy strode out of the bathroom, shirtless, in just a pair of shorts. "You look thoughtful," he said as he slid into bed beside Lola, kissing her cheek.

"I just got this email from a writer," Lola explained, showing her phone.

"She's showering you with compliments," Tommy said.

"And they're working," Lola grinned.

Tommy returned her phone and propped up his head with his elbow, gazing at Lola lovingly. "Are you going to meet her?"

"Why not? I love helping out other writers." Lola cuddled against him, tossing her phone to the end of the bed.

"Shouldn't you charge that?" Tommy cackled.

Lola raised her shoulders. "Ugh. I don't feel like it. I don't have anything to wake up for, anyway."

Tommy turned off the light and soon fell into slumber beside Lola, who, just as when she'd been a little girl, struggled to fall asleep right away. Her mind turned with the beginnings of Claudia's story. She was a woman on the brink of discovering who she was and who her parents had really been. And Lola was eager to help her get to the bottom of it, purely for the love of research.

Chapter Three

1983

Anna led Frederika through the front door of the Sunrise Cove. Lola had gone back to sleep in the stroller, and Christine had nodded off as well, with only Susan bright-eyed and bushy-tailed, happy to greet her father as she hurried around them and up to the counter.

"Daddy! We made a friend!"

Wes had had a stressful morning. Anna could see it in his premature wrinkles, the hair that was tousled from his hands anxiously running through it. Used to his many years of working in hospitality, Wes smiled at Frederika on command. "Good morning. Welcome to the Sunrise Cove."

"Good morning," Frederika said, her accent even thicker this time. Anna still couldn't place it.

Anna smiled at Frederika, touched her shoulder, then said, "This is my husband, Wes. Wes, this is Frederika."

Wes stuck out his hand to shake Frederika's, his eyes

stirring with questions. "Where are you from, Frederika?"

Frederika paused, dropped Anna's gaze, and shook her head.

"Frederika has had a very difficult morning," Anna told Wes, trying her best to maintain a bright and easy tone, despite how tired she was. "And I told her she and her baby could have the free room upstairs."

At this, Wes' smile faltered. Anna could read him like a book. Money was tight, tighter than it had ever been, and Wes pinched every penny to ensure they made a profit during the late spring and summer months. Although his parents were now gone, he felt he had to prove himself for their memory and also to the friends they'd left behind. Plus, his sister, Kerry, had begun a real estate business with her husband, Trevor, and they were already off to the races on cash flow. Wes was competitive about that. Anna understood.

But this was different. She felt it in her bones.

Rather than argue about this in front of Frederika, Wes turned to fetch one of the ornate, iron keys from the back wall, pass it across the desk, and welcome Frederika. "There are fresh towels on your bed. The dinner special tonight is freshly caught trout with mashed potatoes and gravy. We have one of the best chefs on Martha's Vineyard, and our guests often come back to the inn just because of him. If you need anything else during your stay, please don't hesitate to let me or whoever else is at this desk know."

Frederika frowned at him, as though she was quite sure what all the words he said meant. That, or maybe she didn't trust him. Anna took the key from Wes, then eyed

Susan, saying, "I'm going to show Frederika to her room. Will you watch the girls?"

Susan took the responsibility earnestly, closing her book and gripping the handle of the stroller. Wes slid his fingers through his hair, messing it up even more. Anna wanted to tell them both it would be okay, that they could calm down, but she wasn't sure if that was a lie or not. She'd resolved long ago never to lie to her children. Anna led Frederika up the stairs to the second-floor bedroom, with its view of the trees to the west of the inn, upon which was a sliver of the ocean view. Frederika stepped into the room and blinked around her, as though she didn't trust it.

"I'm going to get you a crib from down the hall," Anna said, hurrying away and reappearing a minute later. Frederika had hardly moved. Her baby remained asleep on her chest. With every second that passed, Anna burned with curiosity about Frederika, about where she'd come from, about where her husband was.

"I hope you can sleep," Anna said, setting up the crib in the shadows of the corner. "I know how it is with a baby. Sometimes, you're so tired that your body forgets how to sleep."

Frederika nodded, still standing.

"I just realized you don't have any luggage!" Anna said, her hand on her chest. How hadn't she noticed that? "We have robes and spare clothes downstairs, and there's soap and lotion in your bathroom. Do you need anything else?"

"A robe would be nice," Frederika said quietly.

"Great." Anna set her jaw and went downstairs to find spare t-shirts, a dress she hadn't worn in years, and a robe. As she mounted the stairs, it occurred to her that

Frederika would need new underwear, socks, maybe some bras, and other toiletries. That afternoon, Anna would go to the store and buy them.

Anna dropped off the robe, t-shirts, and dress to a bleary-eyed Frederika, who was eager to close the door. Again, she thanked Anna, her syllables cloudy, and then, Anna was in the hallway by herself, her thoughts swirling. The baby couldn't have been a year old yet, which probably meant she was breastfeeding. But that meant Frederika was probably starving. Anna made a mental note to buy fruit and snacks, as many as would fill a giant shopping bag.

Back downstairs, Wes finished a conversation with a guest, then glowered at Anna. "Can we talk?"

Anna wheeled the stroller into the back office of the Sunrise Cove, what had once been her mother- and father-in-law's office, which now, she supposed, belonged to her and Wes alone. Susan followed them, her chin high, watching the two sleeping little girls as best as she could.

"What is going on?" Wes demanded as soon as the door was closed.

"I found her by the docks," Anna explained. "She was sobbing and couldn't catch her breath."

Wes frowned. "Her accent is different. Why won't she say where she's from?"

Anna shrugged. "She said something about 'them' taking her husband away. I don't have any other information except that she's frightened, hungry, and has nowhere else to stay."

Wes flared his nostrils and gazed out the window, deep in thought. Anna knew his heart and what kind of man he was. He would never throw Frederika out on the street. He also didn't like giving up this money.

"Can you find her somewhere else to stay by tomorrow?" Wes rasped. "Or find her husband?"

Anna frowned. "Yeah, Wes. I can find Frederika's husband. It should be simple since she'll hardly talk to either of us, and she's probably going to sleep for the next twenty-four hours."

Wes sensed her sarcasm and palmed the back of his neck. "We just need to rent that room out. We can't afford to give out too much charity."

Anna stirred with rage. "This woman has nowhere to go, Wes."

Wes stared at the ground. For a long time, neither of them said anything, until Lola shook awake and let out a wild yelp. Fatigue rolled through Anna, and she thought she might pass out. It was all too much to bear.

"I have to take them home," Anna said, drawing Lola against her chest. "If Frederika needs anything, will you call me? I'll come back."

Wes sighed. It was yet another in the seemingly endless, difficult days of parenting— with the added complication of owning an inn. Now, Frederika had brought another dose of chaos.

Wes and Anna didn't say goodbye to one another. Instead, Anna stormed out of the Sunrise Cove and took her girls back home, where Lola finally slept for many hours, Christine drew on the back porch, and Susan helped Anna clean the kitchen, drying dishes and stacking them gently on the counter. When Susan finally yawned after lunch, Anna told her to take a nap of her own, and Susan did, stretched out on the back porch swing as it shifted gently in the breeze. Inside, on the couch, Anna finally fell into a fitful sleep, twitching through nightmares. As a young mother, she was never rested. She was only twenty-five years old, but she felt much older than that, her bones brittle, her hair in strings.

But when Anna awoke two hours later, Susan and Christine were in the living room, their arms ladened with wildflowers they'd picked from the edge of the property, their eyes dancing, and their freckles popping from the June sunlight.

"My girls!" Anna said, wrapping them in a hug. "My darlings. They're gorgeous."

Armed with a new sense of purpose, Anna put the flowers in a vase and set to work in the kitchen, baking banana bread for Frederika and preparing for an afternoon of shopping to ensure she had everything she needed. Life was a constant battle, always apt to get you down. But Anna had to be stronger than that, especially with three little ones relying on her and watching everything she did.

"Today, we're going to go shopping for Frederika," Anna announced after she put the banana bread in the oven. She removed cheese from the fridge to make grilled sandwiches, sure of herself in her own home.

"I'll make a list!" Susan called, tearing one sheet of paper from Christine's pad.

"Wonderful." Anna smiled as Susan selected a dark blue crayon and blinked at her expectantly. "What do you think Frederika and her baby need?"

Susan frowned, digging through her mind for the right answers. "Food?"

"That's right," Anna said, slicing a pad of butter from

A Vineyard Tide

a stick and watching it melt in a skillet, floating across in a shimmering yellow. "What kinds of food, Susan?"

"Cookies!" Christine chimed in, taking another crayon for drawing.

"Not a bad idea." Anna laughed, her heart overflowing as Susan wrote "cookies," the s backward, then informed Christine, "She needs raspberries, too."

This was the sort of mother Anna had always wanted to be: a woman who showed her children the power of kindness and compassion, one who knew that homestyle food like grilled cheese could comfort any belly. And as Susan fought her very young mind, trying and failing to spell "raspberries," Anna placed the first two pieces of bread in the skillet, followed by the orange American cheese, and filled the Sheridan House with soul-affirming smells of toast, melting cheese, and baking banana bread. By the time the grilled cheese sandwiches were finished, the bread a perfect brown and yellow, and orange cheese dribbling from the sides, Susan and Christine had added three more things to the shopping list: a baby blanket, yogurt, and a coloring book. Anna thought it was a pretty good start.

Chapter Four

Present Day

Lola invited Claudia to Martha's Vineyard for a chat the second week of July. Claudia agreed, saying that she and her husband needed to get out of Boston anyway, that the city felt sticky, overwhelming, and hot. Lola, who'd lived in Boston for nearly all of her adult life, remembered that claustrophobic feeling, the nightmares that had plagued her in a hot summer in Boston— many of the dreams ending with torturous memories of her final years in Martha's Vineyard. Back then, she'd been very cagey about her past, hardly telling Audrey anything about her grandmother, Anna, or about what Lola had left behind.

And, of course, Lola hadn't fully understood the entire story. She'd been told that Wes had been the reason her mother had died, when, actually, it had been Stan Ellis— the man her mother had been having an affair with. Lola and her sisters had carried rage toward their father for years, but it had been misplaced.

A Vineyard Tide

Lola couldn't fully comprehend what it meant to be Claudia, who didn't know who her parents were or where they'd come from. But she did know what it felt like to want to fill in the gaps of your own story, if only to get a better picture of yourself.

The evening Claudia was set to arrive for their big meeting, Lola and Tommy went to the sailing bar near the docks in Edgartown, where Tommy liked to chat with the other sailors, discuss boat models and routes, and drink a pint or two of beer. Lola felt jittery with nerves about meeting Claudia, which was a funny sensation, as Lola rarely was nervous. She'd looked Claudia up online and learned she was a highly decorated historian, and she'd even put one of her historical fiction novels on her tablet. A skim of the first few pages told Lola everything she needed to know: she respected this woman's work. She was eager to help.

Before they arrived, Lola chatted with Cole Steel for a little while, a sailor in his late-twenties who often sailed neck-in-neck with Tommy during races, despite often losing in the last leg. Tommy had called Cole a remarkable sailor, "the future." But what Lola liked most about Cole was the way his eyes lit up when his girlfriend, Aria, came down the bar, smiling as she cleaned a bar glass and asking if anyone needed anything else. She had a slight Texas twang. The rumor was that she'd followed Cole to Martha's Vineyard after they'd met in the Caribbean last year— but it was difficult to know what the truth of anything was. All Lola knew for sure was that the two of them were heavily in love. Anyone could see it.

A couple of minutes past seven, Claudia and her husband appeared on the boardwalk outside the sailing bar, holding hands. Claudia smiled nervously as they entered, and Lola popped up from her stool, greeting them with an overly loud," Claudia! Dan! Hi!"

Claudia's curly, blond hair had grown wild from the ferry ride, and her skin was very pale, glowing like a porcelain teacup. Beside her, Dan was sturdy, with a farmer's tan and a big smile.

"You must be Lola," Claudia said, reaching out to shake Lola's hand.

"This is Tommy," Lola introduced him. "And this is the sailing bar. Not exactly a tourist destination, but it's cozy."

"It's fantastic," Claudia said, her eyes shining as she scanned the bar and nodded toward Aria. "We've only been to Martha's Vineyard a few times, and we normally just hit up the touristy fish restaurants."

"Nothing against them," Lola said. "I love those places. It's hard to find a bad restaurant in Martha's Vineyard." She paused, her heart stirring with nerves. "Are you hungry? They have killer burgers here."

Claudia laughed. "I think Dan is. I'm a little too nervous to eat right now."

"I'm nervous, too."

Claudia cocked her eyebrow. "You shouldn't be! I'm the one with a weird, secret past."

"We all have weird, secret pasts," Lola said. "We just don't know about yours yet."

Beside them, Tommy and Dan had begun an easy conversation about the ferry boat that had delivered them to the island, about the engines within them, and about Dan's history with sailing (he'd gone to sailing camp as a kid, apparently). Already, Aria poured Dan and Tommy pints of beer, leaving Claudia and Lola to shrug.

A Vineyard Tide

"Looks like they're preoccupied," Lola said. "Why don't we go outside to talk? It's beautiful today."

"You have burgers here?" Dan asked Aria. "I'd love one. With extra cheese? And fries, please."

Claudia laughed and placed her hand on Dan's lower back. "Lola and I are going to head outside to talk. You'll be okay?"

"I'll save you a fry, okay?" Dan winked.

"Save me two!" Claudia said.

"Aria? I'll have a chardonnay when you get a chance," Lola said.

"Me, too." Claudia nodded and followed Lola outside, where a fresh, salty wind blew through their hair. Aria came out soon with their glasses of wine, placed her hands on her hips, and inhaled, her eyes closed. Lola wondered what she thought about, all alone out here on the docks as the bar grew increasingly raucous, sailors stomping in from their hours at sea, thirsty for pints, hungry for burgers.

"Thank you for coming to the island," Lola said to Claudia, raising her glass.

"Thank you for answering my email! It was a risk."

"I've been intrigued ever since," Lola said.

Claudia grimaced. "I've been up to my ears in questions. I wanted to write a memoir as a way to talk about the foster system, especially in Chicago, and analyze how the foster system came into being."

"From a historical perspective?"

"Exactly," Claudia said. "I went to Chicago for the first time since I left at eighteen, and I was asking questions here and there, which eventually led me to the woman in charge of the foster program when I was brought in."

"How old were you at the time?"

"I was one," Claudia said hesitantly. It was clear she didn't want to show just how upset it made her, having been abandoned like that. "I'm forty now, so this was all a long time ago. The woman in charge of the program back then is now eighty-five, but she's still sharp as a tack, thank goodness. I couldn't believe it, but she was pretty sure she remembered me."

"That's incredible!"

"Especially when you consider how many children she helped through the foster program over the years," Claudia said. "Thousands upon thousands."

"Why did she remember you?"

Claudia sipped her wine as though she wanted to drum up confidence. Her eyes glinted with tears. "Sorry. I haven't felt like myself since I went to Chicago."

"It's okay!" Lola shook her head. "It must be an emotional rollercoaster."

"The thing is, I just always thought I was an orphan," Claudia said. "So many other kids I grew up with didn't have parents at all, or their parents were addicts, or their parents didn't have money to support them. It was easier for me to believe that I just didn't have parents at all. It helped me accept my fate in the foster system."

"That makes sense," Lola said.

"But the woman I spoke to in Chicago told me a different story, one that I haven't been able to fully verify," Claudia went on. "She said that my parents had escaped from behind the Iron Curtain. And that they had to change their names and leave me behind?" Claudia's shoulders fell forward, and tears spilled from her eyes.

Lola's heart jumped into her throat. Nervously, she touched Claudia's hand, at a loss for what to say.

"I just can't imagine the pain they must have gone through," Claudia whispered. "I've heard stories of people escaping from behind the Iron Curtain, from Poland or other parts of the Eastern Bloc— but I never thought it was part of my story. And I can't understand why they couldn't take me with them. Why couldn't they change my name, too?"

Lola bit her lower lip. "She couldn't tell you anything else?"

"She didn't remember," Claudia said. "I put in a request to look at the old paperwork from back then, but that will take a bit of time to go through."

"Everything takes so much time," Lola agreed. "Paperwork is slow as molasses."

"It's driving me insane." Claudia downed half of her glass of wine. "In any case, my memoir has changed considerably since my trip to Chicago. If my parents really did flee Eastern Europe, I want to write a book about that and about all the families who were affected after such an escape. But unfortunately, between all the summer classes I'm teaching, and my responsibilities to the History Department at the university, I don't have as much time as I'd like to dig into this."

"That's where I come in?"

"If it intrigues you at all," Claudia said.

Lola frowned. "You said in your email that they'd spent time in Martha's Vineyard?"

"That's what the woman in Chicago told me," Claudia went on. "That they'd come directly from Martha's Vineyard, out to Chicago. That my diaper bag had a 'Martha's Vineyard Sailing' logo on it."

Lola was incredulous. "So, you theorize that they fled

Eastern Europe and came immediately to Martha's Vineyard?"

"These are the only clues I have," Claudia said. "Is it enough?"

Lola laughed. "Of course not!"

Claudia gave her a confused smile. "Does that mean you don't want the job? It's too hard?"

"No! It means I want it even more," Lola told her. "I've been so bored this summer, just having a good time, attending parties, going to the beach. That's not the kind of woman I am! I need to feel frustrated, in the middle of a writing assignment, pulling my hair out. That's the only way I feel like myself."

Claudia was incredulous. "I think I understand what you mean?"

Lola waved her hand. "I gave up trying to understand myself a long time ago. Suffice it to say, I've never done much research into families escaping Eastern Europe. But the idea that some of them came here, to Martha's Vineyard, after escaping an oppressive regime? That's exciting to me. I have to know more."

Claudia laughed. "That is music to my ears. Have you ever considered writing historical fiction?"

"Why?"

"You've immediately fallen in love with this. It reminds me of the way I get before I start writing a historical fiction book."

Lola thought about this for a moment, about the many years she'd spent digging into real-world issues and stories. "I don't know. Everything I've written about that actually happened is stranger than fiction, you know? I don't know if I need to make anything up!"

Claudia asked Lola about her rate, which Claudia

agreed to pay in installments. After that, they went back into the bar for another two glasses of wine, beaming at one another, excited about this next step. Claudia looked at Lola as though she was about to uncover the secrets of the universe, and Lola looked at Claudia with heavy curiosity, trying to find something Eastern European about her face, her features, or her hair. Ultimately, she looked a whole lot like every other American; her face held no clues.

"How was your meeting?" Tommy asked as he and Dan joined them in a booth.

"I'm terrified of the look in Lola's eyes," Claudia confessed, laughing. "She's about to dive into the secrets of my life. And I don't think anything, or anyone, will stand in her way."

"If I know my Lola, she'll tear through every boundary to get to the truth," Tommy said proudly.

Dan raised his beer glass. "Claudia has been alone in this for too long. We're so grateful for your help, Lola. If there's anyone who deserves the truth, it's my wife."

"And I'm honored she's given me this chance," Lola said.

Chapter Five

1983

Wes' older sister, Kerry, was a superstar. With four young children, a flourishing real estate career, and a healthy marriage, she strode through life with confidence and purpose, often making Anna question her own status. Was Anna a loss leader in comparison? It was very possible. Still, that night, when Anna asked Kerry if she could drop Christine and Susan off for two hours, Kerry leaped at the chance, saying, "I never get to spend enough time with my nieces! Please, bring them by."

With Lola awake yet silent, her eyes enormous as she sat in her car seat, Anna drove to the Sunrise Cove, parked, and met Wes at the front desk. Yesterday, he'd said he needed her help with payroll, and now, here she was, with just enough time to finish it before she had to pick up Susan and Christine and put them to bed. But Anna was glad to be at the Sunrise Cove, if only because she wanted to keep an eye out for Frederika.

A Vineyard Tide

"Will you watch Lola? I want to drop off Frederika's stuff," Anna said, not bothering to explain as she whipped out of the inn, picked up three massive grocery bags from the trunk of her car, and scurried to the second floor. But when she reached Frederika's door, she stopped short. What was she thinking? Frederika had a baby and was going on no sleep. The last thing in the world Anna wanted to do was knock on her door right now and wake her up.

Disappointed, Anna spun on her heel and headed back toward the staircase. But just before she descended, there was a bright cry, followed by the unforgettable sound of a baby's laugh. She turned, staring at Frederika's door, listening hard. The baby's laugh had to be coming from Frederika's room.

Anna was nervous. On tiptoes, she walked back toward the door as the baby's laughter grew louder. Despite whatever horror Frederika and her baby had gone through, the baby still found joy in her mother's smile. That was really something.

"Frederika?" Anna tapped on the door gently with her elbow, still carrying all three bags. "Frederika, it's me. It's Anna."

After a dramatic pause, the sound of footsteps came toward her, and Anna braced herself. The door opened, Frederika gazed through the shadows of the hallway, and her baby was wide awake behind her, standing up with the support of the railing on the crib. Frederika was wearing the dress Anna had brought her that morning, and her blond hair was tousled across her shoulders. She looked natural, rested.

"Hello, Anna," Frederika whispered, then gazed toward the bags.

"I brought you some provisions," Anna explained. "Toiletries, clothes, and food. Have you been downstairs for dinner?"

Frederika shook her head. "We just woke up."

Anna nodded, adjusting the bulky bags in her arms. Immediately, Frederika bolted forward to help Anna, carrying two of the bags to the bed, which was unmade, the sheets strewn back. Anna placed the final bag next to the other two as Frederika pieced through the bag of food — the oranges, the bananas, the crackers, the Diet Coke, and the packages of cheese. Frederika raised a Diet Coke into the light and frowned, unsure what it was. When she spotted the banana, she ripped it out of the bag and cried out.

"I have heard about these! Monkeys eat them!"

Anna laughed because she didn't know what else to do. Who hadn't seen a banana before? Where had Frederika come from?

"They're delicious," Anna said. "Try it."

Frederika struggled with the banana until Anna reached over and opened it with a quick crack to the stem. Frederika's smile was childish, free. Anna watched, captivated, as she took the first bite, her eyes closed as she chewed. In another language, Frederika said something that probably translated just how tasty it was. Anna hoped so, at least.

After she finished the first bite, Anna showed her the banana bread she'd baked, telling her that it was sweet bread made with that very fruit. Frederika smelled the bread, and tears welled in her eyes.

"This is too much," she told Anna.

"No! It's nothing," Anna said.

But Frederika looked at a loss. Slowly, she sat at the

edge of her bed and gazed out the window at the line of trees and the small slot of the ocean you could see just beyond. "I cannot tell if it's all a dream."

Anna shifted her weight. "What's all a dream, Frederika? What happened to you?"

But Frederika couldn't look her in the eye.

"Can I bring you dinner?" Anna asked. "The fresh trout? The mashed potatoes?"

Frederika shook her head. "You've given me enough for now. I really need to rest."

Anna wondered if the woman could really sleep, even after all day spent in that room with her baby, hiding out from the world. But she wasn't in the position to argue with her.

"Maybe tomorrow," Frederika said quietly as Anna stood up. "Maybe we walk?"

Anna's heart shattered at the edges. "Only if you let me cook for you."

Frederika raised her shoulders. "How could I refuse?"

Back downstairs, Lola was still awake, giggling at a customer who made faces at her over the front desk. Wes tugged at his hair as he tried to clear up a problem with another guest, who said he'd overcharged her. Anna wanted to ridicule her, to tell her just how small this inconvenience was when compared to the woman's upstairs— but she knew that wouldn't help anything. It would only make Wes' day worse.

In the office, Anna set Lola up in a playpen with a few toys, and Anna got to work on the payroll, sensing her mind at its limit, her muscles about to give out. She prayed she didn't make any mistakes, as it was up to her to ensure the livelihoods of their employees were safe.

Peter, who worked the desk at night, arrived five minutes before Anna finished payroll. Exhausted and reeling, Anna and Wes held hands and walked out to the car, with Lola babbling happily in her carrier.

"How is Frederika?" Wes asked quietly as he clambered into the front seat, hollows beneath his eyes.

"She isn't saying much. But I think we're going to see each other tomorrow."

"You think she'll tell you more then?" Wes clearly felt guilty about how he'd acted earlier, about how money-driven he'd been.

Anna reached for his face and cupped his cheek. "I hope she does. I really do. And I hope we can continue to help her for as long as she needs."

Wes flinched. "We have to help her. I know that." He cleared the space between them and kissed Anna softly, making her feel woozy, apt to float out of her shoes and into the sky.

"I just can't understand what went wrong," Anna said. "She said they took her husband away. But where to? And how did she end up here, all alone?"

Wes pressed his forehead against hers. "You have such a big heart, Anna Sheridan. I don't know what I would do without you."

Wes drove them in silent concentration, back toward his sister's place, where Christine had fallen asleep on the couch, and Susan was up with her Aunt Kerry, chatting about her expectations for second grade.

"She's such a little lady," Kerry said as she led Susan out of the house, helping her into the backseat, where she buckled her seatbelt.

Tenderly, Wes carried Christine to the backseat, where she yawned in slumber but remained asleep. Anna thanked Kerry again and waved into the back of the house, where Trevor sat with his eldest, Steve. Recently, they'd discussed having a fifth child— an idea that Anna thought was borderline insane.

Back at home, Wes carried Christine to bed and shut the door as Susan brushed her teeth, washed her face, and sang to herself quietly in the bathroom— a song from *The Sound of Music*, "Sixteen Going on Seventeen." Miraculously, Lola fell asleep in Anna's lap, and Anna set her in her crib and hurried downstairs, hoping for a moment alone with Wes. It was a rare thing, indeed.

But Wes was already out like a light. His lips were parted slightly, and his eyes danced behind his eyelids, taking him through dreamlands. Anna sighed and sat at the kitchen table, watching as the evening sky grew dense with rainclouds. It wouldn't be long till they unfurled themselves and drenched the island. She hoped it brought peace to Frederika. She hoped it helped them all sleep.

* * *

The following late morning, as Anna sat on the back porch, Lola babbled in her playpen, Christine colored, and Susan read her book, all with the sunlight spilling through the lush tops of oaks and maples, there was a knock at the door. Anna leaped from the porch swing, unaccustomed to visitors in the middle of the day. And when she hurried through the house and opened the door, she was even more surprised.

"Frederika!"

There she was: the mysterious stranger, dressed in the new clothes Anna had bought for her yesterday, with her baby wrapped around her chest. Frederika smiled nervously, her lips tinted with the lipstick Anna had gotten her and her eyelashes thick with mascara.

When Anna had been shopping, she'd asked herself, *what would make this woman feel normal again?* And one of the answers had been, obviously, makeup.

"I am sorry for dropping by like this," Frederika said. "Your husband told me where your house is."

Anna opened the door wider. "It's not a problem at all! Come in."

As Anna led her inside, Frederika's eyes danced around the mudroom, followed by the kitchen and living room area, until they reached the back porch, with its immaculate and private view of the Vineyard Sound. Anna remembered when this house had seemed impossibly special, when the idea of living somewhere like this boggled her mind. Wherever Frederika had come from, she wasn't accustomed to views like this.

"Hello!" Susan popped up to greet Frederika, drawing her dark hair around both ears. "Would you like some lemonade?"

Frederika's smile was genuine, the easy one of a mother who so often could find strength even in the darkest of times. "I would love that."

"Okay." Susan looked at Anna nervously.

"You know how to make it," Anna said. "Just make sure you stir up enough for everyone."

Susan disappeared into the house, leaving Frederika and Anna to look at one another.

"Won't you sit down?" Anna said, gesturing for the porch swing.

Frederika sat gently, her hand around her baby's head. "I am very sorry for being so rude yesterday."

"You weren't rude! You had had a very difficult day."

Anna took the space next to Frederika, surprised at how easy it was to be with her, despite their brief time together. "I'm sorry if I overwhelmed you a bit."

"The gifts you brought me were..." Frederika placed her hand on her chest. "I cannot thank you enough."

"What happened to your luggage?" Anna asked. "You must have traveled with something?"

Frederika's eyes dropped to the floorboards of the porch. Again, Anna suspected she wanted to shove the truth aside, to hide herself away. Instead, she said, "I had to leave everything at customs. They couldn't trust it. They barely trusted me."

Anna frowned, trying to follow along. "Is that where you were separated from your husband?"

"Yes."

"Have you tried contacting customs?" Anna asked. "Is there a number we can call?"

But Frederika's eyes were piercing. "I can't. I can't let anyone know where we ended up, just in case."

Anna's throat was tight. "Where did you come from, Frederika?"

Frederika couldn't answer that, either. Again, she shook her head, her eyes trained on the water.

"Okay. I understand." Anna's head thrummed with confusion. How could she help Frederika if Frederika was unwilling to open up? "How did you end up in Martha's Vineyard?"

Frederiks sighed. "My husband had a contact here. They wrote each other letters over the past few years. I never was allowed to read them, and they were written in a secret code I was never taught. The man told my husband he would help us once we got to Boston. But the man was not in Boston when we arrived, which was partially why my husband had such difficulties. Because I had no other idea of what to do, I decided to travel to Martha's Vineyard on my own. But when I asked someone at the dock yesterday about this man, the man who'd pledged to save us, he said that the man died two months ago."

Anna placed her hand over her mouth. For a moment, she tried to remember every person who'd died the past few months in Martha's Vineyard, what their names were. But she couldn't remember anyone off the top of her head. Probably, she'd been too entrenched in motherhood and working at the inn to pay close attention.

"What was the man's name?"

"I can't tell you," Frederika said. "I don't want to endanger the rest of his family."

Anna leaned back in the swing, her stomach twisting into knots. "That means you're in danger."

Frederika nodded once and sucked in her cheeks.

"But you can't tell me who you're running from? You can't tell me who has your husband?"

Frederika shook her head. "I'm sorry. I think I've told you all I can."

Anna reached over to take Frederika's hand on the porch swing. It was calloused, as though she'd spent time doing thousands of dishes, or hundreds of loads of laundry, or tilling a garden. It was hard to imagine Frederika anywhere but here, even though she was displaced.

"Thank you for being here," Frederika finally said, her eyes shining. "I don't know what I would have done."

Anna's throat swelled. A long time ago, after the birth of Susan, Anna had fallen into a brief yet tumultuous postpartum depression. Although she'd been there for Susan, ensuring she was fed and cared for and clean,

Anna had struggled to understand her place in the world. How could she be a mother when she had no hope for the future? But during those early days, Wes' sister, Kerry, had come over frequently, sitting with her just like this, watching the water. Anna hadn't needed Kerry to talk to her; she hadn't needed anything but the peace of being alongside someone, someone who loved you. Someone who cared.

Chapter Six

Present Day

Audrey and Max were on the back porch of the Sheridan House, lining up Max's toy cars and then racing them down the porch steps, where they careened to the grass below. Each time, Max squealed happily, eased down the steps, collected his trucks, and set them up again for another race.

"We've been doing this for hours," Audrey told Lola, rising to hug her.

"It looks invigorating."

"It really is." Audrey laughed. "How are you doing?"

Lola winced as she sat on the floor of the porch with her back to the wall. "To be honest, I'm slightly hungover. Only slightly."

Audrey laughed. "Jealous! I haven't gone out in a while. Max, Noah, and I have been playing house."

"And you look like you're handling it well."

Audrey waved her hand. "Max and Noah make it easy on me. Grandpa isn't here very much, which is a bummer, but it's allowed the three of us to find our groove. Some nights, Max demands Noah read him his bedtime story, which is nuts. I thought only you, Amanda, or I would be allowed, maybe forever."

"He trusts him," Lola said.

"He adores his Dad." Audrey's eyes sparkled. "Don't you, Max?"

Max furrowed his brow with concentration, ensuring that each of his toy trucks was in line with one another before the next big race.

"Where were you last night?" Audrey asked.

"I was at the sailing bar. A professor from Boston University wanted to meet me to discuss a project, and I suggested there."

Audrey laughed. "You brought a professor to that dive bar?"

"We had a great time!" Lola insisted. "Her husband and Tommy got along like gangbusters."

"What did she want to talk to you about?"

This was why Lola had spontaneously dropped by the Sheridan House. She had a proposition for Audrey, one that she hoped and prayed she'd agree to.

"She was raised in the foster system outside of Chicago," Lola said, "but has reason to believe her parents fled Eastern Europe and had to change their names and leave her with the system in order to save themselves."

Audrey's jaw dropped. "That's horrible."

"It is," Lola offered. "Although I can't imagine what their lives must have been like in the Eastern Bloc. It must have been horrendous for them to go to such lengths to be free."

Audrey nodded thoughtfully. "Is she writing an article about it?"

"A memoir," Lola said. "And she wants my help researching."

Audrey's eyes doubled in size. "This feels almost impossible to figure out."

"I know. Doesn't that make it even more exciting?"

Suddenly, Max shoved two trucks down the porch so that they leaped from the steps and tumbled into the grass again. Howling, he raised his fists, then bounded down the steps to get them.

"Great, Max!" Audrey said. "Good job!" She shrugged her shoulders at her mother, muttering, "I think he thinks he's doing something really important right now?"

"He is," Lola assured her.

Audrey leaned back, crossing her arms over her chest. "What's the next step?"

"I called the archives in the Boston Public Library. They have a slot open tomorrow afternoon between one and four."

"Which archives?"

"I'm going to research families who escaped Eastern Europe successfully and entered the United States via Boston," Lola said. "It's a start."

"Why Boston? Why you?"

"The professor is pretty sure her parents were in Martha's Vineyard before they went to Chicago," Lola explained. "So, it stands to reason they entered the country in Boston."

Audrey sighed. "You're going to be up to your ears in archives and paperwork."

"You know that's what I love."

Audrey groaned and tugged her hair. "I know why you're here."

"I don't know what you mean?" Lola smiled sweetly, pretending.

"You don't have to put the act on," Audrey said. "Tell you what. I'll come with you. I just have to make sure someone can watch Max tomorrow before Noah gets home."

"And the next day, too," Lola reminded her. "Because we're staying the night in Boston, baby. I already booked us a fancy hotel downtown."

Audrey rolled her eyes into laughter. "You didn't even wait for my answer before you booked?"

"How could you resist something like this!"

* * *

The following morning, Lola picked Audrey up, bubbling with excitement as her daughter kissed Noah goodbye and hustled down the steps, a backpack on her shoulders. Audrey yelped as she slid into the front seat. "We're on the move, baby!"

Lola laughed and drove away, tires squealing cartoonishly.

"Shh! Be careful. You'll get in trouble. Aunt Susan is always watching," Audrey said mischievously.

"I grew up with her watching my every move," Lola said.

And sure enough, after Lola parked the car on the bottom level of the ferry and got out to grab a cup of coffee, Susan had already texted her.

> SUSAN: Was that you driving too quickly down the road?

> LOLA: :P

> SUSAN: Drive safely on your way to Boston! Good luck!

Lola showed the texts to Audrey, who said, "Told you so."

The drive to Boston was mostly uneventful. After a chaotic summer, Lola and Audrey caught one another up on the intricacies of one another's lives, the day-to-day stuff they didn't often talk about. Again, they spoke about Amanda's recent wedding, which had very nearly not happened, along with what Susan had heard about the criminals who'd attempted to rob the Aquinnah Cliffside Hotel during the ceremony.

"I hope the girlfriend gets off with a warning," Audrey said. "Her boyfriend obviously manipulated her!"

"But she still did it," Lola pointed out.

Audrey shrugged. "Love is complicated! Especially when you fall in love with the wrong person."

"Good thing neither of us has ever done that," Lola said sarcastically.

"Right! Good thing." Audrey laughed, tracing her teeth with her tongue. "My dad sounds like he was a really lovely guy!"

"Max's dad sounds like a peach!"

Audrey stuck out her tongue.

When they reached the Boston Public Library, Lola parked in the nearest parking garage, grabbed her backpack, which was filled with empty notebooks, ready to be filled, and led Audrey through the main entrance.

"Remember when we used to come here all the time?" Audrey whispered.

"It was all I could get you to do that one summer,"

Lola said. "You were anti-swimming pool until you were ten or so."

"I was a weird kid," Audrey agreed. "But reading was one thing I could get on board with."

Lola and Audrey signed into the back archives of the library, where a woman with very thick glasses and a dusty turtleneck led them deep into the heart of the three-hundred-year-old building. There, tomes of very old books and ledgers awaited, thick and impressive, holding the secrets to thousands upon thousands of people who'd probably died long ago.

"Claudia was born in 1982," Lola said, setting herself up at a very large desk, where she stacked her notebooks into a tower. "But I think we should look for any connection between Eastern Europe and Martha's Vineyard from the years immediately prior to that. Maybe there was a history of people coming from the Eastern Bloc to Martha's Vineyard?"

"A secret, Martha's Vineyard operation?" Audrey suggested.

"Exactly."

Audrey's eyes glinted with intrigue, and she swept her hair into a ponytail, shivering. "Let's divide and conquer, shall we?"

They decided to opt for the ledgers first. According to the librarian who'd brought them to this dusty archival hall, these ledgers contained within them the names of every person who'd entered the United States from Eastern Europe— including any details those people had been willing to provide.

"But they were probably scared to write everything down," Audrey said. "After such an epic escape, you wouldn't want to put yourself at risk."

"Very true." Lola leafed through a ledger from the year 1979, three years before Claudia's birth, where lines upon lines of names had been written— last names with many, many syllables, indicating Polish or Hungarian origin. Lola's shoulders sagged with the weight of their task.

"Some of them say where they were off to," Audrey pointed out, frowning. "Look. Marc Zolanksy said he was off to New York City. And Marta Kizym said she was going to..."

"Ohio! Wow. Okay."

Not everyone had been upfront about their plans after their Boston arrival. There were entire pages wherein nothing had been written, their next destinations blank. Audrey grabbed a ledger from the year 1981 and began to hunt for any sign of Martha's Vineyard, sitting by Lola quietly.

Nearly three hours later, Audrey finally erupted from her chair. "Here! I found Oak Bluffs!"

Lola burst toward Audrey's book and peered down at the entry, blinking past the dryness in her eyes. Sure enough, three people arrived in Boston in 1981 and stated their next destination as Oak Bluffs. Two women and one man. One of the women's last names was different, which suggested she was the sister of the other.

"I wonder if we can find out what happened to them?" Lola said. "Maybe they can tell us why they wound up in Oak Bluffs in the first place."

"And who their contact was," Audrey agreed.

Lola wrote their names down, thinking about the anxiety of that trip to the United States— a land they'd only heard of, one they hoped meant freedom.

Almost immediately after their discovery, the

librarian entered the archives to say their time was up. Lola furrowed her brow, frustrated. Three names were definitely something to work from— but it didn't feel like enough.

"Thank you so much," Lola said as they left, knowing better than to get on the librarian's bad side. "Do you have any more slots tomorrow?"

Audrey eyed Lola nervously, probably thinking of Max, of who would care for him. But right now, Lola was caught in a vortex of this mystery. She was pretty sure one of the Sheridans or Montgomerys would pick up the slack.

"Let's see." The librarian clicked through her computer, adjusting her glasses so that they hung at the very end of her nose. Probably, she needed bifocals and was unwilling to take that step. "We have a slot tomorrow morning at nine. Three hours again."

"We'll take it." Lola didn't wait to look at Audrey for confirmation.

The Collegiate Hotel in downtown Boston had never been an option for Lola and Audrey. The price had been far outside of their range, and they'd always lived about twenty minutes away from downtown, anyway.

But now, everything had changed. As Lola and Audrey stepped through the revolving doorway of the immaculate hotel, Audrey and Lola took a moment's pause to breathe in, breathe out, and fully appreciate the unique and artistic touches of the old hotel. It had been built in the early 1800s and had kept up its charm of yesteryear, complete with bellboys in maroon outfits with elbow and shoulder pads, charming people at the front desk who looked at you as though you were the only guest in the hotel and a bar that seemed taken directly from the

Roaring Twenties, with a bartender with a fancy, curly mustache.

"This is crazy, Mom," Audrey said.

"Are you still upset that I booked us another three hours in the archives?"

"What! No. Absolutely not." Audrey adjusted her backpack on her shoulder just as a bellhop approached to take their bags. The bellhop gave her backpack a rueful look, as though he'd never carried such a silly thing upstairs before. He took Lola's bag, too.

"I already texted Noah about it," Audrey said, waving her phone. "He's going to take tomorrow off so he can watch Max. He says it's no big deal. And I don't know what we were thinking. Just three hours in the archives? That was never going to be enough time!"

Lola grimaced. "I was overeager and overly optimistic. I assumed we'd breeze in, get all the answers, then have a brilliant night of celebration."

"No, you didn't," Audrey said. "You're a better journalist than that."

Upstairs, their hotel suite was two rooms with a large living area, complete with a small balcony that overlooked the vibrant street. It wasn't difficult to imagine yourself two hundred years ago, standing on that very balcony, looking out at a very different Boston.

"They gave us champagne!" Audrey hustled onto the balcony with the bottle, showing it off, and it glinted in the late afternoon sunlight.

"We'd better pop it open, then!"

Audrey returned to the suite to uncork the champagne and pour them two flutes as Lola continued to stir with thoughts on the balcony, dreaming about these three people from Eastern Europe who'd somehow found their way to Martha's Vineyard. Back then, Martha's Vineyard hadn't been as renowned as it now was. It had been a tourist destination, of course— but it had blown to epic popularity after the Clintons had begun vacationing there. But this begged the question: Why had the Eastern Europeans chosen Martha's Vineyard?

Before Audrey returned to the balcony with the flutes, Lola grabbed her phone and dialed a friend of hers — Matt, who worked in the archives in Oak Bluffs. Whatever she was dealing with, she wanted to get a better sense of it before they hit the Boston archives tomorrow. She didn't want to be as blind.

"Lola Sheridan, as I live and breathe!" Matt laughed into the phone, and Lola could see his face clear as day: big mouth full of white teeth, shaggy ex-rocker hair, and a button-down that didn't quite suit his look. Still, he was a rockstar in the Oak Bluffs records' office, and Lola had been in contact with him frequently since her return. He had a very specific memory. You could tell him bits and pieces about an old story you heard about Martha's Vineyard, and he'd be able to tell you who was involved, what their backstories were, and the exact date it had occurred within the next twenty-four hours.

"Hi, Matt! Good to hear your voice. How's your summer been?"

Audrey returned to the balcony, rolling her eyes. "Workaholic," she muttered, putting one glass of champagne on the balcony table and sipping hers.

After a few pleasantries, Matt dug into her. "What can I do for you, Lola? You don't usually call the archives just to chat."

Lola explained what she'd just learned about three people from the Eastern Bloc, who'd stated their destination as Oak Bluffs. "It was in 1981," she went on. "Maybe you could look up their names in the system? See if they actually made it? My hope is they're still on the island, just waiting for me to come over and pester them."

"Uh oh. You have that wild voice of yours," Matt said. "The one you use when you're entrenched in a story. Sure, I'll look them up. What are the names? I think you're going to have to help me with the spelling, too."

Lola read the names, spelling them out, listening as Matt's fingers clacked against the keyboard. After a very long pause, Matt sighed.

"They're not here, Lola."

Lola's heart sank. "Are you sure? Can you try again?"

Matt did, but still, no luck. Audrey frowned, sensing something wrong.

"What does that mean?" Lola said quietly. "In your expert opinion?"

"Well, it could mean several different things," Matt said. "It could mean they never made it, for whatever reason. Or, it could mean they changed their names by the time they got here."

"They had escaped Eastern Europe," Lola said.

"So, they might have had reason to change their names," Matt said.

Lola groaned.

"This is a tough one, isn't it?" Matt asked.

"I don't know. We're just at the beginning," Lola explained. "We shouldn't get disheartened yet."

"We?"

"My daughter is helping me," Lola said proudly. "And she's looking at me right now like I have two heads, so I'd better get back to her. Thanks for your help, Matt."

"Let me know if I can do anything else. And say hi to Audrey for me!"

When Lola got off the phone, she explained what she'd learned to Audrey— who slumped her shoulders.

"Like you said, it's only our first day," she said. "We shouldn't let this get us down. Besides, we have another three hours in the archives tomorrow!"

"And there will probably be a whole lot more hours where that came from," Lola said, raising her champagne glass.

"I love when you get like this," Audrey said. "You look like you could take on the world."

"Maybe I could," Lola said with a laugh. "Should I run for president?"

"Only if they can move the White House to Martha's Vineyard."

* * *

But the following morning in the archives, bright-eyed, bushy-tailed, and ready for anything— Lola and Audrey spent the first two hours without answers. Disappointment was too small a word for what Lola felt. Slowly, she shifted back in her chair, crossed her arms over her chest, and tried to drum up another way forward, another avenue to find information. Audrey sighed and turned another page, skimming through names they'd never know. Nobody had gone to Martha's Vineyard, apparently.

And then, Lola was struck with a realization.

"Who wrote all this down?"

Audrey turned slowly to face her mother. "What do you mean?"

Lola's heartbeat was frantic. "All of these ledgers! They're written in the same hand."

Audrey's eyes widened. "You're right!"

Lola whipped toward the front page of her ledger, where the man who'd written the names of the escaped Europeans had scribed his own name: Val Gilbert. In Audrey's, he'd done the same.

"Val Gilbert?" Audrey said the name quietly.

"Why does that name sound familiar?" Lola whispered.

"I've never heard it before," Audrey said.

Twitching with nerves, Lola grabbed her phone and again dialed Matt.

"This is coming a lot quicker than I thought it would," Matt answered. "How can I help you, Ms. Sheridan?"

"Val Gilbert. Does that name mean anything to you?" Lola asked.

"Val? Of course," Matt said. "He moved to Martha's Vineyard in the seventies."

"What was his job?"

"Something in government," Val said. "I can search the archives for you. I don't know how many records we'll have on him, though. He died about forty years ago. I believe it was exactly 1983."

Lola's heart pounded. "Yes. Look up anything you can on him, please!"

Matt laughed. "It doesn't sound like you're disheartened anymore."

Audrey blinked at Lola with confusion, pestering her for answers when Lola got off the phone.

"When I was a kid, I had to do a report on a famous Martha's Vineyard figure. I picked Charles Shearer, who was a black man, the son of a slave on Martha's Vineyard.

Back in 1912, he opened the first hotel for black vacationers. I thought it was fascinating! Anyway, a local man had written a book about Charles Shearer, which I used in my bibliography. And I'm pretty sure that book was written by Val Gilbert."

Audrey typed the two names into her phone: Val Gilbert and Charles Shearer. Sure enough, the book existed— long out of print, but with that same dark blue cover Lola remembered from elementary school. One of the photographs on Audrey's phone was of Val Gilbert himself, a sturdy man of approximately six feet, unsmiling, with his arms crossed over his chest.

"I guess we have our next clue," Audrey said softly. "Maybe he has family we can ask about this?"

"I think Matt will help us with this next step," Lola said, taking a photograph of Val Gilbert's name in the ledgers. "Prepare yourself for another chunk of hours in the archives. This time, we won't be far from home."

Chapter Seven

1983

The fire broke out in the Sunrise Cove Bistro kitchen at approximately six-thirty in the evening, smack-dab in the middle of a dinner rush. Anna heard the explosion from the office, where Lola had only just fallen asleep. Abandoning her paperwork, Anna flew up from the desk, grabbed Lola's carrier, and fled the building, calling for all guests in the immediate vicinity to go outside immediately. Smoke billowed out from the kitchen, black and gray and thick, and Anna was terrified for everyone, praying that they got out in time.

Anna wasn't in the bistro when it happened but was told that Frederika had been dining in the Bistro, eating a piece of fish and a pile of broccoli as her baby slept upstairs. As the kitchen staff fled the fire, Frederika dotted her napkin across her lips, hurried to the fire extinguisher, bolted through the door of the kitchen, and put the fire out. It happened in an instant.

By the time the fire engines arrived, all the guests were outside, talking about where they'd been when they heard the explosion and asking if everyone was okay. Just before the firefighters ran through the door, Frederika appeared in the doorway, her baby on her chest, carrying her plate of fish and broccoli.

"It is gone!" she called, waving to Anna before she turned back and re-entered the inn.

Everyone across the grounds of the inn blinked at one another, confused about this strange woman with a different accent. Anna hurried after her, entering the inn immediately after the firefighters. The smoke had cleared considerably, and it hadn't reached all the way upstairs. Frederika was halfway to her room before Anna caught her, breathless, still gripping Lola's carrier.

"Hi! You put the fire out?"

Frederika nodded. "We had many fires where I came from. I lost the fear."

Anna wasn't sure what to say, so she chuckled. "You're much braver than any other person in this inn."

"It would have been useless, losing your inn to that," Frederika explained simply.

"You're right," Anna said. "Humans lose their heads so quickly. I wish I had your composure."

Frederika's eyes widened. "Don't you remember the first time we met? I certainly wasn't composed, then."

Anna waved her hand. That was obviously different. But before she could say so, Wes' voice echoed up the staircase.

"They're saying Frederika saved the inn?"

"She's up here!" Anna called, and, a moment later, Wes sprung up the steps, two at a time, until he appeared, breathless, his hair extra-tousled.

"Frederika! I don't know how to thank you." He smiled at her sloppily. "The firemen are already saying we had faulty wiring! It could have been the end of us."

"Please. It is no trouble." Frederika winced, embarrassed at all this fawning. "Besides, I've lived here the past four days. I need to pay you back somehow."

"You've done it tenfold," Wes assured her. Stuttering, he added, "Why don't you come over for dinner tonight? That fish and broccoli must be cold."

"It isn't necessary," Frederika said.

"I insist," Wes said.

"Does that mean you're coming home for dinner?" Anna asked Wes, hand across his shoulder.

"I have to make sure everything's stable here beforehand," Wes said quietly. "But after that, I have to get out of here. I think I might lose my mind if I don't."

Anna and Frederika carried their babies through the wooded path between the Sunrise Cove and the Sheridan House, shadows of trees licking past them. Both babies slept peacefully, and Anna and Frederika spoke quietly to make sure they didn't wake.

"Where are your other girls?" Frederika asked.

"My sister-in-law is watching them," Anna explained. "She'll bring them back home tonight. Thank goodness they weren't there today! Christine's so sensitive. It would have really gotten to her."

Frederika nodded. "I've noticed that about her. How quiet and frightened she is."

Anna eyed Frederika curiously. She'd only been on the island four days, but already, Anna could tell that she'd cultivated opinions of all of them; she saw them from a very unique perspective.

A Vineyard Tide

"I want to ask you how you see me," Anna said with a laugh. "But I don't know if I can take it."

Frederika's eyes sparkled. "What do you mean? I can't imagine I would say anything you don't already know. You have a very firm grip on who you are, Anna. Far more than your husband." Frederika stalled, sensing she'd stepped in it. "He is a very kind and lovely man. And I see why you fell in love with him."

"But he runs himself ragged with the inn," Anna said quietly, sensing what Frederika meant.

"He has abandoned himself, his children, and you. And I worry that if he doesn't fix that, something in your family will break."

Anna's heart twinged with worry. "I know you're right."

Not long after they returned home, Kerry dropped off Christine and Susan. Christine was sleepy-eyed and eager to spend time alone, especially after her raucous hours with her cousins at the Montgomery House. Susan set the table, watching Anna and Frederika like a hawk.

Frederika hunted through the cabinets for ingredients, explaining she wanted to cook her mother's recipe. Anna reasoned she was probably homesick, that she wanted to give back. Frederika instructed Anna to peel and slice potatoes, which they then boiled, mashed, and mixed with milk and flour. Eventually, they rolled them into little morsels, which Frederika called "gnocchi." Anna had never heard of them before.

"My mother always loved to make them," Frederika said. "They're technically Italian, but she adored Italian food. I always think of her when I eat them."

Just as Wes entered the back door, bringing with him the smell of the fire, the gnocchi finished boiling, and it was time to eat. Wes quickly changed clothes, kissed Susan and Lola hello, and sat at the head of the table, eyeing Frederika nervously.

"Everything is okay up there?" Frederika asked, sitting next to him at the table.

"We managed to feed everyone," Wes said, "and assure them it wouldn't happen again. I have someone coming to check the electricity tomorrow, and the Bistro is closed for the foreseeable future." Wes rubbed his eyes. "Which means we're going to lose a lot of revenue."

"But we won't have to order food," Anna pointed out, sitting on Wes' other side. "We'll save on expenses."

Wes remained quiet, his eyes stirring.

"You really should eat," Frederika interrupted the silence, nudging the bowl toward Wes. "You have had a hard day."

"What is this?" Wes asked, stirring the gnocchi with the serving spoon so that the butter and sage oozed through the mounds of potato dough.

"It's Frederika's mother's favorite recipe," Anna explained.

"Wow." Wes served himself a generous helping, waited for Anna and Frederika to have some on their plate, then scooped several morsels into his mouth. Immediately, he closed his eyes, overcome with the flavors. "It's delicious, Frederika. It's also going to knock me out immediately."

Frederika laughed kindly and ate, her face transforming as she encountered these flavors and textures from her youth. Anna ate, too, and was mesmerized by the sage and the butter and the texture of the potato, something she never would have thought to do.

"I have been thinking," Frederika said, setting down

A Vineyard Tide

her fork. "I would like to work at the inn."

"Oh!" Anna's heart lifted. "Frederika, you're our guest..."

But Frederika looked resolute. "I have lived in your inn for four days, and I have hardly raised a finger."

"You saved the inn from a fire today," Wes reminded her with a laugh. "You've lifted more than just a finger."

"I do not like sitting around, not doing anything. My daughter needs to see me working. She needs to know that, in America, you must be willing to work," Frederika said. "Besides. You are understaffed and running yourself silly around that inn. I'm there all the time. I can help."

Wes stroked his five o'clock shadow. "It isn't the worst idea in the world, honestly."

Anna wanted to tell him that Frederika had just gone through a traumatic event and needed to rest. Then again, what did she know about trauma? Perhaps Frederika needed something to do, a distraction.

"I can work the front desk, or clean, or work in the kitchen when it opens back up again," Frederika said. "I can show people to their rooms, haul luggage, or garden. Really, any task, I am happy to do it."

"A jack of all trades," Wes said.

"I'm sorry?" Frederika frowned at the term, not sure what it meant.

Wes eyed Anna, and over the table, they had a brief, wordless conversation. Anna sensed Wes wanted to overuse Frederika, if only to make his life easier. And Anna wanted to protect her.

"Put me on the schedule," Frederika said. "Let me do something with my hands."

"I can draw up the paperwork tomorrow," Wes said.

"No paperwork," Frederika said quietly.

"I don't know how we can pay you otherwise," Wes said.

But Frederika shook her head.

"I think it needs to be under the table," Anna said carefully. "Due to her circumstances. Am I right, Frederika? You want to be paid in cash?"

Frederika nodded. "I want to pay for the room and food with the job. Whatever is left over can be in cash."

After a long pause, Wes stretched his hand out over the table, and Frederika shook it.

"But you have to tell us if you get overwhelmed," Anna told her. "We don't want you to work yourself ragged." She frowned, adding, "And what are you going to do with the baby?"

"I will carry her with me as I work," Frederika said. "That's what you do with Lola, isn't it?"

Anna smiled, realizing that all this time, she'd gotten so accustomed to having a little girl on her chest— from Susan to Christine to Lola— that she hardly noticed it anymore.

"We're a family inn," Wes said. "Our guests expect that kind of thing."

Susan, the only child at the table, chewed and swallowed a big gulp of gnocchi, blinked at her father, and said, "What is under the table?" She glanced beneath the tablecloth fearfully, as though sure there was something lurking under there.

"It's just an expression, String Bean," Wes said.

"I don't understand it," Susan said with a sigh, as though sensing she still had a lot to learn. Anna wanted to tell her that this feeling never really went away, that regardless of your age, you were always fully aware of how little you actually understood about the world.

Chapter Eight

Present Day

After the big Val Gilbert discovery, Lola and Audrey drove back to Martha's Vineyard, where they were welcomed with piping hot pizzas, vibrant salads (made by Amanda herself, the queen of salads), and iced tea. Noah, Audrey, Amanda, Sam, Lola, Tommy, Max, and Grandpa Wes sat on the back porch of the Sheridan House, eating and catching up. But when Amanda asked Lola and Audrey about their trip to Boston, neither Audrey nor Lola was eager to divulge the information they'd learned.

"It's so early in the process," Audrey explained tentatively. "What we learned hardly has any context right now."

"It would sound like gibberish to you," Lola agreed.

"Ugh! I hate secrets," Amanda said, stabbing a red onion with her fork.

Audrey and Lola locked eyes over the table. Val Gilbert's name was never far from their minds, always blazing through their consciousnesses. It was like a rogue puzzle piece that didn't fit into the rest of the puzzle.

"But you found something," Noah said. "Enough to keep researching?"

"We found something," Audrey assured him. "With Lola Sheridan around, we were bound to crack some kind of code. She wasn't going to let us leave Boston without it."

Lola arranged to meet Audrey at the Oak Bluffs Records Office two days later at nine a.m. sharp. Six minutes past the hour, Audrey stumbled out of her car with an iced coffee and a pair of big sunglasses on.

"I'm sorry! Max wouldn't go to sleep," she said.

Lola hugged her daughter, shaking off any annoyance she'd felt about Audrey's lateness. "Doesn't Max know we're chasing a lead?"

"I tried to explain it to him," Audrey said, "but he wasn't willing to listen to reason."

Lola smiled, remembering that, a very long time ago, Susan had mentioned how difficult Lola had been at bedtime. "Mom went crazy, trying to get you to go to sleep. You always wanted to be a part of the world." Later, when Audrey had been similar, Lola had gotten payback; now, Audrey was the next in line.

It felt wonderful to be a part of the great tapestry of mothers and children. When she thought about it, Lola could practically hear her mother's laughter, as though she was just around the corner, waiting for her.

Matt looked just the same as always, eager with a smile that opened up his face and a button-down that didn't quite work on his frame. He hugged both Lola and Audrey and led them to the basement archives, where he

A Vineyard Tide

said he'd set up as much as he could about Val Gilbert for them to peruse.

"I knew better than to start going through it myself," he said. "I have no idea what you're looking for. And I don't know if I want to know! You're always at the edge of a mess, Lola Sheridan."

Matt left Audrey and Lola in the basement. The air stank of something that was either mold or mold-adjacent, and there was only one very slim window at the top of one of the walls. Lola hurried toward it, opening it to bring in a draft of fresh air.

"All right. Are you ready to dive into the life and times of Val Gilbert?"

Audrey clapped her hands. "I was born ready."

The Oak Bluffs Records Office had numerous newspaper articles that featured Val Gilbert. Most of them had been taken during the late seventies and early eighties, before his death, and featured him as a wonderful pillar of the community. He coached baseball, competed in the Round the Island Race, ate in the hotdog eating contest (and lost miserably), helped his neighbors, saved dogs from the Humane Society, and on and on.

"He's the perfect American guy," Audrey said doubtfully. "I don't see any connection to Eastern Europe from these articles."

"He's almost too perfect," Lola agreed, sitting down. "But the articles only go back to 1977. Where was he before that? Let me ask Matt if we can go through the change of address records from back then," Lola said, snapping her fingers. "Maybe we can find where he moved from? I don't know."

Matt agreed to let Lola and Audrey peep through those records, which, yet again, included miles upon miles of names they didn't recognize, nothing that helped them on their quest.

"Where did he live on the island?" Audrey asked, trying to suppress a yawn. "Maybe that will lead us somewhere."

Lola nodded and hurried back upstairs, where Matt ate an apple and listened to a Wilco album on his computer.

"Matt? Do you know where Val Gilbert lived at the end of his life?"

Matt swallowed a chunk of apple. "Wasn't he out by the Aquinnah Cliffside? Yeah. That little green house about a half-mile from the cliffs. I think that was his place. You should be able to find records of that house downstairs. I think it's somewhere down Moshup Trail?"

Lola pulled up her online street map and hunted for the address of the house Matt talked about, the little green cottage she'd passed hundreds of times without paying much attention to it. The address was 7213 Moshup Trail. But when she looked up the paperwork for that house downstairs, she found another name on the deed: Aleksander Nowak. The house had been purchased by Aleksander in 1976, one year before the newspaper photographs had begun to feature "Val Gilbert" nearly six times per year.

"Who is that?" Audrey asked.

"I'm not sure," Lola breathed. "But look at the handwriting. Doesn't it look the same as Val's?"

Audrey cocked her head. "It's identical."

"Who is this guy?" Lola muttered, placing the house deed alongside the rest of Val Gilbert's stuff. "Is it possible Val isn't his real name? That he's from Eastern Europe, too?"

"Ugh. With all these fake names, I don't know how we're supposed to get to the bottom of this."

"And we're no closer to figuring out who Claudia's parents are," Lola said.

"Why don't we look into this Aleksander guy who signed the deed?" Audrey suggested. "I mean, it's a clue, right?"

"How?" Lola asked.

"Didn't he have to show an ID when he bought the house?" Audrey suggested, her eyes stirring. "Wait a minute."

"What?"

"Had Aunt Kerry and Uncle Trevor already begun their real estate career by 1976? Is it possible they sold him the house?"

Lola's jaw dropped. "Oh my gosh. You're right."

Tenderly, Audrey and Lola returned the "Val Gilbert" items to their folders and tucked the folders into a drawer to the side of the archives, as they'd probably need to return to them later. They flew up the staircase, waving goodbye to Matt as they headed for Aunt Kerry's place. There was no time to explain, no time for proper goodbyes.

Lola breathed a sigh of relief when Aunt Kerry opened the door. "Girls! This is a surprise."

As always, Aunt Kerry was elegant in a pair of black slacks and a slim-cut t-shirt, her hair styled in curls around her ears. A book was sprawled on the couch in the front room, and toward the back of the house, a TV hummed, proof that, more than likely, Uncle Trevor was home, catching up on sports.

"Good to see you, Aunt Kerry." Lola hugged her first, then Audrey.

"Who is that?" Trevor called.

"Lola and Audrey are here! Girls, would you like something to eat or drink? Coffee? Tea? Wine? I've wasted the day away in that book over there. I have no idea who the killer is, and I just have to find out!"

Lola laughed. "Nobody loves crime thrillers like you."

"That's right," Aunt Kerry said. "But usually, I can guess who did it halfway through the book. This time, I'm stumped."

Aunt Kerry led them into the kitchen, where she put a kettle on the stovetop. Lola wanted to just come out with it, to ask the question. But she didn't want to be rude.

Lucky for her, Audrey didn't want to waste time.

"Aunt Kerry? Were you and Uncle Trevor already working in real estate in 1976?"

"We were, honey. We started up in 1975, I believe. I didn't know what I was doing back then. I think I let a lot of clients walk all over me!"

Audrey and Lola exchanged glances.

"Do you still have proof of sales from back then?" Lola asked, her voice wavering. "Documents from people you sold houses to?"

"We have everything," Kerry said, rolling her eyes. "I don't know what on earth we're planning to do with all of it. Presumably, Trevor wants to be buried with our tax paperwork. Bless him. He's the more organized of the two of us. He's also the worrier."

"I've kept us in line all these years!" Uncle Trevor called from the next room.

Aunt Kerry waved her hand. "What's this about?"

"We're investigating someone who may have bought a

A Vineyard Tide

house back then," Audrey said. "But he might have been operating under two names."

Kerry's eyes widened. "I don't even need to read that book! I'm living in a crime thriller!"

"We don't think he committed any real crimes," Lola added.

This slightly deflated Kerry. "Well, let's see. Do you know his name?" Her eyes twitched. "I would ask about the woman's name, but as a woman, it was extremely rare you could buy property by yourself back then. Times have changed so much, Audrey. I'm so happy for the women in your generation."

"Aleksander Nowak," Lola recited. There was no way Kerry would remember it. It had been nearly fifty years since the sale.

But almost immediately, Kerry furrowed her brow and placed her hands on her hips. "A Polish man?"

"It sounds Polish, doesn't it?" Audrey asked.

"We did sell a little house to a man with a Polish accent," Kerry said. "A tiny green house. On..."

"Moshup Trail?" Lola asked.

Kerry snapped her fingers. "It must have been that. A cottage. Just an adorable little place. You know, he was one of the easiest clients I ever had. He really needed a place to live immediately. I think I only showed him that one house!"

Audrey and Lola exchanged glances as Audrey retrieved her phone and brought up the photograph of Val Gilbert.

"Was this the man you sold the house to?"

Kerry blinked at the screen. "I can't say for sure. But it does trigger a memory, I suppose. Trevor? Will you come in here for a moment?"

There was a dramatic silence, during which they listened intently as Trevor turned off the television and creaked down the hallway to say hello. When he saw their faces, his smile fell.

"What's wrong? Did something happen?"

"Nothing happened, darling." Kerry took his arm. "But the girls are asking about a Polish man who bought a house on Moshup Trail back in 1976."

"Goodness." Trevor shook his head. "Our second year of working together!"

Kerry beamed, clearly proud of all they'd accomplished. "Was this the guy? Do you remember?"

Audrey showed Trevor the photograph, and Trevor nodded. "I'm pretty sure it was him. I seem to remember later seeing him out and about. Everyone called him Val at that time, and it threw me for a loop. But I thought, hey. Maybe it was a Polish nickname I didn't know about. I'm not the biggest genius. I don't know much about the world."

"He got married shortly after he moved in," Kerry remembered. "He married an islander who'd lost her husband ten years before that."

"That's right!" Trevor nodded. "Before his death, they seemed really happy."

Lola spun with questions, none of which her Aunt Kerry and Uncle Trevor could answer. But they were getting closer to the story. She could smell it.

"Now, if you don't have any more questions from the distant past, I'd love to serve you some carrot cake," Aunt Kerry said. "Go on! Sit down! I'm sure you've been working so hard that you've forgotten to eat."

Audrey touched her stomach. "You're right about that."

Lola followed Audrey into the nook, where they sat listlessly, listening to Kerry slice the cake and chat to Trevor about the seventies, about what she remembered from their first year as real estate agents.

"What are we going to do next?" Audrey breathed.

"We're going to track down Aleksander Nowak," Lola said. "And figure out where he came from, why he was here, and why he changed his name."

"Sounds easy."

Lola laughed as Aunt Kerry entered the room, armed with cake. Uncle Trevor was hot on her heels with two more plates.

"Put that phone away," Aunt Kerry ordered as Audrey continued to study Val Gilbert's photograph. "You can get back to your mystery soon. For now, let's focus on cake."

Chapter Nine

"Mom! Milk and sugar in your coffee?" Audrey hovered at the kiosk of the ferry as they shimmered across the Vineyard Sound, headed for the mainland.

Lola grimaced. "Just a little bit of milk, please." As she swirled around the topic of Aleksander Nowak and where on earth he'd come from, she felt fidgety and strange. It was probably better to avoid sugar at this junction, even as she ached with desire for it, watching as Audrey tore sugar packets over her little Styrofoam cup, her eyes glazed.

They were on their way back to Boston, with yet another appointment in the library archives awaiting them. It had been three days since they'd learned of Aleksander Nowak and of Aunt Kerry and Uncle Trevor's involvement in his past. Audrey had secured a babysitter for Max, her jaw set. For some reason, now that they were deeper into the puzzle, it didn't sizzle with as much amusement. Lola sensed something dark and sinister at the end of the journey. She wasn't sure she fully wanted to find out.

Audrey did her best to boost their morale in the car. She put on pop songs from her teenage years, not so long ago, as she was only twenty-two years old, and shimmied her shoulders in the passenger seat. "Remember when we made up choreography to this one?" She was speaking of "All About That Bass" by Meghan Trainor, a song Audrey and Lola had belted from car windows, racing all over Boston.

"Oh my gosh. You made us practice for hours!" Lola clapped her hand on the steering wheel.

"We should try it later," Audrey said. "At the hotel."

"As long as you promise not to record it."

"Not even for blackmail?"

"You are my daughter, aren't you?" Lola laughed. "I like your style. I'm also terrified of it."

Back at the archives, the same librarian greeted them with a half-smile and led them to the backroom. There, Lola felt armed with more understanding of the topic at-hand than last time— and went immediately to the documents from the year Aleksander probably arrived in the country, 1976. Sure enough, after about forty-five minutes of searching, they found his name scrawled.

"Why does it say, 'Agent Aleksander Nowak'?" Audrey asked.

Lola cocked her head. "That's strange. Was he a police officer or something?"

Audrey was wordless, bent over her phone, typing, until she pulled up an article from the NY Post.

"Secret Agents In Eastern Bloc May Have

Helped Thousands Escape To The United States."

Lola pinched her eyebrows together. This was truly sensational. "We don't have proof, necessarily, that he did that."

Audrey nodded. "I know. But maybe the librarian knows where we can find more information about that?"

In fact, the librarian did know. She gave them the address for an Espionage Museum in downtown Boston, just ten blocks away from the library. Lola and Audrey thanked her, put everything away in the archival room, and stepped into the sweltering July heat. On their way there, they stepped into a café for chilled green juices filled with spinach and raspberry, where Audrey googled "Aleksander Nowak, spy" and found nothing. Apparently, his story was too entrenched in history to have been recorded on the internet.

Before they left the café, Audrey received a call from her grandfather. Her eyes were alight as she answered it. "Grandpa! How are you?"

Lola watched her daughter's face change and grow slack as she listened.

"I knew it would happen soon, but I didn't know it would be this soon!" Audrey sighed. "I'm happy for you. Really. But we have to have a family party. You know that, right?" She pressed her lips into a paper-thin line, listening, until she said she loved him and got off the phone. "Grandpa's moving out on July 31st. It's official."

"Wow." Lola's heart flipped over. "It's the end of a very long era."

"I know. So crazy, isn't it?"

Lola couldn't help but mourn the loss of her mother all over again. In her mind, Wes and Anna had been meant to grow old in that house, to have their children and grandchildren over, to watch the waves lap up onto the shore forever. But time had had its way with all of them— and it had drawn Audrey, Noah, and Max into that home instead. There was something poetic about it, despite its sorrow.

When they reached the Espionage Museum, the man at the front desk, who wore a yellow sweater to combat the chill of the air-conditioned room, greeted them by saying, "Did you just come from the library?" Apparently, the librarian had called ahead and told him exactly what they were after. His eyes glistened with excitement.

"It's not exactly common that people come to us with specific questions," the museum worker explained, guiding them into the next room. "So, forgive me if I speak too quickly. I'm quite excited."

Lola and Audrey exchanged smiles, grateful to have someone burning with so much knowledge.

"A lot was uncovered about the Eastern Bloc espionage program after the Cold War ended and the Berlin Wall fell," he explained, pausing in front of a collection of photographs. "It seems likely that a resistance was formed in the east and that spies found a way to communicate with American troops stationed in the west. In that way, channels were formed from the Eastern Bloc to allow people to escape, usually under the cover of night, all the way to the United States. From there, many people changed their names due to anxiety about their country coming after them. And it's true that the United States was not always welcoming. If the paperwork wasn't forged correctly, the government wasn't averse to turning people away."

"That's terrifying," Audrey breathed.

The museum worker nodded. "The librarian said you were looking for someone in particular. A potential spy. What was his name?"

"Aleksander Nowak," Lola said.

The museum worker's eyes lit up.

"You recognize the name?" Audrey asked.

"I do!" He turned toward the massive wall of photographs and pointed at a man's face. In it, Aleksander was maybe fifteen years younger than he'd been in the Martha's Vineyard newspaper, and he wore a USSR uniform.

"Aleksander was very important in the USSR government," the worker explained. "From his position in the government, we believe he was able to work undercover and get people out of the Eastern Bloc much faster than other spies. He also delivered information to the West about what was really going on in the East and was instrumental in getting passports made for people coming to the United States— especially those who wanted to completely start over with new names."

"Wow. He sounds extraordinarily brave," Lola breathed.

"He was. But over time, we believe he started making mistakes here and there. He was getting older, and the government was on to him. He brought some people over to the United States and then set up a life here, going by the name of..."

"Val Gilbert!" Lola cried.

"That's right." The museum worker looked deflated, as he hadn't been able to reveal this himself.

"He lived in Martha's Vineyard," Audrey said. "And presumably helped people escape from there?"

"He sent numerous letters to the Eastern Bloc," the

worker went on. "Because all letters were searched and read by the government, he wrote in a secret code."

"How did the people on the other end learn the code?" Lola asked.

"We don't know that for sure," the worker said. "But if you look here, we've cracked it over the years."

He pointed at a codebreaker hanging on the wall, which explained the structure of Aleksander's code. The word "sunshine" meant "passport," and "It's always nice in October" meant "Prepare yourselves to leave in October." But the code was extremely detailed. It would have taken hours to deconstruct a letter from Aleksander—especially considering Lola and Audrey didn't speak Polish.

"We have several of his letters," the worker explained. "But they're not on display."

"How did you get them?" Lola asked.

"They were donated years ago."

"By whom?"

"It was an anonymous donation," the worker said, guiding them toward the back door.

Audrey and Lola exchanged worried glances. Who had had those letters? And why did they want to keep their name out of it?

In the dark shadows of the back room, the museum worker flashed on a fluorescent bulb and showed them the letters from numerous families in the Eastern Bloc, all addressed to Val. Most of the letters had been written by men, fathers in the east.

"We're specifically interested in a family that potentially left the Eastern Bloc in 1983," Lola explained.

"There are plenty of letters dated in late 1982," the

worker said, showing them off. "And even a few in early 1983."

In all, there were fifteen different men's names, all of which Lola wrote down, frustration brimming. It was possible that any of them had been Claudia's father. It was also possible they were barking up the wrong tree.

"We can't thank you enough," Lola said as they prepared to leave, their shoulders heavy with the weight of what they'd learned.

"What's your plan with all of this? Are you writing a book?"

"Yes," Lola said. "A client of mine is. I'm helping her with the research."

"But I can see it in your eyes," the worker said, tilting his head. "You're getting obsessed with it. It's the same as me when I learned about this stuff. I couldn't wrap my mind around all these individual stories, people who seemed to exist outside of time. I don't know why we, as a culture, often don't discuss this era of human history. But if we don't, we're doomed to repeat the same mistakes. Don't you think?"

Lola and Audrey took pictures of the letters, the photographs, and the other various documents, including passports Aleksander had had made for those who'd escaped, and then left the museum wordless. It was only later, when they collapsed in their hotel room that they looked at one another and said, "Wow."

"I can't believe this," Audrey said. "Are you going to call Claudia?"

"Not yet," Lola said. "We still don't know if her parents were any of these people."

"But it seems likely, doesn't it? All the pieces fit together," Audrey said.

"From our perspective, they do," Lola said. "But we know such a small part of the story."

Audrey shifted to her side on her queen-sized bed, rubbing her temples. For a long time, Lola and Audrey were quiet, lost in separate thoughts. It was only later, as clouds burst over the hotel and filled the streets with rain, that Audrey convinced Lola to head to the hotel restaurant for dinner and drinks. There, they found their way to other topics, happier ones, frequently touching on conversations of Max and his development, his wicked sense of humor, and what he would be like when he grew up.

Audrey paused with a French fry in the air. "I hope he's a journalist. There's no better feeling in the world than putting together a story like this, getting to the heart of something that happened."

Lola knew that Max's real father, the man Audrey had interned for in Chicago three years ago, was also a journalist, rather renowned, with numerous accolades. Lola, being nosy, had read several of his articles and recognized his talent. Still, she found Audrey's approach to journalism to be much more nuanced and from the heart.

"You're already showing him a beautiful example of what it means to be one," Lola told Audrey.

Audrey's cheeks were pink. "It's weird how he watches my every move. I have to be really careful."

Lola leaned back in her chair, remembering Audrey as a toddler, how she'd copied everything Lola had done. Even now, across the table from Lola, Audrey couldn't have been anyone but Lola Sheridan's daughter. She'd even stolen the skirt she now wore from Lola's closet, a long jean skirt with a slit up the side.

"Oh." Audrey laughed, her hand over her mouth. "I know what you're thinking."

"And what would that be?"

"That I watched you like a hawk my whole life," Audrey said. "And I turned out just like you."

"I wasn't thinking that," Lola lied.

"You were," Audrey said. "And you're right. But I wouldn't have had it any other way."

Chapter Ten

Two days before Wes was set to move out of the Sheridan House forever, the Sheridan and Montgomery families staged the summer party to end all summer parties. Although Wes knew something big was about to happen, they kept it mostly a secret from him, demanding that Kellan take him out birdwatching that morning. "Don't you dare bring him back until noon," Susan warned her stepson.

Wes had already packed and moved most of his belongings to Beatrice's place. Lola stood in the bedroom he'd moved out of, the one on the side of the house that Scott had built after they'd all come home. It felt so empty. The dresser doors had been cleared; the books had been taken. Even the photographs on the walls had been removed. Lola sat on the bed, thinking of her father, who'd lived in that house alone for so many years after they'd gone away. Now, it was his time to go.

"Hey! Do you want to help me with the guacamole?" Amanda appeared in the doorway of Wes' bedroom, smiling. Just like her mother, she had a knack for ordering around the other members of the Sheridan family— but in a way that sounded kind and optimistic. You just had to say yes.

Lola found Audrey, Amanda, and Christine at the counter, preparing burger patties, stirring up potato salad, and removing groceries from big grocery bags— chips, pretzels, cookies, and Cheez-Its.

"Where are the vegetables I requested?" Amanda asked, looking pointedly at Audrey.

"They were all out," Audrey explained mischievously.

"The grocery store ran out of vegetables?" Amanda rolled her eyes. "That's rich, Aud."

Susan breezed through the back door. "Did I hear someone say vegetables? I already sliced tons to make a big platter. We should be good."

"You saved the day, Susan," Christine said. "As usual."

Susan waved her hand. "Aunt Kerry just wrote. They're on their way. Andy's bringing Will, but Beth's staying home with the baby. And..." She thought for a moment, then snapped her fingers. "Steve is bringing Rita!"

Lola and Christine exchanged glances, thinking again of Rita, of Steve's budding friendship with her in the wake of his wife's death.

"For someone who technically lives in California, she's sure in the Vineyard a lot," Amanda said wryly.

"It's hard to get the truth out of Steve," Susan said. "But they seem happy. And Isabella really likes her. I guess that's all that matters."

"I'm glad he feels comfortable enough around us to bring Rita around," Lola said.

"It takes a lot of bravery not to hide away after something like that," Christine added.

For a moment, the three Sheridan Sisters held their breath, all lost in the memories of their own grief. They'd handled Anna's death in different ways— yet had cast one another and their father aside, bent on carrying their sorrows alone. It hadn't worked.

Lola sliced and diced the meat of the avocados, added lime juice and salt, then mashed the green until the consistency was Amanda-approved. All the while, her sisters, niece, and daughter chatted easily about this and that, all bubbling with optimism for the upcoming party.

Lola went to the fridge to return an unused lime, and when she opened the door, she peered in to see a marvelous, three-tiered cake piled high with frosting and fresh raspberries, blueberries, and strawberries.

"Christine! Did you make that?"

Christine laughed. "You sound shocked."

Lola closed the door of the fridge. "I'm always amazed at how talented you are."

"You know how much I love it," Christine said wistfully. "Baking and decorating a cake takes me completely out of myself. All my worries about Mia, the future, or what the heck I'm going to make for dinner that night fall away. And it's just me and the cake."

"That's beautiful," Lola breathed.

"Did I hear someone talking about how talented my wife is?" Zach's voice came from the mudroom, and a moment later, he appeared, carrying little Mia in his arms. Mia blinked sleepily at everyone and waved as Christine took her in her arms and spoke to her quietly, her eyes filled with love.

Tommy arrived not long afterward, kissing Lola on his

way to the front of the yard, where he, Scott, and Zach planned to set up tables and chairs for the big party. It was up to Scott to start the barbecue, and Zach was in charge of the speaker system, and as the women continued to prep food in the kitchen, they listened to them bicker slightly about the best way to do each of the tasks. Midway through, Scott mentioned that a tree near the shoreline was "nearly dead" and that they had better get it chopped down soon. The other two agreed, then fell into a discussion about whether they should hire someone or not.

"It's funny," Audrey said, taking a pretzel stick from a bag. "This is our house, now— but everyone has a feeling of ownership over it."

"It's the family house," Susan agreed sadly. "Even though I live next door now, I still come over to make sure the flowers are growing all right."

The back screen door screamed, and Aunt Kerry's voice called through the house— the house she'd grown up in so many years ago. "Is my brother here yet?"

"Not yet, Aunt Kerry!" Lola hurried to hug her aunt and Uncle Trevor, taking his six-pack of beer and Kerry's homemade punch and leading them to the living room and kitchen, where they hugged everyone hello and then paraded to the back porch.

"The house is about to fill up," Audrey said.

And sure enough, it did. Very soon after Aunt Kerry's arrival, her children appeared: Kelli with her fiancé, Xander, who'd hired experienced hoteliers for the Aquinnah Cliffside Overlook Hotel, allowing themselves plenty of spare time outside of its walls. Next came Claire and her husband, Russel, along with their twin daughters, and after that came Charlotte and her fiancé, Everett, who were preparing for Charlotte's big move to Orcas Island. Rachel tagged in after them, carrying a big bowl of cookies. Soon after came Andy and his stepson, Will, along with Steve, his so-called friend, Rita, and his daughter, Isabella.

Scott started to barbecue ten minutes before twelve, and the simmering smell of grilled meat filled the air. July sunlight splintered through the tops of trees, and the grandchildren of the family played games in the front yard, tossing frisbees and balls. Kelli's children soon arrived, changed into swimsuits, and went for a dip, and their laughter ricocheted from the house and through the trees. Sam and Noah returned from a trip to the store, ladened with soda, beer, wine, and lemonade, plus several bags of ice. An extra cooler was necessary for such a big crowd.

A minute or two before Wes arrived, Beatrice pulled into the driveway and walked around the side of the house, appearing on the little hill between the road and the water. She wore a bright red dress, and her hair had been styled with a red bandana.

"Beatrice!" Lola waved from the yard, where she held Max on her hip. "Can I get you something to drink?"

Beatrice beamed as she approached, taking in the huge family. "Look at all of you together! Is all of this for Wes?"

"It is," Lola said. "He's lived here for decades. We want to make sure he finishes it out right."

Beatrice's eyes glinted. "I hope it won't be too difficult for him. I have to admit that I'm worried about the transition."

Lola understood. It was difficult to ask anyone to change their entire universe for you. She'd done this when she and Tommy had gotten together. Tommy had been a vagabond sailor, a wild man with his eyes to the wind. Asking him to stay home a little bit more, to build a life with her, had been terrifying. The fact that he'd said yes had been proof of his feelings for her.

Wes arrived at the party five minutes after twelve. From the front yard, they could hear him chatting to Kellan, saying, "Look at all these cars! Did you know this was going to happen? Is that why you invited me to go birdwatching?"

Wes entered the house from the back, then appeared through the screen door of the porch overlooking the water. His binoculars still hung from his neck, and he peered out at his tremendous family with all the love in the world echoing from his face.

"Hi, Grandpa!" Audrey called from the yard, where she and Noah were playing catch with Abby and Rachel.

At this, everyone called out their greetings, and their voices echoed across the yard. Wes' eyes sparkled.

"You want a burger, Wes?" Scott asked from the grill.

Lola hurried forward, lacing her free arm through her father's. Max babbled happily, calling him "Grandpa." Wes reached out to take Max's hand, overcome with emotion.

"It's going to be okay, Dad," Lola said quietly. "We just want to celebrate you and this house."

Wes swallowed the lump in his throat. "Thank you," he said, loud enough only for Lola to hear. "It's perfect."

Not long afterward, the Sheridan and Montgomery families huddled around tables for a feast. Scott, Zach, and Tommy took turns at the barbecue, flipping burgers and brats and hot dogs, and there was, miraculously, enough to go around.

Lola grabbed a seat at the table with her father, Beatrice, Audrey, Tommy, Noah, and Max. Audrey joked that they were lucky enough to sit with the guest of honor, adding, "I can't believe we won't be roommates anymore, Grandpa!"

"You won't miss me a day," Wes teased her.

Audrey stuck out her tongue and turned to look at Beatrice. "When I first moved to Martha's Vineyard, I was a mess. But Grandpa was probably one of the biggest reasons I didn't completely fall apart. All we did was goof around and eat snacks. One of us got bigger and bigger and bigger..." Audrey nodded toward Max. "And Amanda tried her best to keep us in line."

"They sound like gorgeous times," Beatrice said.

"They were," Audrey agreed sadly. "I can't believe they're over."

Wes' eyes filled with tears that he blinked away. Audrey cleared her throat and stabbed her fork through her potato salad. "Grandpa, did you ever know anyone named Val Gilbert?"

Wes' eyes were suddenly very clear. "I haven't heard that name in a long time! Gosh, he must have died when Lola was a baby."

"1983?" Lola asked.

"Thereabouts," Wes confirmed.

"Were you friendly with him at all?" Lola was no longer interested in food, transitioning back into her journalist mode.

"I saw him around quite a lot. He volunteered for just about every charity in town," Wes said. "He was very into Memorial Day and Fourth of July. Sometimes, he dressed up like Uncle Sam. But..." Wes frowned, going through his memories. "But there was a rumor going around that he wasn't actually American. Sometimes, you could hear it in the way he spoke, like he had some other accent. And sometimes, he hung around people who seemed unable to speak English. I don't know."

Susan approached the table with baked beans and prepared to dish them out on people's plates. "Are you talking about Frederika?" she asked.

Wes placed his hand over his mouth and stared at Susan. Shock marred his face.

"Who is Frederika?" Lola demanded.

Slowly, Wes removed his hand from his mouth. "I haven't heard that name in so many years. I can't believe you remember her."

Susan shrugged.

"Who is she?" Lola asked again.

But Wes' eyes were misty. "It's such a long story, honey. Not for today, okay? I just want to enjoy this time with family."

Beatrice reached across the table and took his hand, sensing he was out of sorts. Lola stirred with questions, at a loss. She looked up at Susan, who shrugged again and spooned baked beans on Lola's plate. Lola made a mental note to pester Susan later after her father went home with Beatrice. This conversation was far from over.

Chapter Eleven

Susan and Christine sat on the edge of the dock beneath a low-hanging moon. With their feet in the water, their hair flowing gently in the wind, and their faces out to the dark Sound, it was easy to imagine it was many years ago, that they were teenagers again. As Lola padded through the grass to meet them, she felt ten years old, running out to meet her older sisters. She half-imagined Anna was up on the back porch, gazing out at them, making sure they were safe.

Lola's footsteps made the dock creak beneath her, and Susan and Christine turned to smile at her.

"The kitchen is clean, Max is asleep, and Amanda and Audrey are busy gossiping about a celebrity I don't know about," Lola said, sliding in between her sisters and putting her feet in the water.

"What a successful party," Christine said.

"Everyone played their part," Susan agreed.

"I thought Dad was going to start sobbing at least ten times," Christine said.

Lola crossed her arms over her chest, thinking again of

her father's caginess when it came to Frederika, a mystery woman. Susan sighed.

"You have to tell me," Lola said, laughing. "I've been dying to know."

"Dad was really weird about it," Susan agreed.

"About what?" Christine demanded.

"Do you remember the German woman who lived at the inn for a while?" Susan asked. "You were probably four or five at the time."

Christine frowned. "What? A German woman?"

"She was definitely German?" Lola asked, thinking of Val Gilbert and his Polish past.

"She taught me tons of German words and expressions," Susan said. "For a while, we had conversations that Mom couldn't understand."

"Did she tell you anything in German? Anything you thought was strange?" Lola asked.

"I can't remember," Susan said, "and I wasn't advanced enough for anything like that. She taught me things about food or chores and the weather. I think she liked speaking her native language so far from home."

"Do you remember any German?" Christine asked.

"Nothing," Susan admitted. "Guten Tag, maybe. And how to say thank you and goodbye."

"Why was she living at the inn? And why did Dad act so strangely when you brought her up?" Lola asked.

"I have no idea," Susan admitted. "But she was friends with Mom. She used to come to the house all the time and cook for us."

Lola's eyes widened. "Really! She came here?"

"I have memories of her and Mom sitting on the back porch swing while we played," Susan said.

Lola's mind stirred with questions. On the one hand,

there was no record of this German woman having any contact with Val Gilbert. But on the other, if she was a German-speaking woman, it was possible she was from East Germany— which made it possible she'd been in contact with Val in some way. It was her only lead currently. And Lola decided to take it.

"Maybe Mom wrote about her in the journals," Lola suggested.

"We read so many of them," Christine said.

"But not from those years," Susan said. "Not as much, at least."

It was true. They'd been focused on the years during which Anna had had her affair with Stan, trying to wade through what had really happened before her death. They hadn't considered the early eighties much, if at all.

"So you were seven or eight?" Lola asked Susan.

"Around that," Susan said. "It would have been 1983 or '84." She pressed her lips into a line and considered the dark water before her, thinking hard. "Oh! I can't believe I forgot to mention it. She had a baby."

"Frederika did?" Lola gasped.

Susan nodded. "Yes. Maybe around a year old?"

"She didn't have a husband?" Christine asked.

"I don't know. Not that I remember," Susan said.

Together, the three Sheridan sisters sat in silence for a moment. It felt as though, in sitting at the edge of the dock, they peered into the darkness of the past, asking questions that had no answers.

Toward the house came the sound of the screen door slamming. Amanda and Audrey's voices came next, streaming across the yard and water. A moment later, their shadows were at the edge of the dock.

"Psst! Is anyone out there?" Audrey hissed.

"We're here!" Susan called back, laughing. "What are you two up to?"

"Amanda made me come down here," Audrey said. "She says she has news for everyone."

Amanda walked closer, clasping her hands. Lola's heart thudded with expectation. Even before Amanda said it aloud, Lola felt sure, as though she'd always known her niece would break this news.

"I wanted to let you know that I'm pregnant," Amanda breathed. "I just found out last week. I can't keep it a secret any longer."

Immediately, Lola and Christine popped to their feet to cover Amanda with hugs. Audrey shrieked and leaped on her, wrapping her arms around her, and Susan stood, swiping her hands across her thighs. It was clear from her expression that she already knew.

"Thanks for keeping it a secret, Mom," Amanda said, hugging her mother next.

"You got to know first," Lola said.

"I called her when I was freaking out," Amanda confessed. "I wasn't sure I could handle it."

"Amanda Harris? She can handle anything!" Audrey laughed.

Amanda shrugged. "It doesn't always feel like that."

Audrey laced her fingers through Amanda's. "Whenever you need help, we're there for you. You know that, right?"

Amanda nodded, and tears shimmered down her cheeks.

"You helped me raise Max," Audrey offered. "And now, Max will be a big brother to your baby!"

"And we'll have so many memories, both here and at my place," Amanda said, her voice catching.

A Vineyard Tide

Lola's heart filled with tenderness. Together, she and her sisters, Amanda, and Audrey, sat back down on the dock as the stars crystallized in the night sky above them. Slowly, Amanda's anxiety was swept away with the tides, leaving her shimmering with only excitement and optimism for the future. The Sheridan women were more powerful together than apart. And there, beneath the home where Anna Sheridan had raised them, they were protected and at peace.

Chapter Twelve

1983

It was late July, which meant that Frederika had been living at the Sunrise Cove Inn for six weeks. Due to her incredible organizational skills and her ease with the guests, she'd grown into the greatest resource of the inn, allowing Wes more time off for his family and increasing productivity amongst other staff members. Wes' profits were safe for the month of July, despite his having to "give up" an entire room for Frederika and her baby.

"She's brilliant," Wes said of Frederika often, holding baby Lola for a change, giving Anna a much-needed break.

Frederika had been instrumental in easing the fights between Wes and Anna, as well. Anna was allowed more time to herself, more time to think and dream, and she'd begun to feel more like herself than she had since the birth of Susan. Now that she was twenty-five, the person she was relearning herself to be was much different. She was pretty sure she liked her.

But one afternoon, as Anna breezed through the foyer of the Sunrise Cove with Lola asleep in her stroller, she found Frederika in tears at the front desk. It was a gorgeous day outside, and no other guests were nearby, as they'd taken to the sea or the surrounding beaches, enjoying the island.

"Frederika! What's wrong?" Lola hurried around the side of the desk and hugged Frederika. Her heartbeat was fluttering like a rabbit's.

Frederika reached for a tissue and mopped herself up as quickly as she could. "I am so sorry, Anna. I did not mean to act so unprofessionally."

"It isn't a problem!" Anna waved her hand. "Did something happen? Was one of the guests cruel?"

"No. Nothing like that." Frederika sighed, gazing out the window onto the Vineyard Sound. She looked wistful.

"Is Ricarda okay?" Anna asked, speaking of the baby — who was one of the happiest and easiest babies she'd ever encountered.

"Ricarda is fine," Frederika said. "She doesn't know anything that's happened to her, to us. She is ignorant. And it is blissful."

Anna frowned, heavy with shame. Because her life had gotten so much easier since Frederika had come to the island, she'd allowed herself to forget that Frederika was a woman of secrets.

"You still haven't heard from your husband?" Anna spoke quietly. She didn't want to startle Frederika.

"No. And every night, I stay up thinking about him. Wondering if he's okay." Frederika bit her lower lip.

"Where we come from, what we did was horrific. Illegal. Oh, I do not like to think of the punishments that await us there."

Frederika's face was blotchy. Anna didn't know what to say.

"Is there anything I can do to help you?" Anna rasped.

Frederika shook her head. "I don't know."

"Please, Frederika. Tell me something. Let me help you," Anna begged. "You've done so much for my family. I hate to think you're suffering alone all summer long."

Frederika was quiet for a long time, weighing up the pros and cons of telling her secrets. Finally, she stuttered, "There was that man my husband was writing to. The man on Martha's Vineyard who died."

Anna remembered Frederika saying something about that when she'd first arrived. "Who was he? Maybe I know his family. Maybe they can help."

Frederika closed her eyes. "His name was Val Gilbert."

Oh! Anna knew Val. He adored the island, was seen at every parade, and was often dressed as Uncle Sam, throwing out candy for the kids. Over the previous couple of years, he hadn't been seen as often, and there had been rumors he was sick. Had she heard he'd died? Maybe. But maybe Anna had been too tied up in the chaos of motherhood to remember.

"We should go see his wife," Anna said quietly. "Maybe she can help us find your husband."

Frederika's eyes widened. "Val was married?"

Anna nodded. "He married an islander several years ago. They were both older. She'd been married before, but her husband had died. Anyway, I know exactly where their house is. My sister-in-law sold the house to Val back when he first came to the island."

Frederika was at a loss for words. "You'd really take me there?"

"Why not!" Anna laughed. "It's a fifteen-minute drive."

Frederika stitched her eyebrows together. "Should we call them first?"

"Nonsense. We're all islanders. And here on the Vineyard, just stopping by is a way of life."

All Frederika could do was believe Anna, and honestly, Anna really felt she was telling the truth. She just had never interacted with Mrs. Gilbert before. She couldn't have known the state she was in.

* * *

The following morning, Anna, Susan, Christine, and Lola picked up Frederika and baby Ricarda and drove out to Val Gilbert's old place, where Mrs. Gilbert currently resided alone, as far as Anna knew. Anna hadn't wanted to take all three of her daughters, but Wes was busy with work, and Frederika had insisted on not telling him where they were going or why. Anna understood: Frederika had decided to trust Anna with bits and pieces of her life story — but she still didn't trust Wes, not fully. Perhaps it was because Anna was a mother.

The little green cottage where Val and Mrs. Gilbert had lived out the final days of Val Gilbert's life was located just five minutes from the Aquinnah Cliffs. Because Frederika had never seen them before, Anna parked the car and said, "I have a surprise for you." All Frederika could do was follow.

At the edge of the cliffs, Anna held Christine and Susan's hands as they awed at the crashing waves, the truly staggering rocks. Frederika was captivated. In another language— probably German, Anna decided— she whispered something to herself.

"Do they have anything like this back where you came from?" Anna asked.

Frederika shook her head. "All I ever knew was farmland. I never saw the sea, and certainly not a sea like this."

Anna continued to watch Frederika. Emotion transformed her face, and for a little while, Anna thought she was going to cry again.

"We should go," Frederika said abruptly, turning away from the cliffs, her hand over her baby's head.

"I'm sorry," Anna tried.

Frederika side-eyed her. "There is no reason to apologize. You have shown me something extraordinary."

Anna led her daughters back to the car, with Frederika walking a little ways ahead, her spine straight as a rod. When they reached the car, Frederika remained standing next to the car, catching a last glimpse of the riotous cliffs behind her.

When they reached Val and Mrs. Gilbert's place, Anna was initially frightened that nobody was home. It would have been such a shame, all that drama and preparation for no reason at all. But as they mounted the front steps of the cottage, they could hear the murmur of television on the inside. Anna rang the doorbell. It was time.

The woman who answered the front door was in her mid-seventies. Her white hair hung in coils down her shoulders, and her nightgown looked like a cartoon ghost around her frame. For a long time, she frowned at Anna through the screen.

"Hello, Mrs. Gilbert! I'm Anna Sheridan. We must have met before. Maybe at the parade?"

Mrs. Gilbert cracked open the screen door and took in the sight: two babies, two little girls, and two women in their twenties.

"I'm not buying anything," she told them.

"We aren't selling anything," Anna said, smiling. "We just want to ask you a few questions, if that's okay."

"About what?" Mrs. Gilbert's tone was hard.

Anna wrinkled her nose. She hadn't thought Mrs. Gilbert would be so unfriendly. She'd assumed, as an islander, she would be warm and inviting, grateful for the opportunity to chat with strangers. She'd assumed she would be lonely.

"My friend knew your husband," Anna said, stuttering slightly. "We're so sorry for your loss."

Mrs. Gilbert glared at Frederika as Anna scrambled for a way to get in, to make Mrs. Gilbert more comfortable.

"How did you know him?" Mrs. Gilbert demanded.

Frederika looked pained. Clearly, she hadn't expected such resistance from the wife of the person who'd pledged to help her. "My husband and Val Gilbert wrote one another letters." Her accent was clearly German, and Mrs. Gilbert recoiled.

"You're one of them," Mrs. Gilbert grumbled. "One of the horrific people who stressed my Val out. You know, it's people like you who killed him? He had a bad heart. He couldn't take it anymore, not after everything he'd seen."

Frederika's shoulders slumped forward.

"We are so, so sorry for your loss," Anna repeated, fumbling.

"Your husband was a wonderful man," Frederika whispered. "When I came to the island and learned he died, I knew the world had lost something enormous."

Mrs. Gilbert was captivated by her. She hung on her every word.

"Do you know how many people he helped?" Frederika continued, sounding breathless. "So many people wake up every morning and think of Val Gilbert, of what he did for them. That's immortality, Mrs. Gilbert. He's a hero."

Mrs. Gilbert's eyes glinted with tears. Slowly, she opened the screen door a little bit more, peering down at Christine and Susan.

"Why are you here?" Mrs. Gilbert's voice had softened.

"Your husband helped my husband and I travel to the United States," Frederika explained. "But my husband was detained when we arrived. I imagine your husband would have known where he would be kept, who I can contact for more information on how to free him."

Mrs. Gilbert's eyes swam. "You still haven't heard from him?"

Frederika shook her head.

"How long has it been?"

"Six weeks," Anna answered. "We're very worried."

Mrs. Gilbert stalled for a long time, weighing up whether or not it was worth it to get involved, to let her guard down. In the silence, Christine yawned, her mouth opening wider, and looked up at Anna to ask, "Mama? Can I have a glass of water?"

The sweetness of Christine's voice broke Mrs.

Gilbert. Swiftly, she opened the door and beckoned for them to enter, leading Christine to the kitchen to fetch her water. Anna and Frederika locked eyes for a moment, both fearful. The living room at the front of the house had been decorated with numerous old photographs from the life and times of Val Gilbert. In several photographs, he wore his uniform from his old days in the USSR government. He looked handsome and sturdy, the perfect cover for spying. Probably, everyone believed whatever he said.

This was the way the world worked, Anna knew. People believed in good-looking people.

Anna, Frederika, Susan, and Christine sat in the living room across from Mrs. Gilbert. Christine had drunk her glass of water and was now drawing little patterns in the thick brown carpeting. By the grace of God, Lola was still asleep.

"I am very sorry about your husband," Mrs. Gilbert said to Frederika, pulling her hair behind her ears. As though she suddenly realized what state she was in, she looked down at her nightgown, terrified, and said, "And I must look terrible. Gosh. I am sorry."

"We dropped in on you unannounced," Anna was quick to say. "That was rude of us."

"We used to do that all the time," Mrs. Gilbert said dreamily. "Val just loved this island. He loved how friendly everyone was. He said that back in his home country, people were much cagier."

"Everyone is spying on everyone else," Frederika breathed. "It's impossible to trust anyone."

Mrs. Gilbert nodded. "He told me that, darling. You're from East Germany, aren't you?"

Frederika nodded.

"He just loved Germany," Mrs. Gilbert said. "Of

course, his love for Poland never died. He taught me how to make so many classic recipes. Pierogis were a favorite. I still make them from time-to-time when I have the energy."

Slowly, Mrs. Gilbert reached for a stack of envelopes on the table next to the couch. With a staggering sigh, she said, "I haven't had the strength to open these. Not since he died." She handed them across the room to Frederika, who gaped at them.

"This is from my husband," Frederika breathed. "Before we left the country."

Mrs. Gilbert nodded. "I assumed so, honey."

Frederika opened the envelope and removed the letter within, which she blinked down at, flabbergasted. "He never taught me the code."

"Me neither." Mrs. Gilbert smiled simply, and for a moment, the two women on the other side of this letter correspondence smiled at one another, lost for the same reasons.

"Do you speak German or Polish?" Frederika asked.

"A bit of this, a bit of that." Mrs. Gilbert waved her hand. "Val was such a good teacher. We spent hours hobbling from one language to another. I loved learning new things in my older age." She frowned and dropped her head forward. "I have lost my love for everything now."

Anna's heart flipped over. She imagined herself, many years from now, a widow. What would she do if Wes died? How would she fill her days? Oh, it broke her heart to think about it.

"What are the other letters?" Anna asked.

Frederika handed them over. One was from a records office in Boston, and Anna tore it open and read the information regarding the passports for Frederika and her husband.

"Do you think your husband could be here?" Anna asked, pointing to the address on the envelope.

"I don't know," Frederika breathed.

"We can contact them," Anna said. "As far as they know, you haven't broken the law. They've retained your husband, but that's all we know. And we won't let them take you. No way, no how."

Frederika's chin quivered, and she adjusted her baby on her chest. "Thank you."

Mrs. Gilbert walked them to the front door, where she hugged Frederika and wished her well. She hardly looked at Anna, which was okay. Anna wasn't really a part of this story. She just wanted to help Frederika through it.

Back at the car, Anna surprised herself by asking, "Can you drive?"

Frederika nodded. "Yes. I had to drive often at home."

"Do you miss it?"

Frederika eyed the keys in Anna's hand and rubbed her molars together. "I do."

Anna had the sense that if she had lost all of her power and her entire life, she would want to take a small bit of that power back. Now that Frederika had latched her baby in a car seat in the back, she threw the keys at her. Frederika caught them easily and nodded.

With Frederika in the front seat, there was no radio. She drove over the speed limit but with a sense of power and assuredness, so Anna wasn't nervous, and neither were the children. Frederika drove along country roads for nearly forty minutes, slightly tilted forward, burning rubber, and holding her breath. It was a type of therapy Anna knew. And when they returned to the Sunrise Cove Inn later that afternoon, Frederika turned the engine off and gasped for breath, saying, "I really needed that." It had felt like freedom.

Chapter Thirteen

Present Day

Lola was slightly afraid of Anna's old journals. It was always like peering into her soul, reading her poetic and emotional thoughts, learning of the menial events of her day, and it was always painful, leaving her reeling for hours, gasping for breath. She wanted to know more about her mother and sit with her, here in the middle of her life, and ask her questions about what came next.

For this reason, instead of diving into the diaries first, Lola took to the photo albums her mother had kept in the early eighties. Photos were less painful; they showed happier moments, times when either Anna or Wes had said, "Oh, we'd better get the camera!" You didn't get the camera out when things were going badly, not when you resented your spouse or wanted to hide away in your room and reconsider every decision you've ever made.

And, because Lola and Audrey were now seasoned in

parsing through old documents from the archives, they found what they were looking for really quickly.

"Is this Frederika?" Lola placed the photo onto the table between herself and Susan. It was of a twenty-something woman with high cheekbones and curly blond hair, seated at the edge of the dock with a baby on her chest. She smiled seriously as though she wasn't sure she knew the meaning of happiness. And, on the back of the photograph, Anna (or someone else) had written just one letter: F.

"I believe so," Susan said, picking up the photograph to give herself a better look. They were seated on the back porch of Susan's place, there with Audrey and Amanda, watching the sun drop into the Vineyard Sound.

"How sure are you?" Audrey asked.

"I don't know. Seventy percent? My memories are all in sepia," Susan said. "And remember, I was only seven. Everything is foggy."

Lola shrugged. "Seventy percent is pretty good."

"What does that mean for our next step?" Audrey asked.

Lola wagged her eyebrows. "I've already contacted the Boston Library archives!"

"Oh my gosh." Audrey rolled her eyes into a smile. "Again?"

"Again and again until we get to the bottom of this, baby doll," Lola said. "I'm sure that librarian can't wait to see us again."

"We're the only people who've gone back there in one hundred years," Audrey joked.

"What will you do if you find Frederika again?" Susan asked.

"I'm not sure," Lola said. "But if she was here because

of Val Gilbert, maybe she knew others who came to the island with his help. Maybe she even keeps in touch with some of them. And maybe she once learned about Claudia's parents, about a baby they'd had to leave behind in Chicago." Lola shrugged. "It isn't a lot to go on, but it's all we have. And I'm fully intrigued with Frederika. I wonder what she remembers of our mother. What she can tell us."

Susan nodded, her eyes cloudy. "If you do find her, tell her hello from me. She was a remarkable woman. I remember feeling sad when she went away. I wish I could remember the circumstances."

"Was it sudden?" Lola asked.

"I don't remember," Susan admitted. "I wish I could tell you more."

Suddenly, Amanda erupted from the table and fled into the house, her hand over her mouth. Lola, Audrey, and Susan watched her go, grimacing. Amanda's morning sickness extended across all hours of the day, so that she was hardly able to keep much more than a few crackers down at a time.

"Poor girl," Lola breathed.

"I feel terrible about it," Susan admitted.

"I'll go get another ginger ale from the fridge," Audrey said. "Maybe that will help."

When Amanda returned to the back porch, her cheeks were blotchy, and her eyes were lined with red. Audrey handed her the ginger ale, and she thanked her and cracked it open, collapsing into the chair beside her mother.

"Sorry about that," she said.

"What! You don't have to be sorry!" Lola said.

Amanda sighed. "I'm just glad you guys stopped

chasing after me to make sure I'm okay." She kicked Audrey gently under the table.

"I didn't know what to do," Audrey said with a laugh. "I'm not used to being worried about you!"

Susan opened a package of crackers and slid them across the table. Amanda crunched the edge of one, saying, "I wanted to be pregnant for years! The reality is interesting, to say the least."

"It will pass," Lola told her.

"I'm going to make you so many recipes, the way you did for me," Audrey said excitedly.

Susan and Lola's eyes met over the table as Amanda and Audrey chatted easily, squabbling here and there about what Audrey would cook and whether Amanda would help her. It warmed Lola's heart that their daughters were so close. It wasn't a reality she and Susan had shared back in the day, as their age difference had been too large. That, and Susan had run away.

"Do you think Mom would have known all about Frederika's past?" Lola asked thoughtfully. Her mind was never far from the story at hand. "I mean, if Frederika really was from Eastern Germany like we suspect."

"I have to assume she did," Susan said. "They spent so much time together. Frederika worked at the inn. If she wasn't legally allowed to work here, Mom and Dad must have had to pay her some other way."

"I have a hunch people worked under the table a lot more back then," Lola offered.

Susan shrugged. "Sure. But I don't think it was the norm. And Dad always upheld tax laws or tried to, because he was scared of getting into trouble. He never wanted the inn to be taken away from him."

Lola nodded, thinking of her father, miles away in

A Vineyard Tide

Beatrice's home— building a new life. Lola hadn't yet stopped by since his move-in, but she'd heard the house was small, one story, which was necessary for the approaching years of Wes' tired knees, his aging body. Lola was so grateful he didn't have to go through that alone.

Chapter Fourteen

1983

When they returned home from Val Gilbert and Mrs. Gilbert's residence on the opposite coastline, Anna decided not to waste any time. She called the number on the letter, hoping whoever answered would be able to tell them where Frederika's husband was being kept. Her worst fear was that her husband had been sent back to Eastern Germany, that he hadn't been allowed to contact Frederika at all. This would doom their marriage and their future forever.

But the woman who answered Anna seemed not to know anything at all.

"May I ask who's calling?"

"My name is Anna Sheridan. My friend's husband has been detained due to supposedly inappropriate paperwork. I would like to know who to contact to find out where he is being held?"

"I don't know what you mean. Detained? We handle passports, Ms. Sheridan."

Anna rolled her eyes into the back of her head, frustrated. "Could I speak to your boss? Or someone in charge there?"

The secretary's voice was higher pitched. "I can take a message, of course. What would you like me to tell Mr. Johnson?"

Anna grumbled. "Could I leave my name and number and ask that he call me?"

"Absolutely!" The secretary took Anna's name and number, then chirped, "Is there anything else?"

"Is there any other way to contact him?"

The woman seemed cagey. "I suppose if you send a formal letter, Mr. Johnson would eventually find the time to read it."

Anna brightened at this thought. The letter they'd taken from Mrs. Gilbert had had an address. Perhaps wherever they sent a formal inquiry, they'd reach people who understood how dire their situation was.

But sending anything via mail also felt far too slow. It felt as though they'd never find Frederika's husband. And Anna knew that Frederika felt this way, too.

After Anna got off the phone, she put Lola in a crib downstairs, made sure Christine and Susan were preoccupied in the office within earshot of Wes, and went upstairs to tell Frederika what she'd learned— or not learned.

When Frederika opened the door, her face was streaked with tears, and her shoulders shook violently. Anna leaped into her hotel room, closed the door, and watched as Frederika again slumped onto her bed. She was surrounded by discarded tissues.

"I'm sorry," Frederika stuttered. "I'm getting so tired of crying in front of you."

"You don't have to apologize! And you have every

reason to cry." Anna sat next to Frederika and touched her shoulder. "It must feel overwhelming. Especially after that trip to Mrs. Gilbert's."

Frederika swallowed a lump in her throat. "I just can't help but feel like we're running into wall after wall. Like we'll never find him."

"All we can do is keep trying," Anna breathed. "All we can do is keep calling and mailing and pestering people until they give us answers." After a dramatic pause, she added, "I'm going to send a letter to that address from the envelope, demanding where your husband is. It's all I can think to do right now."

"You already called the phone number?"

Anna nodded. "I left a message, but I don't know if the secretary will be of any help to us."

Frederika's cheeks were slack. "I shouldn't be surprised at any of this. Ever since we got to the United States, everything has been a mess. When they first told me that the baby and I could go through but that my husband had to stay behind, I thought they were making some sort of horrible joke. Who would separate a family like that? We had already traveled halfway around the world! Besides that, my husband had spent almost all of our life savings to ensure Val Gilbert could arrange the passports."

"And they didn't say what was wrong with your husband's passport?"

Frederika shook her head. "No. Val was supposed to meet us there to help us with any problems, but, as you know, he died. It's possible it was random. They didn't want to put me and the baby through another trip back to Europe, but they could easily do that to him. Maybe they wanted to make an example of him. I don't know!" Frederika reached out to take Anna's hand. "I've been so frightened, almost every day and night, thinking that they'll find me here. That they'll take the baby away from me. That they'll send me back."

"You've been working here at the inn for almost six weeks," Anna reminded her. "And nobody has barged down the door. Nobody has demanded any paperwork. Nobody has even caught on that we're paying you under the table!"

Frederika gazed out the window, her eyes glazed. "I know that I relied too much on him, his heart, and his strength. I never imagined we'd ever be apart. And now, I've had to find a power within myself, one that I don't always trust."

"Your baby feels that power," Anna said quietly. "And I feel it, too. You're an inspiration, Frederika. And you're going to get through this. You're going to see your husband again. And you're going to find a way to make it in this country. I promise you that."

Frederika blinked back tears and began to gather up the tissues on the bed. "I can't believe what a mess I made."

"This isn't a mess," Anna insisted. "Why don't you come down to the Bistro with me? We can eat together, maybe open a bottle of wine?"

Frederika looked hesitant, but Anna was resolute. The worst thing in the world Frederika could do right now was hide away. Slowly, she inched toward the side of the room to set up the baby monitor, a gift from Anna. And then, she nodded and followed Anna to the door, where they retreated into the hallway, ready to face the evening. Within five minutes, Anna had taken a gorgeous bottle of German white wine from the bar and opened it at their table, winking as she said, "The perks of owning an inn!" And Frederika closed her eyes as she drank, her hair relaxed around her ears, her face shining from the sweat of the day. Anna's heart lifted at the vision of this woman who'd lost so much. They were only twenty-five years old. There was so much left to gain— and lose.

Chapter Fifteen

Present Day

Lola and Audrey were back in the library archives, up to their ears in documents and names and passport photographs— all for people who, if they weren't yet dead, were quite old, forty years past this traumatic event. As they searched for Frederika, they held up the photograph that Anna Sheridan had taken all those years ago, trying to find similar expressions, similar hair. In truth, a lot of the women from that area of the world looked similar to Frederika, with her high cheekbones and inability to smile with her whole face.

Lola and Audrey's three-hour block of time in the archives finished at two that afternoon. But they hadn't found anything, not one strand of evidence to take them further down the rabbit hole. And so, Lola stalked back to the front desk to speak to the same librarian with her thick-rimmed glasses.

"We need more time," Lola explained. "It's urgent."

The woman slid her glasses up her nose. "We have three-hour blocks of time for a reason."

"I understand that," Lola said, although she didn't, not really. "But we're very close to figuring out something huge. And we can't make it back to Boston for the rest of the week. This is our last chance."

The librarian grumbled and turned to her computer to check something, presumably the schedule. But Lola was pretty sure that they were the only people who ever went into those archives. They'd never seen anyone else.

"Very well," the librarian said. "I can give you two more hours. What do you think?"

"We'll take it."

Lola hurried back into the archives to find Audrey hunched over a large ledger filled with passport photographs and names.

"Anything?" Lola asked, hovering over her own ledger.

"Nothing."

Lola groaned, and Audrey touched her shoulder, this time being the strength that Lola needed instead of the other way around.

"We're going to find her. Or, if we don't, we're going to find something else that pushes us forward," she said. "We have to. We owe it to Claudia."

Lola set her jaw and continued her search, diving all the way through the spring of 1983, through summer, and entering into autumn. Still, every single woman named Frederika wasn't the Frederika in the photograph Anna had taken. There seemed to be no connection.

Audrey leaned back in her chair and rubbed her temples. They'd been in the archives for four and a half hours, far longer than normal, and Lola was beginning to

A Vineyard Tide

understand why the librarian arranged for three-hour sessions only. Your brain gave out eventually. You stopped being able to see things as they really were.

"Didn't Claudia say that her parents probably had to change their names?" Audrey said after a moment.

Lola nodded.

"Do you think Frederika was her original name? Or the one she changed to?" Audrey asked.

"Probably her original name," Lola said. "It sounds really German to me."

"Me, too. She must have picked a more American-sounding name for her new identity," Audrey said, her eyes stirring. "Which must have been after she knew Grandma. Right?"

Lola shrugged. "Maybe. Although maybe Mom preferred to call her by her original name to make things easier."

"But Frederika left Martha's Vineyard at some point," Audrey spoke quickly. "I mean, we don't know when exactly. But we didn't see any more photographs of her after that autumn."

Lola nodded. "You're right. So, we should look later in 1983?"

"For a woman who looks like Frederika but isn't named Frederika," Audrey said with a small laugh.

"It's getting more impossible by the second," Lola offered.

But miraculously, approximately ten minutes before the librarian would assuredly come to kick them out, Audrey shrieked, aligning the photograph of Frederika with a passport photograph of a woman who looked remarkably like her.

"Fiona! She changed her name to Fiona!"

Lola frowned, taking in the surly expression, the sorrow in the woman's eyes. Sure enough, Frederika was Fiona— Fiona Franklin.

"Look! She applied for passports with her family," Audrey continued, breathless. "Luke Franklin and their daughter, Claudia."

Lola's jaw dropped. There, beneath Fiona's photographs, were photos of a handsome man with thick black hair and a square jaw and a little girl, approximately one and a half years old. And sure enough, the little girl's name was listed as Claudia.

"Oh my gosh!" Lola cried, sitting back down in her chair. The world around her had tilted. "Claudia used to live at the Sunrise Cove!"

Audrey was pale with shock. Neither of them had suspected that Claudia's story would align so closely with theirs.

"But it doesn't make any sense," Audrey whispered, interrupting the silence. "Why would Frederika abandon her baby? It looks like they were all set up! Fiona, Luke, and Claudia were an American family! Look, it says here that they were legally born in Bangor, Maine!"

Audrey was right. These documents had been forged expertly. Lola saw them as real, American passports for people who'd been born on American soil. Why, then, had Frederika had to drop Claudia off in Chicago? And what had led them to Chicago in the first place?

"I guess it's possible this Claudia isn't our Claudia," Lola said reticently.

"The years add up. So does the last name," Audrey said.

"You're right."

"And Claudia knows she came to Chicago by way of Martha's Vineyard."

"The woman in charge of foster care told her that," Lola said. "And it's not like she's sure of anything."

Audrey raised her shoulders. "These are the clues we have to go on. We have to take them, if only to move forward."

Lola had heard herself recite this previously. She wasn't sure why, but learning that Frederika had lived alongside Anna, both with babies approximately the same age, had chilled her. For, if it was true, Claudia and Lola had been babies together before Claudia's parents had left her behind.

They'd both had their mothers at the same time, in the same place. And then, later, they'd lost them.

"We have our work cut out for us, I guess," Lola said with a sigh, taking numerous photographs of what they'd found just as the librarian walked into the archives, hitting her watch with her index finger.

"It's ten minutes past!" she called to them. "It's time for you to go!"

Lola and Audrey hurriedly put everything back and whipped past the librarian, laughing to themselves nervously until they were out of her sight. When they left the library, it was pouring rain, and Lola hailed a taxi expertly, grateful that they'd left the car at the hotel.

"Where are we going?" Audrey asked.

"I need comfort food," Lola said.

In fifteen minutes, the taxi dropped them off at the old diner they'd often frequented during their many years as Boston residents. Lola had fond memories of sitting there with little Audrey, as Audrey had drawn pictures or read books, and Lola had written articles for magazines or newspapers or whoever had hired her that week. It was in this diner she'd ripped herself to shreds for her dreams. Always, the grilled cheese sandwiches had helped lift her spirits.

Their booth was open. It felt like coming home, sitting at their old booth, and studying the menus that hadn't changed once, not in the twenty years since Lola had started coming.

"I don't know why I'm even reading this," Audrey said. "I know exactly what I'm getting."

The waitress who approached knew their names, and they knew hers.

"Connie!" Lola jumped up to hug her, inhaling the smell of her French fry hair. "How have you been?"

"I'm doing just fine." Connie placed two iced glasses of water on the table and clapped her hands. "You both look just stunning. How's the island?"

"It's nice," Audrey said, her eyes shining with nostalgia as she raised her phone to show photographs of Max. "This is my baby. We just moved in with my boyfriend, Noah."

Connie's smile was as bright as the sun. "You can't know how happy that makes me, honey. I wish you were here in Boston, close to me. But I'm thrilled you're back with that big family of yours! And I hope you're still writing?" She gave Lola a motherly look.

"We're working on a big project right now," Lola admitted. "It's part of the reason we're here. I'm exhausted! And I need fuel."

"Two grilled cheese sandwiches with extra cheese? Onion rings? Coleslaw?" Connie placed her hands on her hips, reciting their old order.

"You're brilliant, Connie," Lola said. "I don't know how you remember all this."

Connie winked. "They're begging me to bring my skills to the Pentagon, but I think my memory is better served here at the diner. Two coffees, too?"

"Yes, please," Audrey said.

After Connie whisked back through the swinging kitchen door, Audrey and Lola joined hands across the table. They wouldn't comment on what they both were thinking: that Connie looked older now that time had passed. That this meant they were older, too.

"Are you going to call Claudia?" Audrey asked.

Lola nodded. "I'm dreading it."

"Maybe she could confirm or deny if she looked like that as a baby?" Audrey suggested.

"She'd bound to feel very strange about all this," Lola said. "Especially because we still don't know why her parents left her behind if these are her parents."

Audrey winced.

"I was so excited to fall into this story," Lola breathed. "And now, I'm involved in the story. And it feels so intense. So real."

Very soon, Connie returned with platters piled high with three-level grilled cheeses, dripping with cheddar and Swiss, oily onion rings, and vinegar-y coleslaw. Lola and Audrey ate quietly as the jukebox in the corner played the top hits of the 1970s— years before Frederika had come to this country and changed her name. Time was moving forward. And it was impossible to know what would reveal itself next.

Chapter Sixteen

1983

After Anna sent a letter off to the passport office demanding where Frederika's husband was being held and what had happened to him, the waiting was horrific. Every day felt heavy with doubt. She walked to the mailbox with her heart in her throat, praying that somebody had written her back with the information. But August kept going, leaving them empty-handed, and then, it was September, and still, they had no answers.

Frederika had grown into the single most-capable worker at the inn, understanding the ins and outs of the place better than Wes did, sometimes. She was organized and hardly ever got tired, and she insisted on doing everything by the letter in a way that Wes wasn't able to, as he was almost always overworked. The staff members and surrounding islanders respected her, and Anna found in Frederika a wonderful, if often serious, friend. Anna hadn't fully realized how lonely she'd been in motherhood before Frederika had come into her life. A part of her, selfishly, hoped she would remain in their world forever.

In bed one night, Anna finally confessed to Wes that she and Frederika were hard at work looking for Frederika's husband. Wes propped himself up on his elbow and looked at her through the darkness as a September rain pattered across the windowpane.

"Why are you just telling me this now?"

"Frederika swore me to secrecy."

"And have you tracked him down?" Wes asked.

"No," Anna breathed, her voice wavering. "When I called the number, the secretary was very rude to me. I wrote a letter, but I haven't heard anything back."

"I'm going to call them tomorrow," Wes insisted, his voice gritty.

"No! Wes, I promised Frederika I wouldn't tell anyone about this."

But Wes was determined. "Just let me try, Anna. I can't stand the thought of Frederika living out her days broken-hearted. Let me help you get to the bottom of this." In the dark, Wes took Anna's hand gently. "Let me be the husband you deserve."

And so, the following morning, before Frederika got to the desk for her shift, Wes made the same call Anna did, presumably reaching the same secretary. But there was a difference this time.

He was a man.

"Good morning! How are you doing?" Wes sounded confident and sure of himself. "I wondered if you could help me with a problem. A friend of mine was on his way to the United States. I was supposed to pick him up from the train station here in New York City, but he never showed up. Would you be able to tell me where he wound up?" Wes' eyes were illuminated as he listened to whatever the secretary responded. "That would be fantastic. Thank you so much. What was your name? Genevieve. That's a pretty name."

Anna rolled her eyes and smiled. Wes' charms worked on everyone. Not long after that, Wes frowned and scribbled an address on a piece of paper. "That's where he's being held, Genevieve? Okay. And he's going to be sent back home in the next month or two? So, I had better hurry to make sure I see him. Okay. Thank you so much for your help."

Wes hung up and blinked at Anna, who was trying not to cry. Anna hugged him and whispered, "I can't believe you found him. Thank you so, so much."

She couldn't believe she hadn't considered asking for his help before this. It had been so easy for him. It almost made her angry, the walls that were built in front of women that men so easily bolted through. But it was 1983. That was just how the world worked.

Because there wasn't long to wait, Anna requested to Wes that Frederika have the day off. This way, they could go immediately to the facility on the outskirts of Boston.

"I won't be able to watch the girls," Wes said, palming the back of his neck. "Maybe you could ask Kerry?"

"Kerry's busy all week," Anna said. "She's got houses to sell and four children to take care of. But the girls can come along with us. They've been a part of Frederika's journey from the beginning. I hope they'll learn something. Something about human compassion and the spirit of perseverance."

"Let's hope they don't learn something much worse," Wes said with a sigh. "I wish I could come with you." He bent and kissed Anna with his eyes closed, there at the front desk in front of the milling breakfast goers. It had been a long time since he'd shown so much affection for her in public. Anna felt renewed in her love for him.

Frederika appeared at the front desk a few minutes later, her eyes bright and focused on the day ahead. When she saw Anna's face, hers fell instantly. She knew something was up.

"What happened?"

Anna explained what she'd found out, omitting the fact that Wes had been the one to call. She didn't want to complicate things.

"We should go this morning," Anna said. "Apparently, they're planning to send him back in a month or two."

Frederika set her jaw and hurried back upstairs to fetch Ricarda, her coat, and their passports. By the time she returned downstairs, Anna had coats on Susan, Christine, and Lola. They were ready.

Just like all the other times they'd traveled together, they put the two baby car seats on both sides of the backseat and strapped Susan and Christine together in the middle. The girls were so small, cuddled close to one another, Susan with a book always in hand and Christine lost in thought. Anna kissed them on the cheeks and thanked them for being so good. Susan glowed at the compliment, looked up at Frederika, and said, "Dankeschön!" Frederika laughed through tears.

"I've been teaching her German here and there," she explained. "I hope you don't mind."

"Mind? You've been giving my daughter language lessons for free! You're brilliant."

Anna drove them to the ferry, where they let the girls out to run around the top deck as Anna and Frederika hung back, holding Lola and Ricarda. Clouds spit rain, and the horizon of the water was a similar gray to the sky. Anna was grateful when they were back in the car, protected from the whipping winds.

Throughout the drive to the facility outside of Boston, Anna and Frederika were quiet. Occasionally, Susan could be heard in the backseat, reading aloud to Christine. When they parked outside the brown-brick building, Frederika exhaled all the air from her lungs and whispered, "I don't know how in the world I'll be able to keep him here. They already have plans to send him back!"

Anna took Frederika's hand. "He's going to stay in the United States. You hear me?"

Frederika nodded, but her eyes were hard and guarded. She didn't believe her.

Lola had fallen asleep, a blessing after having woken Anna up three times during the night, and Anna held her carrier by the handle and walked on her tiptoes so she wouldn't bother her. Susan and Christine held hands through the parking lot as Frederika charged up ahead, holding Ricarda.

The entry of the facility featured a very long white desk. A woman sat behind it. When she spoke, Anna recognized her voice. She was the secretary she'd spoken to on the phone all those weeks ago. And yes, her name was Genevieve.

"Hello," Anna said, trying to disguise her voice. "We are here to visit one of the men kept here."

Frederika nodded. "His name is Moritz Busenburg."

The secretary looked down at the ledger before her, frowning as she read the very long list of names.

"We allow thirty-minute visits," Genevieve told her. "You won't be able to take your baby."

A Vineyard Tide

Frederika's eyes glinted with tears.

"I'll take her," Anna said firmly. "Go."

Slowly, Frederika removed Ricarda from the strap around her chest and handed her to Anna, who rocked her gently. She'd gotten considerably heavier in the three months since they'd come to the island, and already, Anna's arms were strained. But she remained in the foyer, watching as the secretary led Frederika deeper into the facility toward her husband. Anna thought she might burst into tears.

As they waited, Susan, Christine, and Anna sat on plastic chairs in the waiting room. Anna continued to hold Ricarda, praying she wouldn't start crying, as Lola slept in her carrier. Susan was reading another book to Christine, proud to be able to translate stories to her sister. All the while, Anna stared at the hallway Frederika had disappeared down, terrified for her.

Just now, she was struck with the idea that Frederika would be detained, too. Maybe this was a trap. Her mouth was dry with fear, and Anna closed her eyes. If Frederika and Moritz were sent back, she would raise Ricarda as her own. She would love her with everything she was.

But that would be a tragedy, one Anna wanted to avoid.

There was a payphone on the far wall. "I'm going to call your daddy," Anna told her girls, hoisting Ricarda up and walking away. She dialed the Sunrise Cove Inn and was unsurprised when Wes answered on the first ring.

"Hello! This is the Sunrise Cove Inn, Wes speaking. How may I help you?"

"Wes? Baby? It's me." Anna's voice broke. She was suddenly, overwhelmingly sad. All she wanted to do was be held by him.

"Hi, honey." Wes was very quiet. "Where are you calling from?"

"That terrible place," Anna said. "You should see it. It's like a prison."

Wes sighed. "Did Frederika see him?"

"She's with him now. She left the baby with me. Oh, I'm frightened. I hope they don't keep her back there. Maybe it was a trap?"

"They wouldn't have let her go in the first place if there was something wrong with her paperwork," Wes said.

Anna knew that was logical. But she wasn't thinking logically right now.

"I love you," Anna blurted, surprising herself with how quickly it came out. "Gosh, I'm just sitting here thinking about you. About how frightened I am. And how grateful I am that you're in my life."

"I love you, too," Wes breathed. "I'm sorry I'm so cranky all the time."

Anna laughed gently, tears filling her eyes. "You work so hard. I know it's for me. For us."

"Thank goodness we weren't born in an oppressive country," Wes said. "We never had to escape anything."

"Ours are normal problems," Anna breathed. "They're just like everybody else's."

Wes was quiet for a moment. "I took tonight off. I want to be with you and the girls."

"Good," Anna whispered.

"We can order pizza and stay in," Wes said.

Anna nodded into the phone, squeezing her eyes shut. Nothing made any sense. "I'm going to make sure he can stay, Wes. I don't know how yet. But I'm going to figure it out."

A Vineyard Tide

"I know you will," Wes whispered. "You're Anna Sheridan. You're the strongest person I know."

When Frederika reappeared, she was white as chalk. She collected Ricarda in her arms, closed her eyes, and remained like that, standing as solid as a tree, until Genevieve came into the waiting room and said they were preparing to close.

Back in the car, Anna watched as Frederika latched Ricarda into her car seat and got into the passenger side. With her girls safely in the back, Anna clambered in and started the engine. She knew better than to ask Frederika to speak before she was ready.

It was only when they were on the ferry, the wind off the Vineyard Sound rushing through their hair and the girls running across the deck, that Frederika finally spoke.

"He was so skinny," she whispered. "So, so skinny."

And Anna's heart cracked at the edges, sensing the horror of being a wife incapable of caring for her husband. It was all Frederika wanted to do.

Chapter Seventeen

Two days after their trip to Boston, Anna packed the girls up in the car and drove to the Oak Bluffs Central Library. Susan was enthusiastic throughout the drive, as the library was her favorite place in the world. "How many books can I borrow, Mom? Ten? Fifteen?" And when they reached the front door, Christine burst through and hurried toward the children's section, where there was an enormous selection of crayons, colored pencils, and craft paper. Anna waved to the children's librarian downstairs, who waved back and said, "I can take them from here if you want to browse upstairs. Even the little one!"

Anna removed Lola from her carrier, and Lola whipped toward the table, a speed-demon now that her walking had gotten so much better. Christine showed her how to pull a crayon over a piece of paper, and Lola babbled and squawked as the librarian laughed.

"I promise, Anna. You can go. Take some time for yourself!"

Anna thanked her and hurried upstairs, away from

the sounds of her laughing children and toward the front desk. There, she folded her arms over the counter, smiled at the head librarian, and said, "Gregory! How are you today?"

"Just fine, Anna. I have a few books on hold for you. That thriller you were after is available, as is that historical World War II novel."

"Oh! Wonderful." Anna had completely forgotten that she'd put holds on anything.

"You're not here for them," Gregory said with a smile.

"Actually, could you help me with something? I need to learn everything there is to know about immigration law in the state of Massachusetts and across the United States. But I need it dumbed down, if possible. I never went to law school. Or any college, for that matter."

Gregory led Anna to a section of the library she'd never seen before, where he pulled out three very thick textbooks.

"Law students usually study these when they take the bar," he explained. "Maybe they'll be of help?"

Anna swallowed the lump in her throat and nodded. "Can I check them out?"

With the books under her arm, Anna returned to the children's area, where Lola, Christine, and Susan were playing with the children's librarian. Again, the librarian shooed Anna away, telling her to take a few minutes to read. So, Anna went to a private room, opened to the first page of the thickest textbook, and found herself up to her ears in legal jargon she couldn't possibly comprehend. Tears filled her eyes. This felt like too much for any one person.

But then again, she was all Frederika had. She had to do this.

Forty minutes later, Anna collected her children from the next room. The children's librarian looked vaguely shellshocked, as though it had just occurred to her that three little girls all at once was a whole lot of work. Anna had read the first chapter in a book about immigration law — and she had fifty-seven chapters, plus two books left. It was a start.

"Thank you for watching them," Anna said, collecting Lola into her arms as Christine and Susan danced in the center of the room.

"Of course!" The babysitter looked on the verge of passing out, and her hair had fallen from its ponytail. "Have a wonderful day."

Back at home, Lola remained awake, playing happily with her older sisters. Anna set herself up at the kitchen table with a cup of tea and a bowl of popcorn, where she continued to read throughout the afternoon and early evening. Eventually, her girls reminded her of dinner, of everything she was meant to do, and she hurried around the kitchen, scrambling to make macaroni and cheese. Christine was so tired after a day of play that she fell asleep on her cheek at the table.

With Lola, Christine, and Susan in bed, Anna continued to read, at least until Lola woke up around ten and demanded her attention. Wes ambled in as well, took a look at the legal textbooks on the kitchen table, and shivered.

"Is Lola helping you with that?" he asked, taking Lola in his arms to allow Anna to collapse on the couch.

"Lola is studying for the bar," Anna joked, yawning a split-second later.

"Let's all go to bed," Wes insisted. "How many hours have you spent reading that today?"

Anna grimaced. "You don't want to know."

The following few days went just the same as the first. Anna took every spare minute to read the legal texts, trying to cultivate a plan that would save Frederika and Moritz. And when she finally did come up with something, she kept it to herself for a good forty-eight hours just so she could read up on all the ways it might go wrong.

Ultimately, she was pretty sure this was foolproof. And that terrified her because she felt that something would creep up and tear her plan apart. She had no idea what it would be.

When Anna first explained the plan to Wes, she sat him down at the kitchen table after the girls went to bed and asked him to keep an open mind.

"Uh oh," Wes said. "That scares me."

"I swear to you, it isn't risky," Anna went on. "It's the most obvious way forward, and I really think it will work."

Wes folded his arms. "Come on. Tell me."

"Everything I've read points to this. If a business sponsors a foreigner's visa, it means they can stay. That means, if we at the Sunrise Cove can prove that Moritz is an integral part of our business strategy, the American government legally has to let him stay."

Wes leaned back in his chair. "You want to put the Sunrise Cove at risk?"

"It won't be," Anna hurried to remind him. "It's the most obvious strategy. And I don't think that Moritz and Frederika will want to remain here for long, anyway. Martha's Vineyard was never their final plan, and Frederika doesn't want to keep her name. She wants to distance herself from the Soviet Union as much as she can."

Wes set his jaw, thinking hard. Anna loved him so much, but right now, she wanted to scream at him, to tell him that she'd spent days and days reading those legal textbooks. This was the only way!

Finally, Wes asked, "How are they going to change their names?"

"I'm going to contact Mrs. Gilbert again," Anna said. "I'm sure there's more information at Val Gilbert's place, in one envelope or another."

Wes closed his eyes as Anna reached across the table and took his hand.

"We have to help these people in any way we can, Wes," Anna breathed. "It's the only way."

Resigned, Wes dropped his chin to his chest, exhausted from the day, from the constant need of the girls, from the money that seemed to drain continually from their account. "All right," he said. "If you think it will work, let's do it."

Anna leaped up and ran around the table to hug him, her heart stirring. "It's going to work," she told herself and him. "Everything is going to be fine."

The next morning, Frederika was at the front desk of the Sunrise Cove, bright and cheery with the customers. Anna entered, waved, went to the head office to file some paperwork, then returned to the foyer to say hello. When it was just the two of them, Frederika deflated. She was losing steam and hope at a very fast rate.

"I have a plan," Anna whispered.

Frederika looked unconvinced. "Whatever it is, it's too dangerous. I don't want to put your family at risk."

"You don't want to live in this country without him,"

Anna told her. "You'd rather be sent back with him than live without him. Wouldn't you?"

Frederika's eyes glistened with fear. "I don't know. I really don't."

Anna nodded. Frederika was caught between a rock and a hard place. Perhaps she wouldn't have to make that choice.

Quietly, Anna explained the plan she'd come up with, showing Frederika the paperwork she'd already filled out, stating that Moritz was the perfect Director of Tourism for the Sunrise Cove's new department.

"We need someone to help with hiking tours, boating tours, food tours, and horseback riding tours," Anna explained brightly. "The demand from our guests is huge. And your husband's exquisite talents and experience in the world of tourism will go a long way."

Frederika frowned. "Tourism? He worked as an engineer."

"He's going to have to lie," Anna breathed. "Maybe you can help me write a resumé for him based on past experiences. Maybe we can say he worked at a hotel in East Germany, where he did these sorts of activities."

Frederika bit her lower lip. "It's risky."

"It's all we have," Anna whispered. "If it goes through, you and Moritz can work here for a little while, at least until I figure out how to get you new passports with different names."

Frederika closed her eyes. "I think I have a cousin in Chicago. I'd like to go."

Anna's heart lifted. Frederika had never mentioned a cousin in the country. "You have family here?"

"She left East Germany five years ago," Frederika said. "That was the beginning of our obsession with leaving. She sent several letters from Chicago before we left, talking about what a wonderful country this was. About how much opportunity there was for her husband."

Frederika reached into her pocket and removed a worn and folded envelope upon which someone had written an address in Chicago. Anna understood that Frederika was drawn to that like a moth to the flame. But she couldn't leave her husband out east. She couldn't begin her new life without him.

"We're going to get all three of you to Chicago," Anna said softly, touching her shoulder. "Mark my words."

Frederika nodded stiffly and shoved the envelope back into her pocket. "I need him," Frederika breathed. "I don't want to go on without him."

"And you won't," Anna stated. "It's going to be fine."

Chapter Eighteen

Present Day

This deep in August, Lola knew it was even more difficult to find time to meet with Claudia. As a professor, she was entrenched in her work, preparing for another semester of dutiful students who were hungry for her wisdom— and willing to pay thousands and thousands of dollars for it. Claudia was the kind of woman who did everything to the max, who went out of her way for her students if they asked her to. When Lola emailed Claudia to ask if she had time to meet, Claudia wrote back:

I would love to! I could come to the island next weekend. Just for an afternoon, though. I'm swamped with work, otherwise.

Lola wrote back immediately, saying she understood Claudia was up to her ears in preparations for the new semester. She was happy to come to Boston again. In fact, she'd begun to adore the back-and-forth from the island to the city as she felt more connected to previous versions of herself. She also was so lost in researching that she couldn't sit still, and the drives and ferry rides were wonderful distractions, forcing her mind away from marking endless circles around the same pieces of evidence. She was beginning to drive herself crazy.

"I think I'll go alone." Lola was with Audrey at her little cabin, watching as Max hopped around, playing with the trains and toy cars Lola kept here for him.

"Are you sure?" Audrey tilted her head.

Lola bit her lip. "If it's true that Claudia is Frederika's daughter, then that means we've met before— as toddlers. We were younger than Max!"

"It's a lot to take in," Audrey agreed. "Maybe it's better one-on-one."

"That's what I was thinking," Lola offered. "Especially because, in the end, we both lost our mothers— her as a baby and me about a decade later. And I keep coming back to that. It keeps breaking my heart."

That Saturday morning, Lola woke up at the same time as Tommy and propped herself up with pillows, listening as the shower rained down upon his sturdy frame. When he emerged, his black hair was slicked back behind his ears, and he was shirtless, parading his muscles around the bedroom as he got out his shirt and pants. Lola stretched her arms out to hug him, and he bent down to kiss her gently.

"Good morning, baby," he said.

Lola's heart swelled. "You have a tour today?" Tommy often took tourists around the island by sailboat for extra cash. He enjoyed meeting people from all over the world and regaling his endless stories from his sailing adventures. They lapped up Tommy's charms— and how could Lola blame them?

"I do," Tommy said. "Can't believe you're headed back to Boston."

"I'll be home tonight," Lola said, pressing her nose to his.

"You've been working too hard," Tommy told her. "Sometimes, when I look at you, it's like you're not really here."

Lola wrinkled her nose. "I'm sorry I've been so distracted."

"I'm pulling for you to finish this," Tommy said. "But at the same time, I want at least one more night, just us, before the weather shifts."

"To do what?" Lola teased.

Tommy raised his shoulders. "Lola Sheridan, I want to take you for a wild ride on my sailboat. That thing is a chick magnet! And I can't even get my girl out on it!"

Lola laughed, her shoulders loosening.

"What about tonight?" Tommy pressed it.

"Tonight what?"

"Let's go for a sail when you get back," Tommy urged. "It'll be the perfect way to take your mind off of Boston and the very best way to start a beautiful Saturday night on the island."

"Okay. I think you talked me into it," Lola said.

Tommy snapped his fingers. "Great. After my tour, I'll go shopping for a world-class picnic. Bring your appetite back with you, okay? Don't eat too many hoagies or whatever you eat up in Boston."

"That's Philly!" Lola threw a pillow at Tommy as he raced away from her, laughing. She was so grateful for him, for his sturdy presence in her life, and for his endless laughter. She wasn't sure what she'd done without him—and still thanked the heavens that she'd had the nerve to approach him on the docks back in August 2020, that heinous summer when Susan had had breast cancer, and everything had been in flux.

Lola drove to Boston by herself for the first time in a while, often wishing Audrey was there if only to harmonize with the nineties songs she sang, her vibrato soaring to the sky. Recently, Sinéad O'Connor had passed away, and Lola played her version of "Nothing Compares 2 U," her eyes filling with tears. It had been a favorite of hers when it had come out, and the passion and heartbreak behind her voice was even more painful now. At the end of the song, Lola had to turn it off and sit in silence for a little while, overwhelmed by it.

Lola parked in the Boston University parking garage, paid for her spot, and headed for the History Building. Because the students weren't yet on campus, the stairwells and hallways were empty, echoing Lola's footsteps. Before knocking on Claudia's office door, she went into the bathroom and splashed water on her face, fearful.

The woman who opened the door and greeted Lola was the same woman Lola had met in July. But this time, when Lola looked at her, she saw Frederika in her face: the high cheekbones, the light curls, the blue eyes.

"Hello!" Lola's voice was slightly off-pitch, showing her nerves.

"Hi! I'm so grateful you came up here," Claudia said, showing her to her desk, where Lola sat. "I feel pathetically stressed out. I can't believe I thought for a second I could research this book for myself. I can't begin to thank you."

Lola's throat was tight. As Claudia poured her a glass of water, she glanced around at the walls and walls of history textbooks, the posters of important historical

A Vineyard Tide

moments, and the paintings that seemed to be done by Claudia herself. At least, she was pretty sure that was Claudia's name signed in the corner of each.

"So!" Claudia clasped her hands together. "What did you learn so far?"

Lola couldn't bring herself to smile. Over and over again, she'd practiced how she would explain what she'd maybe learned (or maybe not) about Claudia's parents, but now, she stumbled.

Instead of language, Lola took out the photographs she'd printed, all of which she'd taken in the archives of the Boston Library. The first photograph was of Claudia Franklin at one and a half years old. Immediately, Claudia's face fell.

"Oh my gosh." She was breathless, staring at the image as though it was a snake about to bite her. "Where did you find that?"

"So, it is you?" Lola asked.

Claudia swallowed. "There were three photographs taken of me as a toddler in Chicago. They all look like this." She shrugged. "That, and my last name is Franklin. At least, that's what I've always been told."

"As you've already been told, that's not your real last name," Lola said.

"Do you know what it is?"

Lola shook her head. "Unfortunately not."

"Then how did you find this?" Claudia gasped.

Slowly, Lola moved the passport photograph of toddler Claudia aside to show the passport photos of Frederika and her husband — updated for their new names, Fiona and Luke.

"Fiona and Luke Franklin," Claudia read. "These are my parents?"

"Their new names, yes," Lola said. "And your mother's real name was Frederika."

"How do you know that?" Claudia asked.

Lola shifted through her folder to find the photograph she'd found in Anna's album. "Gosh, I don't even know how to tell this story!"

"Try," Claudia urged. "Please."

Lola did her best. Really, she did. She talked about going through what felt like thousands of ledgers at the Boston Library archives. She talked about Val Gilbert, who was actually Aleksander Nowak. And then, she spoke of Susan's memory of a woman named Frederika, who lived at the Sunrise Cove for a while. She'd had a baby. And she'd spoken German.

"What is the Sunrise Cove Inn?" Claudia asked.

"It's my family's inn," Lola explained. "It's been in the family for a very long time. Generations. And somehow, you and your mother ended up staying there for a while during the summer and autumn of 1983."

"Forty years ago," Claudia whispered.

"This is a photo my mother took," Lola said, twisting it around to show her. "I thought she was a clue to Val Gilbert and his work in helping people escape the Eastern Bloc. My plan was to track her down and pepper her with questions. I had no idea this would turn out to be your mother."

"And have you looked her up? Do you know why she had to put me in the system?" Claudia spoke rapidly.

Lola had been dreading this part of the conversation. Of course, she'd googled Fiona and Luke Franklin almost immediately. But she hadn't found anything about them. Not one social media account. Not one death announcement. Nothing.

"You haven't found them." Claudia looked defeated, as though she regretted having opened this can of worms in the first place.

"No. I haven't. But I'm not done yet," Lola insisted.

Claudia's face was drawn. Again, she stared down at the photographs of her mother and father, taken forty years ago. There was a heaviness to the air in the room that made it difficult to breathe.

"I'm going to keep going, Claudia," Lola assured her. "This isn't over. Not by a long shot."

Claudia tried to smile, but it fell off her face. "Can I keep these photos?"

"Of course," Lola told her.

"Thank you." Claudia tucked them into her first office drawer and blinked away her tears. "And thank you for all your hard work, Lola."

"I have everything written down for you," Lola said. "It should be easy to draw from it for your memoir."

But Claudia seemed to have forgotten that she wanted to write about this at all. In fact, as Lola prepared to leave, Claudia remained in her office chair, staring into space, twirling a pencil between her fingers. She looked lost.

True to her word, Lola agreed to meet Tommy at the docks at seven that evening. She wore a mustard yellow dress that showed a little too much leg and a little too much chest. Fashion was the easiest route to boosting her mood she could think of. And when Tommy spotted her on the boardwalk, he whipped toward her, wrapped his arms around her waist, and whirled her in a circle.

"How did it go today?" Tommy set her down and took her small hand in his.

"Ugh. It was weird. Just as weird as I thought it would be."

"I'm sorry to hear that." Tommy stitched his brows together. "I'm sure she appreciates all the work you've done."

"I don't know if it's always good to learn the truth," Lola said.

"That's stupid," Tommy insisted. "As humans, we always want to understand. Even if it hurts us."

Lola swallowed and dropped her head against his chest. She wanted to curl up into a ball and sleep for days. But Tommy wouldn't let her. In fact, over the next several hours, bit by bit, Tommy helped her fall away from her anxious mind, drawing her into the mysticisms of the beautiful August night. Out in the sailboat, he popped champagne for them and showed off the picnic he'd made containing camembert, sharp Irish cheddar, fresh baguette, strawberries, raspberries, cured meats, hummus, and cannoli, in honor of his Italian roots. In a secluded cove, Tommy dropped anchor, and Lola curled against him, eating a strawberry and watching as the dying light of the evening played out in oranges and pinks across the stone wall of the cliffside. She wondered if, when Frederika had lived on the island, Anna had ever shown her such beauty. She hoped so.

Chapter Nineteen

1983

Due to his mastery of manipulation, after only a few phone calls, Wes arranged for an American visa for Moritz Busenburg to be fast-tracked. Anna listened to him, mesmerized, as he spoke first with Genevieve, then with her bosses over the phone, explaining to them that Moritz had actually come to the United States to work exclusively with the Sunrise Cove Inn.

"I was surprised when he didn't show up to work," Wes explained over the phone, booming with authority. He was seated at the office desk at the Sunrise Cove, twirling the phone code in his fingers, as Anna stood in front of him with Lola in her arms, gaping at this wonderful, lying man. "From what I know of Moritz Busenburg, which is quite a lot, he's a wonderful employee, a true treasure in hospitality. The Sunrise Cove is the tip of the iceberg in terms of our tourism future. Moritz is the secret to that." Wes paused for a moment, listening to whoever spoke on the other line. "You've been to Martha's Vineyard, haven't you? Your father had a house out here! What's his name?" Wes cackled into the phone. "Yes. My father used to play cards with him. I was sorry to hear he passed away. I suppose they both have, now. Yes, they were great men. Truly great."

All the while, Anna shook her head in shock as Wes spun a strong enough web for Frederika, Moritz, and Ricarda to stand on.

Wes and Anna began the work visa paperwork in September, and by early October, it was announced that Moritz could come and work for them legally. Anna couldn't believe it. When she told Frederika, she walked out of the foyer of the Sunrise Cove to hide in the office and sob on her knees. Anna hurried after her and hugged her until she stopped shaking.

"Wes did everything he could," Anna explained happily. "And it worked!"

"You're the one who studied immigration law," Frederika reminded her, wiping her tears. "You're the brains behind the operation."

"But we never could have done it without him," Anna reminded her.

"I just don't know what to say. I feel like I might float away."

For the first time in a very long time, Wes took the day off from the Sunrise Cove to join Anna and Frederika to pick up Moritz. The other employees at the inn breathed a sigh of relief, grateful for a day off from their boss and his obsessive instructions. Aunt Kerry came to the rescue to babysit, and before they left the island, they dropped the girls off at the Montgomery House, waving at them as they left the driveway. Even Ricarda remained behind, chatting happily with Lola as they played with large plastic toys on the carpet. It was the first time Frederika had been separated from her daughter since they'd come to the United States, and she was flush with panic about it. But she knew it was for the best.

All the way up to the facility on the outskirts of Boston, Frederika remained quiet in the backseat. When Anna glanced back at her, her eyes were closed, and her lips were moving as though she were praying. Between their seats, Anna and Wes held hands, united in their mission. Anna remembered the beginning of the summer when she'd felt they were separate, exhausted with life and one another. This had brought them together.

As soon as they parked, Frederika burst from the back of the car and walked toward the facility as though she was drawn by a magnet. Wes and Anna hurried up after her, as they had to show the correct paperwork to ensure he could leave. Anna burned with curiosity about this mystery man. He'd been her raison d'être for so many months— and now, he was coming to live at their inn. Still, she didn't know anything about him or even what he looked like.

Privately, Anna still hoped Moritz and Frederika would decide to stay on Martha's Vineyard. But she knew better than to ask for that. Chicago awaited.

Wes swaggered into the foyer with the same confidence he'd shown on the phone, handed over the appropriate paperwork, and chatted with one of the bosses of the place about the weather as one of the guards went back to retrieve Moritz. Anna was silent, watching Frederika.

The minute the door opened to reveal a very handsome man with a square jaw and a thick head of black hair, Frederika sprung forward and wrapped her arms around him. She shook violently but emitted no noise. Throughout, Moritz kept his eyes open and his strong arms around her. They were back together again. The air in the room was very dense, and Anna found it difficult to breathe, her throat tightening and loosening. As their hug continued, Anna forced herself to look at the ground, trying and failing not to imagine how she would react if she didn't see Wes for many months. She would be inconsolable.

When their hug broke, Moritz came toward Anna and Wes. In German, Frederika quickly explained to Moritz what had happened — presumably that Anna had studied immigration law and Wes had made all the right phone calls. The handshake that Moritz gave Anna that day was one she would remember for the rest of her life. His grip was powerful.

"Thank you," Moritz said, looking both of them in the eye. "I cannot wait to work for you, Mr. and Mrs. Sheridan. The Sunrise Cove Inn will be my life's work."

This was exactly what the man working at the facility wanted to hear. Wes nodded.

"Your resume is astounding, Moritz. We look forward to the future."

The man behind the counter at the facility rubbed his palms together. "We love this sort of thing. European culture is finding its footing in the United States. You know, my great-great-grandfather was German, and he set up a wonderful life for my family here in Boston."

Moritz forced himself to look at the man, a man who had more-or-less served as his prison guard for the past several months. Anna wouldn't have been surprised if he'd bucked up and punched the man in the mouth. Restraint was key.

"Thank you for your help as we worked this situation out," Wes spoke through the strained silence. "You must come to the Sunrise Cove sometime."

"I'll see both of you there," the man said.

Outside the facility, Moritz raised his face so that the October sunlight played across his cheeks. Frederika raised herself up on her tiptoes and kissed his cheek, then spoke quickly in German.

"Let's get out of here," Wes muttered to Anna, taking her hand as they walked to the car. "This place gives me the creeps."

Moritz and Frederika got in the back and held hands on the seat between them. When Wes started the engine, Frederika laughed gently and placed her head on the seat rest.

"I can't believe that worked," she managed to say, trying to calm herself down.

Anna turned and locked eyes with Frederika. "Everything is going to be smooth sailing from now on."

Moritz wasn't as good at English as Frederika was. It took him quite a while to assemble sentences, and he gave Frederika many confused glances when he forgot a word or phrase. Finally, he managed to say, "I thought I was going to be sent home next week. I was so upset, thinking I'd never see my daughter or wife again."

Anna's heart swelled.

"This was a brilliant idea," Moritz said as Wes drove them across Massachusetts, back toward the island. "Even Val wouldn't have thought of it."

After they parked on the ferry, Frederika and Moritz walked ahead of Wes and Anna, holding hands as they strode across the top deck and leaned against the railing. The wind was chilly, and clouds lurked, dark and heavy, across the horizon. Wes wrapped his arms around Anna as the ferry dragged them back to the island, back to their children. Under his breath, he said, "You can see how in love they are."

Anna turned and gazed into Wes' eyes. "They can see the same about us."

At the Montgomery House, Kerry stepped onto the porch with Ricarda in her arms, smiling broadly. Moritz rushed from the car and up the steps to take his daughter in his arms. She yelped happily and laughed as he hugged her. His eyes filled with tears. Frederika joined him and hugged them both, her shoulders shaking. Beside them, Kerry struggled to keep it together.

"I've made dinner," Kerry called down to Wes. "Come on in!"

"You didn't have to do that," Anna scolded her.

"All the kids were hungry," Kerry said. "And you four have had quite a day."

As was her habit, Kerry had made a gorgeous feast— roasted lamb, potatoes, asparagus, fresh bread, and pumpkin pie. As Moritz walked into the dining room to take in the view of the piles of food, his jaw dropped, and he looked back at Frederika to say something in German. Frederika laughed.

"What did he say?" Kerry asked.

"He said it looks like an American movie," Frederika said. "And it really does."

Kerry beamed, clearly pleased with this response. "Sit down, everyone. Please."

They did. Anna found a place between Lola's highchair and Wes, with Susan and Christine seated across from them. Frederika and Moritz sat on either side of Ricarda's highchair, doting on her as Kerry poured them glasses of wine and chatted about the games they'd played. Kerry's children were intrigued with Moritz, especially when he spoke in German to Frederika or Ricarda.

"What does that mean?" Steve asked as he tucked his napkin into his shirt.

Frederika rubbed Moritz's shoulder. "Back where we came from, we don't speak English. Moritz's English will get better quickly, though. Mine certainly did."

Anna remembered how wonderful Frederika had been at English from the very start. How had she gotten so good? Had she taught herself? Or did she just have a way with languages— a skill that should have been furthered in a university setting?

When Kerry finally sat, she bowed her head, and Trevor said a prayer, blessing the work they'd done to bring Moritz home, blessing all three of their families, and finding light in the midst of what had been a terribly dark time. And when they opened their eyes and began to eat, Anna noticed that Moritz blinked back numerous tears, often glancing over at his wife and daughter as though he couldn't believe he'd made it out.

Chapter Twenty

Present Day

It wasn't Lola's favorite thing to ask for help. She was stubborn, preferring to put herself through pain and torment if it meant that she could pat herself on the back at the end and tell herself she'd been able to do it alone. Unfortunately, the "new" passports for Fiona, Luke, and Claudia Franklin had forced her into a dead end. And, the Monday morning after she returned from her meeting with Claudia, she dialed an old friend who could maybe help.

"Lola Sheridan? Is that really you?"

Lola rolled her eyes into the back of her head, hating how quickly a smile spread across her lips. "Colin. How are you?"

Colin had been Lola's boss back in Boston back in her early days of journalism. More than that, they'd had a fling that hadn't lasted very long but still lived on in Lola's memories as being quite romantic. She'd last seen him three years ago when he'd wanted to date her properly and had even come out to the island to prove his love. Unfortunately for him, Lola had met Tommy that very same summer— and she'd followed her heart into Tommy's life instead of Colin's.

"I'm doing just fine," Colin said. It was clear he'd lost any anger he felt toward her and now remembered her fondly, perhaps even as the woman who'd gotten away. "I've been waiting for you to call me."

"You figured it would happen?"

"I figured you'd need something one of these days," Colin said with a laugh. "Am I right?"

Lola groaned. "I am in a pickle, to be honest with you."

"Hit me with the details. What do you need?" Colin asked. "You know, I'm always there for you. Whatever it is."

"I appreciate that, Colin."

Lola explained what she'd learned so far and gave him the names she currently knew: Fiona, Luke, and Claudia Franklin, plus Fiona's real name, Frederika.

"I think they left the east coast at the end of 1983," Lola went on. "And at some point, they abandoned their child. But I don't know when or why."

"Sounds tricky," Colin said. "I'll do what I can to track them down and call you back."

After Lola got off the phone, she felt fidgety and strange, and she donned a pair of tennis shoes and did something she rarely did— she went for a run. There were several forest paths that weaved out from the cabin she shared with Tommy, and she ran hard and fast, her tennis shoes flapping against the soft soil. After a while, she lost track of her anxious thoughts and found herself at the edge of the woods, very close to the sea, and so she kept going all the way to the beach, where she stripped to her underwear and waded into the water. Nobody ever came to this beach, as it was rather secluded, surrounded by rocks and trees and not offering as much sunshine as the others. Lola floated on her back and gazed at the sky above, thinking hard about Colin, about the phone calls he was making as he got deeper into Claudia's story than Lola could manage. He had contacts in law enforcement. He knew people with files that weren't kept at the Boston Library.

At five-thirty that afternoon, Lola met Audrey in downtown Oak Bluffs. Noah was back home with Max, and Audrey was bright and happy, chatting about a freelance article she was writing for a local magazine.

"You're quiet," Audrey pointed out, frowning. "Is there something going on with Claudia?"

Lola raised her shoulders. "Colin's looking into it for me. I'm so nervous, thinking he'll call at any time."

Audrey touched Lola's shoulder. "Now that Claudia knows so much of the truth, we have to give her the rest of it. She's probably going insane, thinking about all the missing pieces of the puzzle. I hope Colin can put it together."

"I hope so, too."

"Hey, you two!" Amanda appeared on the other side of the street, waving. Susan bucked up behind her. Both were still in heels from the office, and they clacked along happily, adjusting the collars of their suits. They could have been sisters.

The four of them exchanged hugs. Susan and Amanda confessed it had been a very difficult day at the office and that they were so excited to be free.

"Where's Christine?" Susan asked.

On cue, Christine's car turned the corner, and she waved from the front seat. After a brief perusal of the street, she found a parking spot and jumped out, waving. Lola felt herself breathing easier than she had all day. Her girls were with her. She was okay.

For a little while, the five of them walked downtown in the heat of the August afternoon, talking about their days and discussing what they wanted for dinner. Toward the end of the block, a pop-up store opened its doors, advertising baby clothes, and Audrey shrieked, grabbed Amanda's hand, and dragged her inside. The rest of them followed, laughing. It was never too early to get excited about Amanda's pregnancy. It was a new era of hope.

"Look at these little socks!" Audrey sighed, removing a bright red pair from a stand near the front of the store. "I remember when Max was so little. Everything he did broke my heart! Now, we're in the middle of the terrible twos, and my head is spinning."

"Three is even worse," Susan said, smiling.

"You're just used to the twins," Amanda reminded her, speaking of her brother's children. "They were always double trouble."

"Still can't believe you were going to move in with them," Lola said.

"I think I would have lost my mind by now," Susan admitted, remembering her initial life plan from three years ago, before she'd decided to come to the island.

As Amanda and Audrey continued to peruse the baby clothes and toys, Lola's phone buzzed in her pocket. Terrified, she ripped it out and stared at the name: COLIN. It was time.

"I have to take this," Lola told Christine.

Outside, Lola leaned against the brick wall. Her heart felt like a butterfly.

"Colin! Hey." She steadied her tone, trying to sound calm.

"Hey there. I have some information for you."

Lola sighed. "Already? I thought I had at least twenty-four hours to calm down."

Colin laughed. "Unfortunately, my guy out in Chicago is fast. Those names came up in the system, all right."

Lola held her breath. She could hardly bear it.

"During December of 1983, Fiona and Luke were arrested under suspicion of forged documentation," Colin explained. "They had applied for an apartment, and their paperwork came back faulty. When the apartment management demanded to know who they were, Luke got very angry. It says in the file that he threatened management. After this, the manager called the police, and Luke and Fiona were taken into custody. Their baby was put into foster care."

Lola's mouth was very dry. "They didn't abandon her."

"No," Colin said. "But they were sent back to Europe. It looks like they petitioned to bring their daughter with them, but they were denied by the state."

Lola closed her eyes. "I can't believe that."

"It's truly evil," Colin agreed.

"They just wanted to build a new life," Lola breathed.

Colin remained silent. This was his first day in the midst of this story, but it had already taken a toll on him.

"I found out their real names," Colin said. "They admitted to them when they were forced back to Eastern

Europe. Frederika and Moritz Busenburg. Their daughter's real name was Ricarda."

Lola's heart flipped over. "I don't know how to thank you, Colin."

"Don't thank me," Colin told her. "If I were Claudia, I wouldn't know how to carry this."

"Imagine learning your real name after living as another your entire life," Lola said.

"But her parents technically gave her this one, too," Colin pointed out. "They thought Claudia was a perfect name for her American life."

"I didn't think of it that way, but you're right." Lola bit her lower lip and tried to smile as Audrey stepped out of the baby store, frowning.

"Can I help you with anything else?" Colin asked.

"I don't think so. But I owe you dinner next time we see each other."

"That better be sooner rather than later. Take care, Lola. Miss you all the time."

After Lola hung up, she fell into Audrey's arms and cried quietly. Audrey didn't demand answers until she calmed down and dried her cheeks.

"That was Colin?"

Lola nodded. "Everything fell into place. But it's not pretty."

"It was never going to be, I guess," Audrey said.

"You're right," Lola said. "I got distracted by how exciting it was to research. I forgot that we couldn't change the past."

"We can't," Audrey whispered. "But we can help Claudia make sense of her life. And that is worth so much."

Chapter Twenty-One

1983

Anna Sheridan and Frederika drove to the Christmas tree farm on the outskirts of Oak Bluffs with a full car of very excited little girls. It was early December, and fluffy snow sat in piles on either side of the country road. Houses were decorated with Christmas lights and wreaths, and the radio station played Christmas songs that Susan and Christine sang along to. All six of them were bundled up in coats, hats, and mittens, their cheeks bright red from the brief walk from the house to the car. Anna wanted to remember everything about these days, the final before Frederika, Moritz, and Ricarda went out west to join Frederika's cousin in Chicago. It broke her heart.

Once they reached the Christmas tree farm, Susan and Christine bolted forward to look at the options, Lola hobbled after her sisters, and Frederika lifted Ricarda against her to keep her from getting away. Anna laughed and said, "I'm so jealous! Lola refuses to be held very long these days."

"She's a vivacious one," Frederika said. "My Ricarda watches everything she does and mimics her. It's slightly scary."

Anna laughed and wandered through the trees, keeping her eyes on her children. After a few minutes, Susan yelled that they'd found "the one" and stood in front of it with her arms extended to ensure that nobody took it before her mother claimed it.

"What do you think, Frederika?" Anna said, standing in front of the tree with her daughters.

"That's the one," Frederika said. "I just know it."

Anna asked one of the twenty-something employees at the Christmas tree farm to chop it down for her and drive it over to her house with the truck they had on-hand. After that, she and Frederika took the girls to the grocery store for supplies. The plan was to decorate the tree and have a wonderful feast. It was Christmas two weeks early — a necessity, as Frederika was itching to get on the road.

"I'm broken-hearted you're leaving," Anna said as they stocked the car trunk with groceries. "I know I keep asking it. But won't you consider staying?"

Frederika laughed. "We have to go, Anna. You know that."

"Why can't your cousin come here?"

"There are only so many jobs on this island," Frederika explained. "And too many people know me here. I want to be anonymous. I want to feel safe."

Anna understood, although she didn't want to. She wanted to argue more, to remind Frederika that she was the single-greatest friend Anna had had in many years.

When they got home, Anna checked the mail to find a

very thick and large yellow envelope. Her heart thudding, she tore it open on the back porch and checked inside to find three passports, just as she'd arranged for— one each for Luke, Fiona, and Claudia Franklin. They'd had a fun time deciding on these new "American" names. When Frederika learned that Claudia worked as an American name, she nearly wept with joy. "That was my mother's name," she explained. "Spelled with a K instead of a C."

Anna knew that giving Ricarda her mother's name was essential for Frederika. She wanted to be connected to her roots, even as they moved into a new era.

Anna found Frederika in the kitchen, prepping for the feast. Susan led the charge of decorating the Christmas tree, ordering Christine to hang various ornaments in specific locations. "A little to the right, Christine. And one inch higher." When Christine didn't get it exactly right, Susan sighed and stepped forward to do it herself.

"Look at what came in the mail!" Anna placed the passports on the counter.

Frederika's knees gave out from under her. In German, she muttered to herself and gaped at Anna before she threw her arms around her. "It's happening. It's really happening."

"You're American citizens," Anna said. "Just like everyone else!"

"Just like everyone else," Frederika repeated. It was music to her ears.

As the ham baked in the oven, Anna and Frederika helped the girls with the Christmas decorations. Anna put a Christmas album on her record player, and the songs crackled against the windowpane as another December snow fluffed against the windows. A little bit before Moritz and Wes were set to return home from the inn, where they were doing some repairs, Anna opened a bottle of wine, and she and Frederika toasted the holiday season.

When Moritz returned home, Frederika showed him their new American passports, and he grabbed her waist and lifted her into the air in a beautiful circle, her dress whipping out behind her. Their joy was palpable. Moritz picked Ricarda up from the ground and covered her with kisses, saying, "My little Claudia! Look at you! You're Claudia Franklin! You were born in the United States of America!"

* * *

Two days later, Wes and Anna helped pack up the car that would take Moritz, Frederika, and Ricarda to Chicago. Moritz and Frederika had bought it with their earnings from their months of working at the Sunrise Cove, plus a small loan Wes had given them. Although it was used, it was sturdy and safe. Anna watched as Frederika leaned into the back to buckle Ricarda in safely, kissing her on the forehead before she pulled back out.

When Frederika turned toward Anna, time stopped. "I don't know what I would have done without you," Frederika admitted, tucking a curl behind her ear.

"I feel the same way," Anna said, stepping forward to hug her friend. "Promise you'll get there safely. And that you'll call us as soon as you feel comfortable."

"Of course," Frederika promised.

"And promise this won't be the last time we see each other," Anna continued.

"I promise."

Wes wrapped his arm around Anna's shoulders as they watched Moritz back the car out of the driveway and head toward the ferry, turning out of sight. Susan, Christine, and Lola were behind them, calling out "goodbye" over and over again. Anna turned to press her face into Wes' chest, overwhelmed. She suddenly felt very, very alone.

"It'll get easier," Wes breathed.

"What if they're not safe?" Anna asked. "What if something goes wrong?"

"Their passports look perfect," Wes assured her. "I think they'll live deep into old age as American citizens. We'll probably laugh about this twenty years from now. They'll be more American than us by then."

Anna tried to laugh off her fear, to fall into motherhood and Sunrise Cove Inn tasks in a way that kept her mind off of whatever was happening out west. Christmas was a wonderful distraction. This was the first year that Lola could participate in much of the festivities, and she was mesmerized, especially as Susan and Christine told her about Santa Claus, Christmas cookies, and the traditions Anna and Wes had created for their children over the past few years. Anna beamed proudly as Susan and Christine told Lola everything. Their version of the world was the one she'd given them— and she was happy with it.

Anna had convinced herself everything had gone okay out west. She'd told herself a story of Frederika and Moritz that allowed her to sleep at night.

And so, when the call came late at night on December 20th, long after her girls had gone to sleep, Anna didn't think for a second it would be them. She thought it was most likely a prank phone call, or maybe Trevor or Kerry, asking for a favor.

"Hello? This is the Sheridan residence." Anna was groggy, and she leaned against the kitchen counter for support, cradling the phone between her shoulder and her cheek.

"This is a collect call from the Chicago Police Department. Do you accept the charges?" The voice was hard and medicinal. Something cold dropped into Anna's stomach.

"I accept," Anna said. She wanted to run to the staircase and call up to Wes to tell him to come help her. But she didn't want to leave the phone.

"Anna. It's me." Frederika's voice was rattly and strange.

"Fiona! Are you okay?" Anna was careful to use her new name.

"They figured us out," Frederika whispered. "And they took her away! They took Claudia away!"

Anna stood up straight, her heart pounding. "What? What are you talking about?"

"They're sending us back," Frederika rasped. "But they won't let us take Claudia with us! They won't let us bring our baby girl!"

Anna's head spun with questions. How had this happened? Hadn't they been careful?

"You need to find her," Frederika continued. "You need to get her out of their system and send her back to me!"

"Is there someone we can call to get you out of this? Wes is very good with people! We can come to Chicago tomorrow. We can..." Anna spoke quickly.

But suddenly, the call was cut, and all she heard was the dial tone. Stricken, she put the phone back in the cradle and stared at it for a long time, willing Frederika to call her back. A part of her wondered if that had been a dream, if she'd accidentally fallen asleep on the couch and was sleepwalking.

But when Wes returned downstairs and found Anna on her knees in the kitchen, she shook violently, and tears streaked her cheeks. For a long time, he held her there, asking her what had happened, who had called them. And Anna struggled to make sense of something so heinous in a world she no longer recognized as her own.

Chapter Twenty-Two

Present Day

The day after Colin learned of the fate of Frederika and Moritz, Lola again contacted Claudia to arrange a meeting. Claudia wrote back within a minute, saying she would come to Martha's Vineyard this time. She wanted to spend a few days by the ocean. She needed time to think.

The suite in the back half of the third floor of the Sunrise Cove Inn offered the very best view of the Vineyard Sound and was often booked, especially this late in the summer and especially on the weekends. But when Lola stopped to talk to Sam about arranging a room for Claudia's trip at the very inn she and her mother had lived in for the better part of 1983, Sam told her there had been a cancelation that weekend. The suite was available. Lola booked it for Claudia immediately. It felt like fate.

Exhausted and fearful for the weekend, Lola went to the Sheridan House to visit Audrey. It was strange to park in the driveway and know that the house held only three people— Noah, Audrey, and little Max, especially after so many people had come in and out of its doors over the previous three years. Lola took a deep breath, trying to be grateful for the passage of time and the wisdom it brought.

Lola knocked on the back door and let herself in when Audrey called, "Mom? Are you here?"

Lola removed her shoes and stepped into the kitchen, where Audrey wore an apron and stirred a bowl of dough. Lola had never seen Audrey bake like this before, and the sight made her laugh in a way that surprised her.

"What?" Audrey demanded. "I wanted banana bread! And Amanda has been so busy with work this week."

"Is she your normal banana bread provider?" Lola asked.

Audrey grimaced, placed the bowl back on the counter, and scooped a bit onto a spoon to taste. When she did, her eyebrows rose, and she said, "You know what? It isn't that bad."

Lola stepped up to taste-test. "It's really good, Aud!"

"Amanda would kill us for eating raw eggs," Audrey said. "But she's not here to find out."

Lola watched as Audrey poured the batter into a bread dish and slid it into the oven. Her eyes danced as she stepped back.

"Domesticity is easy," Audrey said. "I don't know why I let Amanda make me think it was hard."

Lola laughed and tugged her fingers through her hair.

"You're nervous about something," Audrey said, sensing it immediately. "Did you talk to Claudia?"

"She's going to stay at the Sunrise Cove this weekend," Lola explained. "I'll tell her then."

"Is she staying in the same room she was in back in the eighties?"

"I don't know," Lola said. "The inn doesn't have those records anymore, unfortunately." Lola burrowed her teeth into her lower lip, terrified of what she'd come to the old house to do. "It's time to look at Mom's journals again."

Audrey's eyes were shadowed. "Are you sure?"

"I don't know. It's not that I want to, necessarily. I'm just so curious if she ever knew about Frederika's fate."

"How would she have known?"

Lola shrugged. "Maybe Frederika reached out to her once they got back to East Germany?"

Audrey's eyes glinted. "Have you looked their names up? They can't be any older than Grandpa, right? They might still be alive!"

Lola's eyes widened at the thought. "We could bring them back together again," she whispered.

"You look at the journals," Audrey said. "I'll research where they ended up."

Lola retrieved her mother's journal from the years 1983 and 1984 and padded back downstairs to sit with her daughter on the back porch. Max was napping, and the only sound was the rush of the wind through the leaves and the lapping of the water across the sands. Audrey was slightly bent over her computer, diving through pages and pages of the internet, hunting for Frederika and Moritz Busenburg.

Meanwhile, Lola opened her mother's journal.

December 28, 1983

I haven't been able to sleep since I found out about it. Frederika and Moritz were taken. And Claudia is out in Chicago all by herself, probably frightened. I told Wes that first thing once the new year starts, I'm headed to Chicago to search for her. I'll do anything I can to bring her back here. After that, we can deal with taking her back home.

It seems like such a waste. We worked for months to make sure they could move west safely. I was so sure it would work.

And I can't help but blame myself. Maybe the passports were off. Maybe I contacted the wrong people to make them. Maybe everything I did was a rookie mistake.

Wes says I shouldn't be so hard on myself. I can barely look at him right now. All I can do is pretend to be joyful for the girls. It's Christmastime. But oh, I've never been more broken-hearted.

January 11, 1984

I'm staying in a crummy hotel on the outskirts of Chicago. I flew here from Boston all by myself, without the girls and without Wes, and I cried quietly the entire way. I have to be brave for Claudia, but I'm beginning to lose faith in myself.

Chicago has a train system, which I'm able to use to get to the foster care office. I plan to go first thing tomorrow. Until then, I will eat this package of crackers I bought from the drugstore and sleep on this horrible, crooked mattress. I will dream of home.

January 12, 1984

I went to the foster care offices. They wouldn't even see me. They told me to go home.

January 13, 1984

I went back to the offices and said I wouldn't leave until I spoke to someone. I waited for eight hours, watching as children without their parents were taken in and out. Most of them were crying. I tried to tell the woman at the front desk that I was there to take one of these children from the system, to care for her myself. She then asked me *to fill out a form, which I handed back to her. She said I would hear back from them in six to eight weeks— if I was a match. I was furious. It was then I was asked to leave by the guard! He said I was loitering.*

January 14, 1984

Again, the office. Again, no answers. I wasn't allowed to meet with anyone higher up. I'm thinking of Wes, of how easy it was for him to manipulate his way into getting Moritz out of that facility. But I'm just a woman alone in the world right now. I have no power against these people.

Wes is begging me to come home. And it's true what he says. We have to focus on our own family. We've done all we can for theirs. But I can't help but think it's entirely unfair. We were born with all the luck in the world. And Frederika and Moritz are left to mourn their daughter, all because of an oppressive system I don't understand.

Lola sniffed and closed her eyes. She could feel her mother alone in that hotel room in Chicago, her heart broken. She could feel the loneliness within Anna as she sat on her crummy bed and wrote in her journal. It was heavy on her arms and shoulders. It made her stomach twist.

"What did you find out?" Audrey asked, turning toward her mother.

"Mom knew. She fought to find Claudia, but the system didn't cooperate. It looks like she went home after a while, broken-hearted."

Audrey's eyes were dark. Lola realized, with a jolt, that Audrey was no longer typing furiously on her computer, which meant one thing.

"What did you find?" Lola breathed.

Audrey turned her computer around to show a German website, which she'd translated from German to

English. On it were two obituaries— one for Frederika and the other for Moritz. Lola's heart stopped.

"Frederika passed away in 2002," Audrey said, her voice cracking. "And Moritz died two years later."

"Goodness." Lola's shoulders shook. "Frederika died just six years after Mom did."

Audrey nodded. "But that's not all." She clicked on another tab to show a social media profile for someone named Raphael Busenburg, then another tab to show Maria Busenburg, and then another to show Daniela Busenburg. Lola gaped at them. They all seemed to be in their thirties. And they all looked very, very similar to Claudia.

"Don't tell me..." Lola breathed.

But Audrey nodded her head. "Moritz and Frederika had more children. And they're all still in Germany."

Chapter Twenty-Three

Lola leaned against the railing of the harbor, gazing out across the glittering blue as Claudia's ferry approached. Claudia hadn't been very talkative since they'd arranged this meeting, probably because she assumed Lola only had bad news for her. But Claudia could have never dreamed of having siblings. And now, it felt as though Lola was showing her something that actually mattered. Something that would help her with the grieving process and move on to the next chapter.

Lola was no longer sure if Claudia would want to write a memoir about this experience. If she did, Lola had a hunch it would be a top-selling one, as it delved into both personal and world history in a way that was sure to captivate readers. But Lola knew that it often wasn't easy to reveal such personal details to strangers. She would understand if Claudia wanted to keep it to herself.

The ferry docked, and the massive ramp was pulled down to allow both cars and people to skirt from the vessel. Lola spotted Claudia in the masses, a backpack slung over her shoulder. To Lola's surprise, Claudia had come alone, without her husband. And when Claudia beelined for Lola, she looked at her with haunted eyes.

"Welcome back," Lola said gently.

Claudia tried to smile. "It's so beautiful here. I think I forgot what the world looked like away from my university desk."

Lola smiled. "Your husband didn't join?"

"I told him I needed some time to myself," Claudia explained softly. "I've probably been hard to be around." Claudia dropped her chin to her chest. "I hate that I haven't been able to handle this emotionally, you know? When I approached you about this, I was sure I was strong enough. I didn't even think twice about it!"

"You shouldn't be hard on yourself," Lola said. "It's all a big mess. And you never had a say in any of it."

Lola and Claudia walked along the harbor for a little while, both wordless. When they reached the Sunrise Cove Inn, Lola paused at the fence and gestured up toward the beautiful place, explaining, "You and your mother lived here when you were one."

Claudia's eyes glinted. For a very long time, she stared at it, then stuttered, "Now that I know what she looked like, I can almost picture it. I'm imagining her standing on the porch with me in her arms. I'm imagining us playing in the sand."

Lola closed her eyes. How many times had she imagined that, with herself and her own mother? It was natural to want to escape into the past.

"I don't know which room you lived in with your mother," Lola explained as they entered the foyer. "But I booked you the very best room. The view to the ocean is gorgeous."

Sam waved from behind the counter. "Good afternoon! Welcome to the Sunrise Cove Inn."

"This is my niece's new husband, Sam," Lola explained as they walked toward the counter. "Sam, this is Claudia. She used to live here at the inn."

Sam's eyes widened. "Wow! When was that?"

"1983, apparently," Claudia said.

Sam was solemn. "When I started working at the Sunrise Cove, I knew I was entering a place with a long-standing and beautiful history. I love meeting people who were a part of that."

Claudia swallowed and tried to smile again.

"I'll show her to her room, okay, Sam?" Lola stepped around the counter and headed for the line of iron keys, which hadn't changed at all since the eighties.

"Let me know if you need anything at all," Sam told Claudia.

"Thank you."

Lola led Claudia around the side of the desk toward the staircase that led them to the second floor. The back suite's entryway was ornate, carved in patterns of leaves and flowers, and the doorknob was golden and glowing in the sunlight that swept in from the hall window. Lola opened it to reveal the beautiful room, with its king-sized bed and glistening white sheets, its antique furnishings that Anna herself had picked, and its paintings from local artists. Out the window, a white beach stretched along the turquoise water of the Vineyard Sound, and a young boy tried to skip rocks, slamming them against the surface. Very soon, a young woman approached, adjusted a stone in his hand, and showed him a better technique. Lola was captivated by the image for a moment, although it was one of thousands of times a week that mother helped her son. It was like breathing to her, just as it was for all mothers.

"It's beautiful," Claudia said, leaning against the side of the bed. Her face was stoic. "It's hard to imagine living here for six months. She must have been so frightened here. She must have felt so far from home."

Lola nodded. "I think my mother and yours struck up a wonderful friendship. They helped each other through difficult times." She paused. "Of course, my mother never had to escape a country. But I think she was really lonely in motherhood, especially because my father was always working here at the inn."

Claudia turned toward Lola. She looked on the edge of breaking down. "Women go through so much, don't they?"

Lola nodded, at a loss for what to say. Claudia seemed to grasp the weight of this meeting. It was beyond words.

Finally, Claudia managed to add, "I don't know if I can wait any longer. You have to tell me what you learned."

Lola led Claudia to the balcony attached to the suite. Claudia watched Lola like a hawk as she folded her hands on the wooden table and said, "Your mother and father were named Frederika and Moritz Busenburg. They traveled out to Chicago in December of 1983, using false identities. When they arrived, they applied to rent an apartment, but were immediately arrested for falsifying documents. You were put in foster care, and your mother and father were sent back to East Germany. My mother went to Chicago to try to find you, but unfortunately, the system was too convoluted. Nobody could tell her where you'd ended up or how to adopt you. Eventually, my father asked that she come back here. But her diaries go

A Vineyard Tide

on to say that she continued to try to find you for many years after that."

Claudia furrowed her brow. Lola could imagine Claudia growing up in the system, sleeping on dirty bunk beds as children squabbled beside her, keeping her awake at night. All that time, someone in Martha's Vineyard had done her best to bring her here, to the heaven that was the Vineyard Sound. But, as it did with so many other children, the system had failed Claudia. Maybe her paperwork hadn't been adequate; maybe whoever was in charge simply hadn't bothered to try to help. This was something Lola wasn't sure she would ever uncover.

Lola went on. "Unfortunately, I have to tell you that your parents passed away several years ago. Frederika died in 2002, and Moritz died two years after that."

Claudia's chin quivered with sorrow.

"But we also learned something else," Lola continued, pulling up the photographs of Claudia's siblings on her phone and turning it around, her heart thudding. "Your parents had three children after they returned to East Germany. All of them reside in Germany. And I'm sure they would be very eager to meet you."

Claudia gaped at the photographs. After a very long silence, she whispered their names, almost as though she'd forgotten that Lola was there in front of her, listening. "Raphael? Maria? Daniela?" She shook her head. "I can't believe this. I cannot believe this at all."

"It's true," Lola affirmed. "And don't they look like you? Especially Maria."

Claudia continued to stare at the photographs, spinning with questions. "All this time, I thought I was alone in the world."

"You were never alone," Lola told her. "And your

parents never abandoned you. It was a horrific event, something that should have never happened."

Claudia raised her chin, looking resolute. "But it did happen. This is my story. And for the first time since our last meeting, I feel like writing that memoir again." She laughed gently as her eyes glistened with tears. "It's gotten so much more complicated since I put you on the case."

"I can't imagine what you're feeling right now, Claudia. I can only thank you for allowing me to go on this journey."

Claudia returned Lola's phone and dabbed her cheeks with a tissue. "What now?"

Lola laughed. "I have your siblings' email addresses."

"Email! Isn't that funny? I barely know what to write. Then again, that's how I contacted you, isn't it?"

"Just speak from the heart," Lola told her.

"You're right." Claudia exhaled with a mix of frustration and relief. "It's so bizarre that you and I met forty years ago. Isn't it?"

"It really is."

"We were just little girls together," Claudia said. "I wish I could remember it. And I wish I could remember my mother. Maybe my siblings can tell me more about her." She paused for a moment, her eyes trained on the ocean. "You wouldn't like to come with me. Would you?"

Lola's heart opened at the thought. "To Germany?"

Claudia nodded. "You're a part of my parents' story, too. I'm sure my siblings would love to meet you."

Lola was never one to say no to an adventure. She didn't give Claudia a chance to change her mind before she agreed. Now, she just had to wait for Claudia to make the big leap— and email her siblings out of the blue.

A Vineyard Tide

There was no telling what they'd think of all this. But, if Lola believed in anything, it was the power of families, especially as they came together again. She'd witnessed it firsthand when Susan, Christine, and Lola had returned to the Vineyard to repair what had once shattered.

Chapter Twenty Four

When Lola awoke the morning after her meeting with Claudia, there were fifteen text messages and four missed calls listed on her phone. Beside her, Tommy slept gently, his chest rising and falling as the morning light filtered out from behind the curtains. Lola skimmed through the texts, all from Claudia, to read over what had happened.

> CLAUDIA: Apparently, Maria's up with a baby (a baby!) and read my email immediately. She called at four a.m. her time— and we both cried!

> CLAUDIA: Frederika and Moritz only ever spoke of me using my given name, Ricarda. So, when my siblings tried to look for me in the United States, they didn't get far.

> CLAUDIA: They have spent so many years wondering about me! And I didn't even know they existed!

> CLAUDIA: Best of all, my maternal grandmother's name is Klaudia! Can you believe it?

Lola hurried to the kitchen to brew coffee and call Claudia back. Claudia was breathless on the other line.

"I was just on the phone with my husband," Claudia explained. "He couldn't believe any of this, either. Anyway, I'm about to book my tickets to Germany. How's a week from now for you?"

Lola laughed. She felt as though she floated a few inches from the ground. "What about Boston University?"

"They can wait," Claudia said. "I've already informed my students I'll be missing their first two classes. Given the fact that I'm a history professor, dropping into my own history, it's understandable. Isn't it?"

"Completely," Lola agreed. "I'll buy our tickets today."

One week later, Lola, Audrey, Claudia, and Claudia's husband, Dan, eased through the security line at the Boston Airport and grabbed seats at an airport coffee shop. Claudia glowed with excitement and spoke a mile a minute about the spontaneous plans she'd made with her siblings, a trip that would begin in Berlin and ultimately end at Raphael's lake cottage.

"That was where my mother and father raised the three children," Claudia explained, showing a photograph of the house. Raphael had sent it over.

"It's beautiful." Lola took her phone and swiped through the photographs of the house.

"My father was able to get a steady job after they returned to East Germany. He was an engineer, which

East Germany was in dire need of at the time," Claudia explained. "My parents purchased that house about a year after they left the United States."

"They didn't get into any trouble for escaping?" Audrey asked.

Claudia's face was shadowed. "Apparently, my mother and father were never open with the details about the year after they returned, before they bought the house. My siblings believe there was a sort of punishment. Perhaps they had to pay a lot of money. Perhaps they had to work for the government." Claudia's face went pale. "But the important thing is, they were able to reintegrate back into society and build a life that, for them, was worth living."

Lola swiped to the last photo in the series, which was taken of a framed photo hanging on a paneled wall. In it, Frederika held a beautiful little girl.

"Apparently, that's always hung at that house," Claudia breathed. "They've always known about me and what I looked like at that age. And they've always known to mourn the loss of their older sister."

Over the table, Dan held Claudia's hand for support.

"I hate that I can't stay in that house longer," Claudia stuttered. "But my siblings have said they can prove I was born in East Germany, which means I can definitely get a passport."

"We're going to spend a lot more time in Germany," Dan affirmed. "It's time you get to know your roots."

"But not until next year," Claudia said gently.

"Maybe you could work at a German university!" Audrey said.

Claudia's eyes sparkled. "That's my dream."

A Vineyard Tide

"And we've already started learning German," Dan added. "Badly."

"Your mother taught my older sister to say a few things here and there," Lola remembered. "She missed speaking her mother tongue so much."

Once on the plane, Lola and Audrey selected the same film to watch side-by-side, *Palm Springs*, a romantic comedy that made them belly-laugh. Even after the stewardesses dimmed the lights and encouraged everyone to sleep as they cruised over the ocean, Lola and Audrey struggled to calm down. Lola was shivering with adrenaline, excited to watch Claudia meet her siblings for the first time.

Unfortunately, this lack of sleep during the flight left Lola scattered and quiet when they landed. For a long time, she and Audrey waited for their baggage with glazed eyes as Claudia and Dan spoke quietly together. Both had slept on the plane. Both looked much better than Audrey and Lola.

"Why don't you join us for lunch later?" Claudia suggested, breaking Lola's reverie.

Lola nodded. "We'd love that."

In the cab to their hotel in Mitte, Berlin, Lola leaned her head on Audrey's shoulder. "It's good that Claudia will meet her siblings without us. I can't imagine having some straggler along for the ride when I met back up with Susan and Christine three years ago."

"You're right," Audrey said. "But they want to meet you. You're the spitting image of Grandma Anna. And they've heard all about her over the years, I'm sure."

"You're one to talk," Lola reminded her. "You're the one who looks the most like my mother."

Audrey was quiet, probably because she couldn't refute the truth.

The cab drew them deeper into the center, toward the TV Tower that stuck out from a city that, eighty years ago, had been destroyed in a war that had changed everything. That war had been the beginning of what had ultimately divided West Germany from East Germany, resulting in Moritz and Frederika's failed search for freedom. Yet, on a beautiful August morning, it glistened beneath the sun. Gothic church steeples splintered the blue sky, and people on bicycles bounced on cobblestoned alleys.

At the hotel, Lola and Audrey hauled their suitcases into the lobby and checked in with a very kind woman with a brisk German accent. Their hotel room had two lush beds and a view of a downtown street, where a yellow tram whizzed past. In every way, it was different than Martha's Vineyard.

"It's hard to believe all that research we did in the Boston Library led us here," Audrey pointed out, yawning into her hand.

"It's extraordinary," Lola agreed.

"What should we figure out together next?"

Lola laughed gently and stretched out on the bed, pointing her toes so that her calves tightened. "Let's try not to do anything too close to home next time. I don't know if my heart can take it."

Claudia texted during their nap to tell them the place and time of the lunch plans. They were to meet at Max and Moritz restaurant in Kreuzberg at 1:30 p.m. for a German feast. After that, they'd head to a beer garden to sit in the splendorous summer sun and chat some more. Claudia and Dan would head back to the family home on the lake tomorrow afternoon, at which time Lola and

Audrey planned to explore Berlin, go dancing, and eventually take the train to Munich, where they'd see castles and hike in the Alps. "But not too much hiking," Audrey had explained to her grandfather before they'd left. "You know I'm not keen on exercise."

When Lola and Audrey had explained everything they'd learned about Frederika, Moritz, and Claudia to Wes, Wes had turned gray. For a very long time, he'd stared out the window of the Sheridan House, watching the water as it lapped against the sailboat. It had been his first trip back to the Sheridan House to visit since his move, and he looked like a ghost.

Finally, he'd said, "Your mother worried about Frederika and Claudia endlessly. It cursed her for the rest of her life. Sometimes, I made phone calls to the Chicago foster program, demanding information. But eventually, they told me it was a lost cause. I didn't have the authority they needed to tell me anything. And no lawyer we ever spoke to could reveal what we needed to know."

In a way, Claudia was the long-lost sister Lola, Christine, and Susan had had for the briefest of eras.

Audrey and Lola woke up from their naps around noon, showered, changed, and struck out on a journey to Kreuzberg, where Claudia, Dan, and her siblings awaited. They'd spent all morning walking the Landwehrkanal, drinking coffee and eating pastries and talking themselves silly. Lola couldn't wait to see what they all looked like together.

As Lola and Audrey entered the restaurant, an explosion of laughter came from the back room. Very soon, Lola could parse out Claudia's laughter in the chaos as it rose higher than the others.

"I think that's our table," Lola explained to the server, guiding Audrey back.

For a moment, Lola leaned in the doorway and took in the sight. Claudia sat at the far end of an oval table, her elbows up on the wood as she sat, captivated, listening to what her brother, Raphael, said. Raphael spoke with his hands, with an energy you could imagine Moritz had passed along to him. And as he told his tale, Daniela teased him about it, saying, "You are telling the story wrong!"

"Does he do that often?" Claudia asked her sister.

"All the time!" Daniela sighed, her eyes glinting.

"Oh! Lola!" Claudia had spotted her, and she stood to wave her over. Immediately, her siblings and her husband rose and turned to watch her and Audrey come closer. Claudia looked like a little kid on her birthday. She was having the best day of her life. "Everyone, this is Lola and her daughter, Audrey. They were instrumental in helping me contact you. Audrey, Lola, this is Raphael, Maria, and Daniela."

Lola and Audrey offered their hands for handshakes, but the three Germans refused, hugging them and thanking them for all they'd done.

"When I read that email in the middle of the night, I shrieked louder than my baby!" Maria said. "My husband thought there was something really wrong."

As Lola and Audrey found chairs around the table, Daniela pulled a photograph from her purse and passed it nervously across the table so that it sat in front of Lola and Audrey. Lola's heart dropped into her stomach. It was almost too much.

In the photograph stood Frederika and Anna. Both wore classic eighties puffed sleeves, and their hair was big

A Vineyard Tide

and elaborately curled. They smiled as though they'd just told each other secrets they would take to their graves. And each of them held a toddler girl— one of whom reached across the space between them to touch the younger on the arm.

"My gosh." Lola could hardly breathe.

"We found it in Mom's things after she died," Daniela explained. "She never kept Anna and Wes a secret from us, of course. But we never knew what Anna looked like."

Raphael's eyes were shadowed. "I helped Mom look up the Sunrise Cove Inn after we set up internet at their place. That must have been one year before she died, 2001, and the images on the internet were grainy and bad. Still, she looked at those photographs for hours. And I'll never forget what she said when she read the information panel." Raphael paused, staring down at the table. "She asked why the website didn't say anything about Anna. 'Why does it just say Wes? He was always taking too much credit for everything!'"

Lola laughed gently, sensing herself on the verge of breaking down. "She didn't know my mother died."

"I didn't think to look that up," Raphael admitted. "She ranted about your father for a while and talked about how wonderful your mother was. And after that, I printed a photograph of the Sunrise Cove for her to have. It was grainy and terrible, but it hung in her sitting room for the rest of her days. She always called it a safe place. She hoped she would be able to return one day."

Lola's heart cracked at the edges. There wasn't a dry eye at the table.

"I stayed there last week," Claudia admitted quietly, looking at each of her siblings. "I had never felt closer to her than I did when I sat on the balcony of the inn and felt the breeze over my face. But now, in this restaurant half the world away from everything I've ever known, I feel her even closer."

Over the table, Raphael, Maria, Daniela, and Claudia joined hands. There was a sense of purpose burning in their eyes, as though, now that they'd found one another, they wouldn't let go. Lola understood that. And a part of her burned to run out of the restaurant and call Christine and Susan to remind them, perhaps for the millionth time, that their mother had lived on this earth, that she had loved and lost, and that she was still affecting people nearly thirty years after her death.

But there would be time for those conversations— glistening last days of summer as Lola gathered with her sisters at the Sheridan House. But now, here in Berlin, was a time to take Audrey's hand in hers, squeeze it, and thank the stars above for allowing them a front-row seat to the reunion of a lifetime. It was time to order food, to fall into the decadence of the recipes that Frederika had once cooked for Anna at the Sheridan House. It was time to find solid ground after a long flight across the ocean, to open their hearts to a new chapter, and feel at peace.

Coming Next

Pre Order Vineyard Winds

Other Books by Katie Winters

The Vineyard Sunset Series

Secrets of Mackinac Island Series

Sisters of Edgartown Series

A Katama Bay Series

A Mount Desert Island Series

A Nantucket Sunset Series

The Coleman Series

Made in United States
North Haven, CT
02 January 2025